Adventures with Children
in the Early School Years

ELSA BARNOUW
& ARTHUR SWAN

Adventures with Children

in the Early School Years

AGATHON PRESS INC.

Published by
Agathon Press, Inc.
111 Eighth Avenue
New York, NY 10011

Library of Congress Cataloging-in-Publication Data

Barnouw, Elsa.
  Adventures with children in the early school years.

  Rev. ed. of: Adventures with children in nursery school and kindergarten. 1959.
    1. Nursery schools. 2. Kindergartens.
I. Swan, Arthur. II. Barnouw, Elsa. Adventures with children in nursery school and kindergarten.
III. Title.
LB1140.B2915 1986   372'.216   85-15784
ISBN 0-87586-070-2
ISBN 0-87586-069-9 (pbk.)

Printed in the United States of America

To RUTH DAVIS PERRY

A Necessary Preface

When *Adventures with Children in Nursery School and Kindergarten* was first published some twenty-five years ago, it was our hope that it might be of some use to parents, as a lively and accurate picture of what good nursery and kindergarten experiences might provide for their young children; and to teachers in training, as an exploration of attitudes and activities that contribute toward the healthy development of children from two years old to six.

Since that time, it has become evident that this book has touched a far wider audience than we could have foreseen, and that through its focus on the needs of young children it has something of importance to contribute to current efforts on behalf of this significant but defenseless segment of our population. *Adventures with Children* is being used by Directors of many Head Start and full-day programs across this country, and has served as a guide for the setting up of several private nursery schools. The present edition, retitled and revised, is published in order to make the book available to those who have looked for it recently in vain.

Readers familiar with previous printings will see at once that the book sports a new title: *Adventures with Children in the Early School Years.* The long respected terms "nursery school" and "kindergarten" seem to focus more on the youth of the learners than on the quality of their learning, much as the unfortunate label "pre-school" implies that these years comprise a kind of Never-Never Land prior to the time when "real learning" begins. The exciting and enriching experiences lived so fully by the children we observed are not "pre"-anything! They represent the children's first and formative years at school.

The present edition offers much new material which reflects, as do updated topical references, some of the profound changes that have taken place in our world across the last two decades. While many of our earlier observations about young children and the ways in which they learn hold as true today as they did when this book was first published, the society around the children of the 80's has reshaped itself in some evident and important respects. We can no longer assume, as we could when we took our original notes, that Mother stays at home to see to children's needs, while Father goes out to work to provide the family income. We cannot even assume that Father is in the home. Further, if a child can look forward these days to suppertime with both parents, we can be fairly sure that the grownups will have little energy to share after their full days of work outside the home. For many a young child, school days begin as parents set off for work; and the long hours away from home may extend well past the end of the grownup's working day. New school programs have been developed in order to meet the needs of new family styles—not always in the best interest of the child—and the present edition of *Adventures with Children* reflects these changes.

It has been heartening for the authors to take note of the increasing numbers of men who now work in classrooms for young children. The many references to teachers as "she", which we have permitted to stand as originally written, may remind the reader, as they reminded us, of the present trend toward the lessening of sex-stereotypes at school, as well as in homes and working-places across the country. This relaxation of role-definition has been a healthy one for children, as it has been for the adults around them.

In these days, when young children are coming in for more attention than ever before, and when too frequently their lives are being shaped by people who have had little or no experience with them or their contemporaries, their chances for healthy growth are beset by real dangers. They run the risk of losing out on childhood altogether. "Learning experiences" appropriate to the six- or seven-year-old are being forced upon the three- or four-year-old before his life has been sufficiently enriched by the active, first-hand, sensory experiences that are the essence of his learning style. While it is evident that children of three or four or five or six differ from one another as individuals—as do people in any other age bracket—some general statements can be made about what young children are like at any of these ages, about how they learn, and about the role of adults who wish to be their co-explorers in this complicated and ever changing world. Many such observations are included in this book, and we hope that through following the adventures of teachers who have shared their energies and special skills with young children, something of the flavor and importance of this early school world can come alive for new readers.

It is of prime significance that we take time to listen to these children and to let them tell us about themselves and the world as they see it, and that we give them time to grow at their own rates and to be what they are—little children—during these brief and crucial early years.

ELSA BARNOUW
ARTHUR SWAN
1986

Contents

Introduction   *1*

1   The Child Comes to School   *5*

2   The Teachers   *21*

3   Some Rules   *35*

4   Dramatic Play   *49*

5   Physical Development   *63*

6   Conflicts   *75*

7   Routines   *87*

8   Creative Arts   *107*

9   Music   *125*

10   Language   *139*

11   Original Stories   *160*

12   Nature   *173*

13   Kindergarten's Wider World   *193*

14   Deep Thoughts and Special Days   *210*

15   Birthdays and Good-bys   *231*

Our Thanks to

Ruth Davis Perry, who suggested the writing of this book, and who gave unstintingly of advice and encouragement.

Rose Wachter, whose insistence on making the book of value to teachers in Waukegan and Walla Walla helped widen its scope.

Dr. C. Ivar Hellstrom for his wise counsel and friendly support.

The teachers, especially at The Gardens Nursery School-Kindergarten and The Riverside Church Nursery School, who willingly shared anecdotes and experiences.

The countless parents and children who have enriched our lives and whose experiences make up most of this book.

Introduction

"Why isn't my shadow here when it rains?"

"Are you my friend?"

"Why do I have to eat *that?*"

"Why does Brucie have a little thing to make wee-wee out of, and I don't?"

"Why doesn't Daddy love us any more?"

Such questions may perplex or embarrass or charm or annoy us, but asking them is as necessary for young children as it is typical of them. There are so many things to learn, so many mysteries to unravel!

Now full-grown, supposedly in wisdom as in stature, we adults still find ourselves plagued by unresolved questions. We may use three-syllable words to phrase them, but they generally prove to be only grown-up versions of some queries we could not answer when we were younger. Like the children's questions above, our adult problems fit into one of these six perennial questions:

1. Who am I?
2. Why am I here?
3. Where did I come from?
4. Where am I going?
5. Who are you?
6. What kind of world is this?

As soon as we look at this list, various answers present themselves, but the further we pursue them the more distant any sure conclusion appears. Wise men and women spend their years in search of conclusive solutions to these riddles, only to be contradicted by other sages with answers equally convincing. The nature of our existence seems to leave such issues eternally up in the air, and search or study as we will, we shall end our lives as much in wonderment as when we started them. Yet search and study we must. The questioning adult, like the questioning child, is on the road to maturity and understanding.

Some of the children with whom this book is concerned have not even the simple vocabulary needed to ask these questions, yet their lives are already devoted to a wide-eyed exploration for answers that will make sense to them. Particularly among two- and three-year-olds, for whom words are still unwieldy tools, this questioning process is closer to the emotions than to the intellect. Adults must discern and follow the child's silent, inner research, for by the time such feelings can be spoken about, he is already well on his way to forming his own answers.

Neither nursery school nor daycare is a "must" for every child, but they often serve as valuable supplements to the home. Such agencies present young children with a variety of experiences through which they can make discoveries about themselves, fellow beings, and the world around them. The school atmosphere is compounded of freedom and guidance. For the finest blend of these ingredients there are no formulas or recipes except the ones prompted by insight and a healthy sensitivity. In the chapters ahead, children and their parents and teachers will live through actual experiences, observed in a number of early childhood settings. Not one of the six important questions is going to be asked point-blank, nor will any be answered in an explicit way, since dogmatic replies have a habit of stifling further inquiry. Yet the unspoken questions form a framework within which the children's accomplishments and defeats might all be catalogued, and upon which the teachers' goals might be said to be based. The reader who keeps them in mind will see the most commonplace event invested with special value and the simplest learnings of childhood touched with the wonder of fresh discovery.

The Child Comes to School

Mrs. Hammond looks down at her son as the elevator door closes. His hair, usually a tousled mop, is slicked down, and his suit (for a wonder) is still clean. Jeremy might fool anyone into thinking that he was a real gentleman. Anyone but his mother, of course, who has begun to entertain serious doubts. Time was when he could be trusted to beam cherubically at adults and win the most stubborn heart with his guileless "Hi!" That was before his birthday last winter. Now Jeremy is four.

The elevator stops at the second floor of the parish house, and a woman gets on. Mrs. Hammond is too busy with her apprehensions about the approaching interview with the nursery school director to notice this newcomer. Not so Jeremy. He studies the woman intently. Her smock and her fingers are spotted with red paint, for she has been retouching some children's toys. Angular features and stray wisps of hair emphasize a bizarre appearance. Mrs. Hammond suddenly notices Jeremy's close scrutiny of this apparition. "Oh, no!" she thinks desperately. "Don't say anything. You may not be Mother's sweet helper these days,

5

but you *won't* insult a hard-working woman." She mentally implores the elevator to rush to the fifth floor. No more delays! This four-year-old is not to be trusted.

And then it happens. Jeremy looks directly at the lady and asks in a voice that is clear and rather sweet, "Are you a witch? You look like one."

The lady smiles helplessly. Jeremy awaits her answer. Mrs. Hammond prays for a speedy delivery. After an age, the door opens, and she grabs her son forcibly, propelling him toward the director's office. Will they accept a monster in this nursery school? Is it possible that Jeremy can top this latest, frightful moment? Her hot blush has hardly subsided before the director, Mrs. Williams, is standing before them. Mrs. Williams' clear blue eyes and friendly smile set Mrs. Hammond more at ease. She looks at Jeremy and sighs. After all, he is a handsome child. And he is clever, too, if only he will behave sensibly. One can't expect that either, these days.

"How do you do, Mrs. Hammond," Mrs. Williams says. "And this is Jeremy, I suppose."

Act calmly, Mrs. Hammond counsels herself. He has played his ace for today. "Say 'Good morning' to Mrs. Williams, Jeremy," she urges in a sweet tone.

Her gentlemanly four-year-old retreats, scowls and says, "I don't want to go to your stinky school!"

What manner of beast is this? No beast, really. Just a four-year-old. Mrs. Williams, fortunately, is neither abashed nor hurt by this uncouth remark. In a few minutes Jeremy is happily building a house with some large blocks he has discovered in the playroom outside her office.

While he busies himself, his mother tells Mrs. Williams several tales of woe about the painful moments her son has caused her in recent weeks—his bloodthirsty language, his rough and tough manner, his unpredictable moods and comments. "He never used to be like that. What have we done to make him such a little fiend?"

Mrs. Williams listens and nods her head sympathetically.

"You don't need to feel so guilty about him," she says. "There is nothing unique about Jeremy's behavior. We hear the same story over and over again from parents of four-year-olds. Children aren't exactly comfortable living companions at that age. Their moods and struggles remind me of adolescents. One minute they seem almost grown-up, the next they are infants again."

Mrs. Hammond agrees that Jeremy does seem very grown-up sometimes. "He asks the most amazing questions. Just the other day he came to me in the kitchen and stumped me with this one: 'Mommy,' he said, 'where do yesterdays go to and where do tomorrows come from?' "

As the interview proceeds Mrs. Hammond forgets that her son is a fiend incarnate, sent to earth only to put her in embarrassing positions. He now seems an interesting person. After a while she is helped to regard the "witch" incident in a clearer light. There was no insult intended on Jeremy's part. His question was quite sincere. He really wanted to know if she was a witch. He had been told the story of "Hansel and Gretel" and had been frightened by that sinister character. He was not at all certain about witches, for the line of demarcation between fact and fancy is still shaky at the age of four.

"But why did he have to tell you in that disagreeable way that he didn't want to come to school?" Mrs. Hammond finally asks. "Look at him out there. I'm sure he's going to love it."

"He had no way of knowing if he would like it or not," Mrs. Williams assures her. "He has never been to school. He was voicing his uncertainty."

"Maybe I put him on the spot by making him greet you," Mrs. Hammond suggests.

"I think you probably did. It isn't a good idea to try to put words in a child's mouth."

Mrs. Hammond leaves the interview with a hopeful feeling that she may enjoy her four-year-old a bit more in the future. Perhaps she had unconsciously been yearning for those days gone by when he was a cuddly three-year-old who used to clamber into her lap in such a winning way. Yes, she needed to face the fact that her Jeremy was growing up.

Jeremy is only one of thousands of applicants who troop in for interviews with directors like Mrs. Williams as a preliminary step to enrollment in nursery schools all over the country. In this first interview parents are given some idea of the basic philosophy and curriculum of the school, and they, in turn, have a chance to express their own particular needs and concerns, all of which may be important for the staff to know. Most nursery schools admit children a year younger than Jeremy and a few contain groups for children who are still two.

"Well," you may ask, "ought such young children to be at school at all?"

Experience has shown that a half-day program, carefully adapted to the child's stage of development, can be of great value, especially in an urban environment. Nursery school should never be regarded as a substitute for the home, but rather as an agency which supplements what the home cannot provide. Further, in today's complicated society, a full-day program may be required even for the very young. Single parents, as well as couples who find that both partners must hold down full-time jobs, have to scour their neighborhoods for settings that provide the care and the sensitivity, warmth, and attentiveness appropriate to the needs of such young children.

What brings two-year-old Paul to school? There are many reasons. He is an only child. His father is a young college instructor. Paul's room is a small one and looks out on a sunless courtyard. As he wakes one morning he clambers out of bed and hustles into the living room, which also serves as his parents' bedroom. He starts to romp and slide off their bed, but is immediately warned not to do this because Mrs. Hudson downstairs objects to the noise.

While Mommy prepares breakfast, she calls out a series of admonitions to her young hopeful:

"Don't throw the ball in the house! Stop pounding! No, you can't visit Charlie just yet—it's too early. Maybe we'll meet him in the park."

But Paul has to wait a long time to see Charlie. First Mommy has to cook, wash dishes, make the beds, do the vacuuming, take the laundry to the basement, telephone, and do a hundred other little chores which confront the housewife. Paul helps a bit but then starts exploring on his own. His toys begin to bore him. He climbs onto the window sill in the living room so as to get a better view of the traffic eight floors below. There is a protective railing, but Mother has a moment of terror. She gives him a good shaking to remind him never to do that again. Next he examines the electric outlet under the table and begins to poke his finger inside. This experimentation is cut short by an anguished cry from his mother. Because of his intelligence and lively interest, Paul wants to find out about everything. He opens the kitchen gas jets, flushes some toys down the toilet, sprays Mommy's perfume over himself, powders his nose, and drapes her necklaces around his neck. He is so busy that he forgets to go to the toilet. A puddle spreads in the middle of the best rug. There is no evil motive in any of his pursuits, yet they are a terrible source of irritation to his mother, who soon finds her temper strained to the utmost.

"Stop that!" "No!" is her constant refrain. Finally she is ready to go out.

"Go to park?" asks Paul hopefully.

"Not yet, dear," says Mother. "First we have to do the marketing. I haven't anything for lunch."

While his mother waits in long queues, Paul continues his explorations. He sees no reason why he can't help himself to fruit and candy so lavishly displayed on the counters, but again he is told not to touch anything. Suddenly he vanishes. His mother has a terrifying five minutes while she hunts for him up and down the avenue. She finds him by the curb, watching open-mouthed as the traffic thunders by. At last there is a half hour left for the park. But by then both are in such an ill humor that they don't have much fun. Paul gets into several fights with other children, and their mothers call him a bad boy.

That evening Mother consults Father about enrolling Paul in nursery school. They agree that that would be a good plan. What a relief to have Paul in a place where he can explore safely, under the guidance of experienced teachers, with regular playmates, without worrying what the neighbors will say! And while Paul is at school, reasons his mother, I can get my housework done more quickly and then we can have a good time together in the afternoons. After making certain that there is room in the two-year-old group, she tells Paul about nursery school. The fact that his parents are so enthusiastic will make it easier for Paul to cross the threshold into this new adventure when the time comes.

Though Paul's is a fairly typical situation, nursery school is not merely a solution for the busy housewife. It often serves to alleviate a trying home situation. Mark, for example, is by nature a happy, constructive child. Recently, however, his life has become a misery because his one-year-old sister demolishes whatever he starts to construct. Yowls and complaints are the order of the day. At nursery school Mark may still have to contend with would-be vandals, but at least he will be dealing with his peers instead of a baby sister whom he has been sternly cautioned to treat gently.

The case of three-year-old Michael is even more urgent. He is a late-comer in his family. There is a gap of seven years between him and his next older brother. The two girls are already in high school. Michael is a misfit in this household geared to a pace of living far beyond his level. In his desperate desire to make himself one of the family, he strives for accomplishments far beyond his reach. Meanwhile he is losing out on normal childhood experiences. He has won praise for mastering the alphabet, for counting up to twenty, and for being able to pick out "Frère Jacques" on the piano keys. But the strain of keeping up has made him a nervous, irritable, high-strung little fellow who sucks his thumb constantly. Three hours a day in nursery school should give Michael a new outlook on life and on himself. Only among his contemporaries will he be able to discover his real capabilities and inner resources. Once he has found that he need not always be on the receiving end, the pendulum may carry him from extreme submissiveness to efforts to boss the entire class. There is no doubt that it will take many months before Michael can establish a proper balance, but nursery school can help him to work through his particular problem.

Joanna is the only child in a household with four doting adults, each of whom tries to exert a different system of discipline upon her, yet waiting on her hand and foot. In her many attempts to become independent, Joanna has been continually frustrated. She is subject to frequent temper tantrums and often speaks to adults in a hostile tone. Visitors describe her as a "spoiled brat." The parents turn to nursery school for help. Not only can the classroom assist by allowing Joanna a chance to try her wings in the way that she needs, but it can give the family practical suggestions on how to deal with Joanna at home.

Danny's parents are financially secure and can afford full-time domestic help. He has a room full of toys and plenty of play space, so why does he need nursery school? His mother is puzzled about her little boy because he hardly touches his nice toys. He wants to look at television all day or badgers her to read him a story. Furthermore, he whines continually. She had done all she can for Danny but he doesn't seem happy. Perhaps he is lonely. Danny doubtless needs contemporary companionship but he needs more than that. He is bored in his over-protected, well-oiled household. He yearns to be a brave hero, courageous and tough like the characters on TV. Actually he is so timid that the children next door call him a baby. Danny has never had a chance to cope with simple everyday problems. He needs to venture forth in a setting not altogether free of hazards. Real living includes a few hard knocks and bumps. Life in nursery school is down-to-earth. It can offer Danny some of the adventures he craves, but on a level with which he can cope.

The applications which pour in year after year are sufficient proof that a half-day nursery school, for countless reasons, is a boon to children and their families.

On the other hand, a full-day setting may be a vital necessity for some. Ms. Ellison, a single parent, has just found a satisfying and reasonably well-paid position in an architect's office. She now requires a humane and well-organized setting, geared to the needs of her three-year-old son, Victor. She has begun to despair, for in her search for an alternative to a full-time baby-sitter, she has failed to find a day-care program that comes anywhere near her expectations. The first one she visited was orderly and clean, but the people there seemed oddly impersonal and unimaginative. The children were cared for, but they went from one activity to another without much spontaneity. What would happen to Victor there? She didn't want him to lose his sense of humor or get into trouble for wanting to have some fun. Further, their whole day had to be spent indoors.

Her second visit brought her to an entirely different setting. It was a noisy and untidy place, where the adults were well-meaning enough but never seemed to notice when a squabble broke out or when a nose needed to be blown. Free play was allowed, but there appeared to be no guidance or control. Many of the books were torn and the toys broken. Ms. Ellison had begun to think that she would have to settle for the safe but limited companionship of her baby-sitter, or reluctantly give up her job and look for part-time work.

Now, after a talk with the director of The Child's World Day Care Center, she feels that she has found just the place for Victor. The director has explained the general philosophy of the school and has gone through the day's schedule with Ms. Ellison. There seems to be enough flexibility to allow Victor a long afternoon nap when he needs it, or some quiet activities to pursue when other children are resting.

Ms. Ellison has taken an immediate liking to the director. She has discerned a twinkle in her eye, which bodes well for Victor's sense of humor, and she has found an optimistic spirit in the other members of the staff. Ms. Ellison is allowed to spend some time observing, both indoors and outdoors. She is impressed with the variety of sensible equipment and the well-planned play space. The children all seem happily occupied. Furthermore, she can stay with Victor, until he feels comfortable in this new setting, for half an hour each morning before she goes to work!

Entering nursery school is an important event in a young child's life and may be attended with difficulties. If Mother has been a constant companion since her youngster's birth the tie may be so strong that both will dread the parting. Allowing for a gradual adjustment to nursery school, with mother staying by, is likely to produce a healthier start than insistence upon an abrupt leave-taking. Once the child is assured that his mother will not leave, he is more able to devote himself to the business of examining the classroom and warming up to his new teachers. Many nursery schools begin with short sessions and arrange to have only a handful of newcomers together at first, with their mothers sitting by. Although this may not be easy for the teaching staff, there are advantages in the long run. While getting a first glimpse of nursery education and becoming acquainted with each other, the mothers can also observe their children taking their first steps toward independence. Furthermore, confidence in the teaching staff is of major importance if a mother is to entrust her child to the school's care. A few days of visiting in the classroom may do wonders in this respect.

When a child seems ready to face the school situation on his own, his mother may leave for brief periods at first, "to make a phone call" or "to drink a cup of coffee." One thing which is insisted upon is that the child is made aware of the parent's departure. Now and then a mother, dreading a scene, will suggest leaving quietly while her young one is absorbed in play. This might work out smoothly for the moment, but think of the devastating effect on the child when he discovers that she has gone without warning! How can a child trust anyone who behaves in this way? Mommy might leave at any time without letting me know, would be the child's obvious conclusion. No, it is far better for both to face the facts—even if it means tears. Most young children have lived so short a time that they have not had sufficient experience to know that Mommy really will come back. By undergoing the daily process of having her leave and return, the child gradually gains assurance that he will not be permanently deserted. This period can present real problems for the working mother. Compromises must sometimes be made, but one must be aware that they are likely to have an impact on the child's adjustment to school.

The more a parent understands, trusts, and feels at ease in a school situation, the better it will be for the child. For this reason, preliminary discussions and parent-teacher workshops for the upkeep of school equipment are standard practice in many a nursery school. Friendly visits to the family by members of the teaching staff may also make it easier for children to cross the hurdle from the familiar security of home to the bigger world beyond.

The child's initial adjustment to nursery school can have enormous bearing on his future attitudes toward school and society in general. The discovery that there are people beyond the family circle who care deeply about him and will stand by him at all times may be the most far-reaching lesson he can learn during his first year at school.

Two-year-old Beth, whose parents had just been transferred from Japan, was a mournful little creature when
she first came to school. For several days she refused to let
anyone take off her hat, jacket, and leggings in the classroom—perhaps fearing that she would have to stay forever
if these were removed from her. Later, when her mother
left the room for short periods, she wept copiously and
needed frequent reassurance that "Mommy will be back
soon." A teacher noticed that Beth needed to urinate one
morning and invited her to go to the toilet. But Beth pro-
tested that she didn't want to go. "I don't need to," she
sobbed. "I went already—I went in Japan." A week later it
was heartening to hear Beth telling various classmates who
needed comforting, "Your mommy back soon." Beth was
speaking from experience. She now took pride in hanging
her wraps in her locker and no longer dreaded using the
unfamiliar toilet.

Now and then a child comes to school for a week or two
without demur, goes through all the routines and activities
apparently satisfied, and then suddenly begins to protest.
What has happened? He may have been deeply unhappy
from the start but too controlled to let anyone know about
it. Until such a child can be helped to release his inner
feelings he will have difficulty. Though it may be upsetting
and embarrassing to his mother to have her child fling
himself wildly on the floor at her departure, teachers usually prefer this sort of performance to the complete sup-
pression of feelings. The child who gives vent to his emotions and is assured that the adults understand how he feels
has a head start on the one who maintains an outward
calm for fear of censure or being considered "a baby." It is
a strain always to be "a big boy" or "a good girl," so often
expected by parents. There is nothing wrong about crying
when one is unhappy or hurt. It is an outlet provided by
nature.

One three-year-old showed marked antagonism toward
school, saying, "I don't like the ladies there," and making
life miserable for himself. This resistance proved to have

arisen out of his parents' disappointment that their bright son had not been placed in an older group. When they became reconciled to the arrangement, his feelings were promptly reversed and he turned into an enthusiastic group member. Any doubts, disagreements, or feelings of apprehension on the part of parents are easily transferred to the child and can stand in the way of his adjustment. Sometimes it is discovered that Father doesn't really approve of letting his small son go to nursery school, or Grandmother has accused Mary's mother of shirking her duties, with the result that feelings of guilt stand in the way. Without knowing it, some parents are subconsciously reluctant to have their children separated from them, so that it may take weeks, even months, to make the break. This occurs at any of the nursery age levels. Four-year-old Dicky, who habitually went through an agonizing departure scene with his mother, entered the group one morning without a tear or lingering glance. That afternoon he apologized to her for his abrupt leave-taking. She was suddenly aware of the fact that he had been prolonging his behavior more for her sake than his own. Teachers must take into account the fact that placing a child in school for the first time may be as great an emotional experience for the parent as for the child.

Even established school-goers may have temporary setbacks. Four-year-old Sylvia had attended nursery school for a year without special difficulties, but during her second year she began to put up daily resistance against coming to school. She feigned illness, wept when her parents insisted on bringing her, and moped almost all morning in the classroom. Her mother's immediate impulse was to lay the blame on Sylvia's present teachers. But after more honest consideration, she realized that Sylvia's problem had coincided with the arrival of a new baby brother. Sylvia had been the center of attention at home for four years. Now she felt she had to compete for time and affection from her parents. It was suggested that her mother arrange her schedule so as to have an undisturbed lunch with Sylvia when she came home from school. While the baby rested, Sylvia received the undivided attention she craved. Efforts in the classroom are necessarily limited unless the school understands a child in relation to his family.

Teachers soon come to recognize that the influence of home is stronger than that of any outside agency. School may be able to deal with certain problems in the immediate group situation, but to be really effective in the lives of growing children, a working partnership should exist between parents and teachers in which knowledge and insights are shared.

During recent years the status of children as a group has risen tremendously as a result of a vast amount of research and writing in the fields of psychology, psychiatry, education, and allied sciences. It has been impressed upon parents and others that children must be respected. Not fully comprehending this term, and trying hard to live up to the advice of experts, some earnest parents have confused "respecting the child" with catering to his whims. Some of the present-day bumptious conduct of the younger generation is doubtless one of the factors resulting from the exaggerated prominence given to their needs. Impudence, friction, and hostility are often the disappointing outcome of placing children in the limelight.

Whereas children have been riding high during recent decades, their parents have been in the doghouse. Accusing fingers have been pointed at them. Their egos have been sorely punctured because research findings in psychiatry inevitably trace the source of troubles in later life to mismanagement in early childhood. It is all your fault, has been the battle cry. Parents have lost confidence in themselves, have begun to mistrust their common sense and judgment, and snatch hopefully at any advice handed to them.

Although it is well for people to be open-minded to new

ideas and to welcome help in as difficult a task as rearing children, there is nothing more deleterious to the relationships within a family than constant indecisiveness on the part of parents. Children need to look up to their elders—to find in them a rock of dependability and sincerity. If there is any great need nowadays it is for parents to regain their self-respect and confidence.

It is an unfortunate paradox that books which urge parents to be relaxed with their children frequently produce the opposite effect in their readers by making them more self-conscious. Am I doing the right thing? Would Dr. So-and-so approve? Each step must be analyzed and dissected. No act is spontaneous or natural. The result may be that outward conduct will have little relationship to inner feelings. Mrs. Andrews, for example, is speaking in a sugary tone to Jackie, but there are undercurrents of anger. The most annoying part of it all is that Jackie senses quite well how his mother feels and would prefer to have her come out with it. Parents need to trust their common sense and act naturally. Of course, serious efforts to become better parents by the reading of articles and books, by attending meetings and discussions, and by doing some honest self-appraisal are to be lauded. But people should act according to their best judgment and not go about all the time with feelings of doubt, guilt, and uncertainty.

How can parents achieve this emotional balance? For some it may seem a remote goal. Teachers can sometimes help by being trustworthy friends who have time to listen sympathetically, who are available when specific needs arise, and who sense not only when to give advice but when to withhold it.

Parents often require bolstering. Many feel inadequate in their task of rearing children although they may actually be doing an admirable job. This is especially true of those who sense the importance of the early years and take their responsibilities much to heart.

Some parents need to be encouraged not to be afraid of

their children. They hesitate to say "no" for fear of stirring up enmity and losing their child's affection. Yet children seldom harbor grudges. In fact, they feel infinitely happier in the long run with adults who won't let them do things they should not do. It is especially upsetting for an intelligent child to be allowed to do everything he desires, because such a child has enough sense to know he is stepping beyond the bounds. "Someone stop me, please!" is an unverbalized plea one can often recognize beneath a child's outward conduct.

Nowadays, special problems beset homes where both parents hold down full-time jobs, or where the single parent must be out all day at work. Returning home after a long day, they may find themselves too fatigued to deal with the frictions or demands with which their children confront them. The children, too, have spent long hours away from home. Exhaustion aside, these parents may feel that in some way, they have "deserted" their children by entrusting them to other adults for so much of the day. The result of this conflict of needs and feelings may be that the parents settle for giving in to their children's demands, even unreasonable ones, simply in order to keep peace or to make up for having been unavailable all through the day. Often, a frank talk with an understanding teacher or director can help a parent set the course straight again.

Parents are sometimes chagrined when their recalcitrant offspring respond readily to the requests of their teachers. Should teachers ever run the risk of feeling smug because of their undoubted success with certain children, they should be reminded that they have the advantage of objectivity which is very difficult for parents to maintain. It is a relatively simple matter for a teacher to remain cool and unperturbed when pupils throw tantrums, because such behavior is no disgrace to herself. It is interesting to see what happens when a nursery school teacher gets married and has a family of her own. Some find that rearing one's own family is different from dealing with someone else's children. Others are able to use the wisdom they have acquired through years of training and experience.

A few decades ago it was not unusual to hear a teacher say, "I don't have any trouble with my pupils, but oh! the parents!" At that time people sometimes voiced the opinion that children would be happier if they were brought up in institutions under trained personnel where no harm could come to them from their parents' mismanagement. The findings of research and actual experiments in institutional living have proven the fallacy of such ideas. Furthermore, drastic innovations of this nature are antagonistic to the democratic way of life. The home is still the mainstay of our type of civilization. And though school may be an important subsidiary, the family unit remains first in the child's life.

A small group of four-year-olds were discussing with their teacher what they did when they were frightened.

Laura said, "Do you know what I do? I stay as still as a rock."

Some other children gave their own contributions. Then Laura continued, "Do you know what I do when I'm really, *really* scared? I climb up on my Mommy and stay there."

In simple words Laura had expressed a universal need. The understanding teacher knows that when mothers are no longer close at hand a comforting lap on which to climb may be needed all the more.

"Jack shall have a new master" **2**

The Teachers

"How can you go on working with small children year after year?" "Don't they drive you crazy?" "I should think you would have to carry aspirin with you all the time!" Such comments are not unusual from parents and others outside the field of nursery education.

It is true that children are often noisy, tiring, irritating, and unappreciative of one's efforts. They can drain one's energies to the last ounce, yet there is an eternal fascination about them that makes one forget their exasperating qualities. The truth is that they force grownups to grow up. They shake us out of our self-centeredness, make us plumb the depths and look with fresh eyes on our complacent attitudes. Their trust in us forces us to be more trustworthy. Their unprejudiced minds make us ashamed of our prejudices. Their need for love makes us more loving. And in our efforts to understand their troubles we adults gain deeper insight into ourselves.

To meet the varied individual needs of young children, nursery schools and daycare centers provide more than one teacher to every group. Sometimes three or even four workers find themselves teamed together, some well-

trained and experienced, others less so. The example they
set in cooperative teamwork is of tremendous importance
and has its impact on the group.

Among staff members who have worked together successfully for a period of time a kind of sympathetic understanding can be built up so that a gesture or a single word
suffices when something needs to be done. Each teacher
finds her place where the need seems greatest at the moment; once one of the staff has taken responsibility for any
situation, none of the others interferes or offers help unless
it is asked for. Needless to say, teamwork is not achieved
overnight. Frequent changes in staff are not only confusing
to the children; they also make impossible a solidarity of
approach and a smooth meshing of minds. It is much easier
all around if teachers stick together as a working group for
at least a year.

On a stormy morning toward the end of January, a
whirlwind of squabbles and tears broke out in a four-year-
old group. Stewart, long under the thumb of his insepara-
ble crony, Edward, came to the staff in real distress.
Edward had been teasing him since the moment they entered the room together. Not content with sly jabs and
pokes, Edward had thrown his playmate into a sad state by
taunts and threats, all of which were taken at their face
value by credulous little Stewart. He wept frantically and
returned again and again to his teachers for help. Miss
Brown decided that for the time being the best thing to do
was to separate them, until Stewart was in some condition
to cope with his problem, and Edward had thought of a
more constructive way to play with his longtime pal. Accordingly, the folding doors were pulled to, and the large
room divided into two play areas of equal space. Stewart
was invited to use the large hollow blocks on one side, in
the company of some industrious children under the supervision of Miss Brown. Edward and his rather obstreperous
gang of toughs took over the other side. Keeping an eye on
this group was Mr. Stern, the assistant teacher, busy with

note pad and pencil. The boys were continuing to conspire against Stewart, and bits of their subdued conversation were audible: "Let's scare him." "We should smack his eyes out." Gradually, however, most of this group drifted toward the unit block shelves and began to build a garage. Edward continued to stand near the door, intending to rush into the other room and terrorize Stewart the minute Mr. Stern's back was turned. Philip, a tense little fellow who looked up to Edward, stayed close to his idol and invented new ideas for doing away with Stewart. When after fifteen minutes had passed and Mr. Stern saw that these two showed no signs of seeking constructive activity, he asked if they would like to dictate a story. They promptly decided that what they wanted to do was write a letter to Stewart. With obvious relish, they dictated the following message:

We're going to tie Stewart's hands in back of him. (Edward)   And then we're going to follow him with a rifle. (Philip)   And shoot him. (Edward)   I'm going to bring a lot of guns, and we're going to shoot him. (Philip)   Then we're going to bring a horse to school, and he'll scare Stewart. (Edward)   Kick him! (Philip)   We're going to ride our horses. (Both)   My horse is going to bite Stewart. (Edward)   Stewart broke Margot's gun with his hands. He ripped the Scotch tape. That's all that made us mad at him. (Both)

Mr. Stern looked the letter over and after a moment suggested that they might slide it under the dividing wall. With whoops of delight, Edward and Philip slipped the letter along the floor, under the folding doors, and into the other room. Almost at once a mad scramble near the wall and cries of "Miss Brown! Miss Brown! A letter!" told them that their frightening note had been discovered. They hopped around Mr. Stern in glee. He, in turn, was wondering exactly how Miss Brown would carry the project through. Nothing quite like this had turned up before, but he knew that it was not likely to stump her. He crouched by the wall with Edward and Philip, listening and waiting for some response.

On the other side of the wall, Miss Brown had seen the folded paper as it slid under the doors, and had only a moment for vague speculation about it before it was presented to her by a crowd of excited children. "Miss Brown! A letter!" they shouted, crowding around her. "Read it to us! What does it say?" She glanced at its contents.

"It's from Edward and Philip," she said, "and I guess it's mainly for Stewart." An idea popped into her head, but she decided to hold it until she could gauge Stewart's reaction to these additional threats. He clung to her, trembling with anxiety, as she read it aloud. It was obvious that he believed every word, and could see himself being bitten by horses and shot in a million places. He stood by her silently when she finished reading it.

It was time to try her idea, she decided, since Stewart was in no condition to cope with the situation himself.

"Wouldn't you like to write them an answer?" she asked. The other children welcomed the suggestion, and soon even Stewart was smiling as he contributed his replies:

I'm going to get an elephant to kill him—Edward, not Philip. I'm going to get a tiger. (Stewart)   And I'm going to get a big, bad wolf. (Susan)   And I'm going to get a lion. (Roberta)   And I'm going to get a hundred guns. (Susan)   I would get a rifle and scare them away. (James)   I'm going to get a tiger. (Stewart)   And I'm going to get the whole wide world. (Susan)   I'm going to get a big, big, sharp knife and poke them in the eye. (George)   That's all. (Stewart)

This message was, in turn, passed across the way. A few more threats were tossed back and forth, but their venom soon ran dry. Before long, everyone was laughing at the idea of exchanging letters via the crack under the sliding doors. The content became mildly jocular, and toward the end, rather meaningless. The teachers stood by until they were convinced that the children did not need their moral support any longer. By the end of the morning, tension had relaxed and the two boys were pals again.

Without complete confidence in each other, neither Miss Brown nor Mr. Stern could have brought the problem into the open so easily or settled it in such a satisfying way. There was no worry about catching Miss Brown off guard, nor was she annoyed at having been involved in a project started by Mr. Stern. This kind of give-and-take is vital to a creative school program.

In a very real way, the ability of the staff to have fun together and appreciate each other's company has its effect on the group. Children are quick to sense a comfortable camaraderie among their teachers, and unconsciously respond to the friendly spirit they feel around them. A staff composed of cold or suspicious adults is likely to find a similarly unpleasant atmosphere developing within their group. Naturally, one does not expect that each co-worker is going to prove a bosom friend, or even that day-to-day relationships will always be smooth, but given a certain amount of maturity on both sides, friction can be reduced to a minimum and a pleasant working relationship maintained.

A healthy sense of humor is a prerequisite of this profession. Children are delighted when an adult responds to their silly talk and clownish behavior. It is no crime for the teacher to unbend now and again and add her bit to a session of nonsense patter. Nor does it hurt if she laughs at a particularly odd grimace. Why not relax and enjoy such things with the rest of the class? A teacher in a group of four-year-olds once fell dramatically to the ground after being "shot" by a gang of desperadoes. Everybody got a laugh out of it, and no one was worried about loss of dignity. Once when Miss Brown put her head into the doll corner to see what was going on, she was ousted by Pegeen, who shouted at her in a raucous but jolly voice, "We don't want you in here! Get out!" Allowing her own carefree mood to get the better of her, Miss Brown put on an exaggeratedly woeful expression and pretended to weep. "Boohoo!" she wailed, in an overdrawn imitation of a rather frequent four-year-old response to rejection. "Pegeen won't let me play! Mr. Stern, make them let me in the doll corner!" What laughs went up! An encore was requested and the tragic scene was repeated. After that day, Pegeen evidenced a chummier feeling toward Miss Brown than she had before.

An impasse can often be averted by timely humor on the adult's part. One day a group of young fours began chanting in loud, insistent tones:

> "We want cookies! We want cookies!
> We don't want old graham crackers."

Though a mere whim had prompted this chant, the demand began to snowball rapidly and it looked as if a revolution were imminent.

"All right, all right," said the student teacher who happened to be in charge of refreshments. "I have some scrumptious cookies for you! Wait till you see them. They have coconut and marshmallows and pistachios inside, and lots of fudge frosting on the outside. Would you care to try one?"

"Yes, we would," came the chorus.

As she solemnly served the familiar graham crackers, each child, with a knowing grin, pretended to relish this luscious repast.

Joining in children's make-believe often strikes a responsive chord between adults and children. A kindergarten group in a large church-sponsored school had the following conversation one day while seated at their snack table.

ADELE *[to the teacher]:* I looked in your house yesterday. My
       mother took me there.
DOUGLAS: I did too. I went in the back and hid.

ROB: I was playing Santa Claus and I left a present at your house, but you won't see it until Christmas.

EDWIN: I went down your chimney.

DOUGLAS: Me too.

TEACHER: I thought I heard someone—did you see each other?

DOUGLAS: Yep.

TEACHER: It's a wonder you didn't get burned. Oh, that's right, I didn't have the fire going.

DOUGLAS: It wouldn't make any difference, because we have a hose that you can't see or hear the water.

ROB: I have special shoes, my Sunday ones, and you couldn't hear me when I walked around.

MARK: They are just fooling.

DOUGLAS: I went on my magic carpet.

TEACHER: Do you have a magic carpet? I do too.

EDWIN: Where is it?

TEACHER: I park it on top of the church when I come to school.

ADELE: Maybe the bells will knock it away.

TEACHER: I don't part it too close to the bells, because it might hurt the carpet's ears. *[Children all laugh.]*

MARK *[jumping up and going to the teacher]:* You're only fooling.

TEACHER: I always go home on my carpet. I saw Nancy yesterday, because I go down Riverside Drive.

NANCY *[grinning]:* I saw you.

BOB: I saw you at 102nd Street.

MARK *[hitting at the teacher]:* It's not true.

TEACHER *[whispering in Mark's ear]:* It's only make-believe. *[To the other children]* Nancy was so surprised to see me, weren't you?

NANCY: That's right. I was surprised.

But working with young children is not always fun. Anybody entering the teaching profession must be prepared for innumerable bad moments. These always seem to come at times when one is most desirous for a smooth morning. Things get out of hand, hostilities flare up, bumps and bruises have to be attended to, and nerves are stretched to the breaking point. All nursery school teachers are familiar with such days and they sometimes wonder why they go on in the profession. Sharing their troubles with fellow staff members does a lot to revive their enthusiasm and confidence.

Miss Blackburn, a young teacher, was notified that her five-year-old group was to be visited by a distinguished educator. This great lady entered just as twelve children were filing into the book corner to hear a story. Miss Blackburn welcomed the guest and invited her to join the group. As the children pushed and shoved for seats and waved books at her, saying, "Read this one!" she selected what she hoped was a sure-fire hit. "Nothing can go wrong if I read this," she reasoned. "It has always been their favorite." She opened the book and announced that she was ready to begin. She read well, and secretly hoped that her visitor would be pleased with her choice and her presentation. But it soon became apparent that the story was not going over. Titters and laughter kept interrupting the train of thought. Laura and her cronies were whispering, their voices gradually growing louder and louder until Miss Blackburn could ignore them no longer.

"Laura," she said, "are you still interested in hearing this story?"

"Yes," came the response, but it did not sound very convincing.

Miss Blackburn picked up the narrative again, this time doing her utmost to make it interesting. But once more she was thwarted. Several children around Laura had become so engrossed in some private discussion that they were totally unaware when their teacher's voice stopped abruptly. Miss Blackburn listened. One or two sentences were audible through the babel of jabber.

"It's so funny!" A man gets hit on the head!" "Ha-ha!"

Soon the whole group had forgotten the story. Everyone was involved in lively conversation except Miss Blackburn and her visitor. It seemed hopeless to cope with this uproar.

The visitor leaned forward and said with a sympathetic smile, "You seem to have mutiny on your hands."

Miss Blackburn agreed and managed a wan smile. She was determined to establish order and end the period with something constructive. She raised her voice and said, "Laura!"

Laura looked up.'

"What are you all talking about? What is so funny?"

"My comic," said Laura. "A man gets hit on the head."

"Have you had enough of this story?" Miss Blackburn began. Before she could get any further, a great cry of "Yes! Yes!" came from all her restless audience.

"Well, what would you like to do?" she asked.

"Read my comic," Laura piped up in a determined voice.

"Yes!" "Laura's comic!" "I'm tired of that story!" "Laura's comic!"

Miss Blackburn was stunned. Read a comic book? That hardly seemed like suitable nursery school literature. And there was the visitor to consider, too. What would *she* do in this dreadful position?

"I don't care to read comics at school," she said at last. "Laura, you ask your mother to read it to you at home."

"My mother won't read it to me," was the disconcerting reply.

"You read it! You read it!" shouted twelve persistent voices.

What else was there to do but accept the majority opinion? Miss Blackburn gave Laura permission to get the comic from her locker. A troop of jubilant friends followed her and soon returned in a riot of delight with Laura at the fore, waving a gaudy magazine. Miss Blackburn accepted it with feelings of misgiving. She opened it. At once a great silence descended on her group. Not a whisper was heard. Every face was turned toward her, every eye bulging with anticipation. She began to read. Her audience was rapt, breathless, awed. Never had she received greater attention. And never had she read literature on a lower plane. She became hopelessly confused. Every other word was "Biff!" "Bang!" or "Zowie!" She lost the thread of plot, apologized, retraced her steps in hopes of making better sense of it. No matter. No one cared. Her group was entranced. The comic ended, she ushered her blissful children into the rest room, where they lay down like lambs and rested without demur. Miss Blackburn brightened up. Her guest departed, after letting drop some words that fell like balm on a tender wound: "You handled that situation nicely. You have a fine group of children. Thank you so much. Good-by." As she watched her walk down the hallway, Miss Blackburn took stock of the situation. She concluded that if she had not been so desirous of impressing her visitor, she would have had a better relationship with the children from the start. Over the lunch table an hour or so later, she shared her sad tale with the staff and laughed as much as anyone over the story of her discomfiture.

The needs of two- and three-year-old children bring staff members into frequent physical contact with them, but the warmth and attention these youngsters require must be balanced by good common sense and objectivity. Great danger lies along the pathway of emotionalism. Mrs. Kennedy, a student teacher, stated frankly at the first of the year that her inability to have children had caused her much unhappiness. She soon became so attached to Robbie that he deliberately played tricks on her, conscious that his hold on her was so strong that she would take almost anything. This relationship was unsatisfactory on both sides, and was still unresolved when Mrs. Kennedy left the group. Shortly before her departure, she came to Robbie and said, "I won't be seeing you after this week. This is one of my last days at school." Robbie, sensing her wish for a fond good-by, jumped into the air, and shouted, "Goody, goody!" Satisfaction of her own need for love would have been better worked out away from school.

On the other hand, objectivity can be carried to such an extent that it robs the teacher of any personality at all. One mother, after observing in a New York school, said with some surprise to the director, "Why, they're not like teachers! They *love* the children." It is sad to think that this profession has gained a reputation for lovelessness or lack of human warmth. To find the balance between the two extremes calls for more than book learning. A happy frame of mind, good health, and serenity are almost indispensable.

Even seasoned teachers may find themselves developing a special interest in one or two children, taking notes on their behavior and observing their actions almost to the exclusion of the rest of the group. Honest analysis may show that the teacher has identified herself with these favorites. Perhaps she was shy in her childhood: she may watch Sheila with great sympathy, for Sheila has had trouble in making friends of her classmates. Miss Harrison's mother died when she was a child: this year she finds herself writing note after note about Lilian, whose mother died a few months ago.

There are many pitfalls along the way—habits one may have fallen into unconsciously—and it is refreshing to be put wise to them through the clear-sighted mimicry of the children. They are quick to pick up vocabulary, tone of voice, posture, manner, and habits of dress. Miss Feldman laughed when she heard Tony say to another child, "Now be *steady*, or you'll have to leave the doll corner," but she was careful not to overdo her use of "steady" from that day on. Teachers' habits, dress, and idiosyncrasies are discussed around the dinner table in children's homes, and parents often bring back accurate second-hand accounts of happenings at school.

Knowing that their classroom behavior is under constant scrutiny is likely to make teachers uncomfortable unless they feel sure of their ability as teachers. Call it self-confidence or the courage of one's convictions or whatever you will, this quality is of tremendous importance. One calls upon it in periods of waiting, when a child's progress seems to be at a standstill. Without the long-range vision that comes with a knowledge of the factors that affect children's growth, weeks of patient observation would be hard on many a conscientious teacher.

It is when adults do the planning alone, when they maneuver children and treat them as things, that programs meet with disaster. In contrast with older traditions in which the teacher carried full responsibility, modern classrooms try to allow everyone to carry his own share of the weight in a democratic way. Children should be allowed to give what they can, and to make choices where they are able to choose wisely. Giving too many choices only confuses and frustrates children, but care must be taken to give them enough of the simple decisions they are capable of making.

A six-year-old alumna of a small nursery school came back one day for a visit. The director asked how she was getting along in first grade.

"I don't like my new school," Katy replied. "It isn't very much fun." She gave three interesting reasons for her disillusionment: "Well, Miss Stone talks all the time. She just says everything, and we don't ever get a chance to say anything. . . . Remember last year, when we cut out that pumpkin? I used a big, sharp knife, and we smelled the insides when it was open. And we took the seeds home and they grew! Well, Miss Stone made our jack-o'-lantern all by herself, And she put it on a high shelf where we couldn't touch it. She said it was just to look at. . . . We used to be silly sometimes in your school. Miss Stone won't let us do anything. She says we have to behave at school."

More than likely Miss Stone is unhappily aware that her methods are too dictatorial for an ideal school situation. Faced with an overcrowded room and no assistance, what else can she do but crack down when things threaten to get the least bit out of hand? This is not the school she studied about in college. No doubt she feels drained and dissatisfied when she locks up her classroom and trudges home.

No teacher finds her situation perfect. In every school, problems arise that were not touched upon in education courses. It is hard to reconcile reality with the ideal. And yet, the struggle of bringing the two closer together carries with it rewards far richer than those hinted at in the texts.

Faith, both in her ability as a teacher and in the potentialities of her pupils, characterizes the mature teacher. Confidence in her work should not be confused with complacency or a refusal to look beyond her classroom walls for fear of innovations. She is open to new ideas and looks upon her fellow workers not as rivals but as co-workers in a common enterprise. She willingly shares her findings and knowledge for the universal good.

The mature teacher can also be recognized by the respect which she shows her pupils. This means that she recognizes them as individuals with need for a balance between carefree play and responsibility. She allows each child to progress at his own particular rate. Instead of rushing in eagerly with answers and information, she encourages children to search for themselves, even if this may be a slow and laborious procedure. She needs to be well-informed but should not set herself up as an Answer Man. Her task is to participate in joint inquiry. "Let's find out," should be her motto. This is particularly important when philosophic or religious topics arise. The dogmatic individual is a dangerous leader, for such a person gives no chance for speculation. Young children are likely to accept whatever they are told because they do not have sufficient experience to challenge statements.

Because the teacher's attitudes are so easily transmitted to her small pupils it matters a great deal what her philosophy of life is. How does she feel about the world of nature, for example? Does she only accept its more pleasant manifestations evident during springtime when blossoms burst open and birds return? How does she feel about the insects

in her garden and the hawk hovering overhead? Does she*
judge the predator and scavenger from a moral point of
view, or has she learned to recognize tht all creatures have
an important place in the delicately balanced, intricate
web of life? They are all part of the wonder of nature.

Although the mature individual avoids forcing her opinions on others she is not a flabby, vacillating creature. She
stands on firm ground in her beliefs, yet is open to further
learning. She can accept suggestions and criticisms. She
does not claim to have the final answers but will state her
point of view if this is asked for. Discouragements and setbacks do not make her falter or give up, for she has a long-
term viewpoint which recognizes that growth in children
may be very slow. She maintains a deep-seated trust in
each child's desire to grow toward maturity and provides
the friendship and moral support which are needed for this
long, uphill climb.

---

*We hope that here, and throughout the book, the always
implied—and intended—"she or he" is clearly understood.

"Red light! Green light!" 3

Some Rules

A good school is an example of democracy at work on a small scale where teachers, children and parents are all learning together. "To each according to his needs, from each according to his ability" might well be the nursery school motto. Each person, whether child or adult, is encouraged to develop the best that is in him. This naturally implies recognition of the rights of all the others to do so too. Limits are necessary for safety, comfort, and the general welfare. Each school has some understood "rules" which govern conduct. These are not inflexible but serve as helpful guides in social relationships and the use of equipment. They undergo modification as the children gain in maturity.

For example, a general rule in nursery school is that prior use gives prior claim. "You had it first. It's yours," is a theme often repeated by staff members, particularly for two- and three-year-old children. A child should be allowed to finish what he is doing without fear of having his possessions snatched from him. But once he has gone off to something new, the equipment is available to anyone else. Pupils are encouraged to defend their property against encroachment. This may seem like a self-centered philosophy to some readers. How do the children ever learn to share? They do learn to share willingly if the sharing is not forced down their throats before they are ready for it. The term "sharing" to some children merely denotes giving up what they most want to use. A story comes to mind of gentle-manly Dean, who had received a much-longed-for tricycle on his fourth birthday. Dean was allowed to take his new possession outdoors where a number of children had gath-ered to play.An hour or so later he came upstairs with tears in his eyes and asked his mother, "Will it be all right if I have a turn now on my bike?" He had been "sharing," but at what price? Frustration and resentment simmered be-neath the surface.

Children soon discover whether or not adults are fair and consistent in their dealings. Even at the age of two, children begin to sense that just causes will be defended. "Da's mine—I had it first" also implies "Da's Johnny's—he had it first." This is a tremendous lesson to learn. Once this basic idea is established, other steps follow. In the ensuing months and years one may hear teachers saying, "You have been using that wagon a long time, Jimmy. Billy would like a turn too," "Could Phyllis have one of your dolls, Cyn-thia? You have four and she has none." In a setting where justice prevails and children have gained a sense of security, it is very likely that Jimmy will relinquish his wagon (after two or three more rides around the court), and that Cyn-thia will give Phyllis one, or even two, of her dolls. Even before the children are five, these suggestions may not need to come from the teachers. Children will remind each other and will bargain among themselves. That does not mean, however, that all children will be gracious about sharing—even at the age of five.

Almost every year a handful of "hoarders" appears on the nursery school scene. They remind one of misers who gather their possessions about them and guard them zeal-ously. The possessions give no real satisfaction and all en-ergy is consumed in defending them against possible theft.

A most persistent case of hoarding was that of three-year-old Eleanor who would daily sit upon a huge pile of toys like a hen above her chicks. She collected so many things that her classmates were sometimes short of play equipment, yet they were too afraid of Eleanor to do much about it. The staff tried to steer a halfway course. They set some limits upon Eleanor's mania for collecting while still allowing her to satisfy her tremendous urge. Fortunately, the room was well stocked, so that no one really suffered deprivation. Eleanor had had a hard time in her short life. A climate of increasing violence had forced her parents to leave the Middle East in a hurry. Most of Eleanor's toys had been left behind. She had visited people here and there across the whole breadth of America and, as a consequence, lacked a feeling of permanent roots. It was no wonder she felt urged to cling to the entrancing playthings she discovered at school. Her problems were aggravated by her parents' distress at her behavior. They could regard her only as a selfish little girl. When they were helped to understand the reasons for her conduct a marked change for the better took place, and when Eleanor found by experience that the adults were sympathetic and sensitive to her needs, she began to relax. She realized that the toys would always be there, day after day, and there was no need to stand guard over them all the time. Eventually she could enjoy herself in spontaneous play.

Though basic rules are kept in mind, each individual requires somewhat different treatment. Teachers expect more of one child than another because no two are quite alike. The staff pretends not to notice Julie's first aggressive acts. They are a sign that she is gaining courage to stand up for her rights. But Michael's rough behavior has gone on too long. He needs to gain control over himself. The teachers may step in to put a stop to his continuous fighting and to steer him toward more constructive activity. Bookish Walter takes refuge each day in the library. In order to encourage him to take more active part in full-bodied play, it may be necessary to limit his time there. Other children, who have found a happier balance, are permitted to go in and out at will. Most children accept this variation, recognizing the need for flexible treatment.

There are times when staff members find it necessary to be arbitrary and to take a firm stand. Although the children are encouraged to settle their own differences as far as they can, situations sometimes overwhelm them. The teacher needs to know when to assume a leading role and when to take a back seat. A new piece of equipment is likely to cause stormy weather. If a dozen children demand the same object, what can be done about it? During World War II, Miss Hellman spent a year as supervisor of daytime activities in a residential nursery in England. Equipment was extremely limited, yet she discovered a very good doll carriage carefully hidden away in a closet where the children could not reach it. "We had to put it away because the children fought over it so much," was the explanation. Not daunted, Miss Hellman brought it out one day, after she felt established in her new setting. The children were told beforehand that the carriage was going to reappear, but with the understanding that each person would be allowed to use it for five minutes. A wrist watch was used as an impartial reminder. Though there were many impatient demands for a turn, the day wore on without too much tragedy or conflict. By the end of a week it was no longer necessary for the staff to take a prominent lead in the matter. The children were getting accustomed to having the carriage as part of their everyday equipment and were no longer so desperate to claim it. Though most schools are seldom faced with a situation as extreme as that, now and then there is bound to be a scramble for a favorite plaything. Teachers then institute the same sort of temporary policy.

One morning a strange kitten wandered onto a school playground. The hapless creature was promptly pounced upon by a host of eager fours who happened to be near at hand. They fought for a chance to pet her—one grabbed her head, another her body, a third her tail. A teacher hurried to prevent damage. "One at a time!" she kept reminding. Jamie, the boy who had first caught the kitten, took it upon himself to decide who might hold her next. The others accepted his leadership—oddly enough, this often happens. He proved to be unusually fair, so that each child eventually had a chance to hold the kitten. The teacher merely stayed by to keep an eye on events.

Obviously, in supervising children, safety comes first. Many a nursery school teacher has wished she possessed eyes at the back of her head as well as in the front. No matter how conscientious and alert she may be, mishaps do occur. Bloody noses, scratches, bites, cuts, bumps, and bruises seem to be an inevitable part of childhood. Hazards are not entirely eliminated from the program. It would be a very unreal situation if they were. The world is a hazardous place and children need to learn how to take increasing care of themselves in it.

Swings, seesaws, climbing frames, shovels, hammers, saws, ropes, and scissors offer some obvious hazards, but many other things, if misused, can also cause accidents. For example, a block if thrown can be a painful weapon, and so can sand. Hence rules are enforced to insure that only balls and beanbags may be thrown. Only specified places may be used for climbing or jumping.

Ropes offer endless ideas for play, especially to fours and fives. In addition to being used for skipping, they serve as props in many a dramatic enterprise, as a fireman's hose, a fishing line, a lasso, a gas pump line, or a cable by which to fasten a ship to its moorings. While these fascinating games progress, teachers are alert to dangers involved, and establish rules for safety when the need arises. Every year children start tying up one another. The staff then makes sure that the rope is tied in a safe place, never around the neck. The children see the sense in this and cooperate remarkably

well. If they continue to exercise similar control and caution when allowed to handle ropes outside the school situation, their teachers have passed the real test of good teaching. Unless the desired attitudes and habits are carried
beyond the school walls they have not really been learned.
The teacher whose group goes haywire as soon as she leaves
the room is not a good teacher no matter how impressive
her control may appear to be when she is present. Her type
of discipline has not taken firm root because it was imposed
from above. Self-discipline is the only type which can be
relied upon. Although two- and three-year-olds of necessity
lean more heavily upon adult guidance and direction, they
are gradually gaining habits of self-control. As the children
grow in experience they can be expected to take more and
more responsibility for their actions. People who are old
enough to handle tools can be expected to use them properly. Children must be reminded when digging in the earth
to keep shovels below shoulder level to protect heads
nearby, and a prompt stop is put to ambitious woodsmen
who take a notion to use the shovels for chopping down
trees or shrubs, for property also needs to be respected.

Unfortunately, very few city nursery schools have playgrounds that include the restful beauty of grass lawns,
trees, shrubs and flowers. In this respect, suburban and
country schools have a distinct advantage. In hot weather,
especially, even a little grassy spot is an oasis for city children, and if they are lucky enough to have a garden and a
tree or so, they are fortunate indeed. Of course, if they
were permitted untrammeled use of such grounds, the
place would soon be bare. Climbing has to be restricted to
the playground jungle gyms and monkey bars, for trees
would eventually perish under the weight of a large flock
of junior Tarzans. Digging is restricted to the earth plot
(which may best be left as a "digging patch" all year
around, without flowers, so that city children can enjoy
working with the earth) and sand play takes place only in
the sandbox. Lawns are a delight, but these too must be

used with discretion. In summer, fall and winter months young feet cannot do great damage, but in springtime when tiny shoots are struggling for existence in soggy soil, it is wise to rope off the grass plots. "Keep off the grass" signs, fashioned by kindergarten carpenters and painters, serve as helpful reminders to parents as well as children.

At the kindergarten level the alert teacher can find opportunities to encourage beginning self-government within her group. One five-year-old group had a rule that the door to the small library in the corner of the room should be left open except when a teacher was there with the children. Despite the fact that this regulation was quite well understood, the door had a mysterious way of closing frequently during the morning. As reminders were of no avail, the teacher called a group discussion. Everyone knew the rule and recognized the reasons for it. What could be done to enforce it? Severe penalties were suggested by some children, but were rejected by others. Then somebody thought of a plan of keeping the door open by placing an adult chair in front of it—and, as an additional precaution, piling a lot of building blocks on top of it. This suggestion was unanimously accepted. The teacher agreed to let them try this plan but added the suggestion that a committee be assigned to attend to the details. The following day the chair was set in place as a doorstop, and a pile of blocks was loaded upon it. At the close of the morning the blocks had to be replaced on their shelves. This procedure was followed for three or four days, but finally a boy announced, "This is silly! It takes too much time and it uses up blocks we need for our building." His classmates agreed. "You could write a sign and put it up with Scotch tape," suggested someone. This was considered a fine idea. So the teacher printed a sign—according to instructions— and a child stuck it on the door. Though it is doubtful that anyone could actually read it, everyone knew what it said, and the "Open Door Policy" was established once and for all. By encouraging the children to work out their own solution, this problem was mastered far more successfully than if autocratic methods had been attempted.

In the kindergarten group in a large city church, in which the trip to and from the playground entailed various hazards, an incident occurred which led to the following discussion.

TEACHER: Yesterday, you know, Rosemary and Ellen ran out of school to the street. Do you think that was good thinking?

ELLEN AND ROSEMARY *[giggling]:* Yes, it was.

CHORUS: No!

TEACHER: Why not?

PAUL: They could get hit by an automobile.

TEACHER: Exactly.

CHUCK: Even sometimes when the light is red, fire engines might go through.

ELLEN: Sometimes cars too.

TEACHER: You're right. The drivers see the red lights, but they don't always stop.

BOBBY: You shouldn't go on the street.

ROSEMARY: And there are kidnappers too.

BOBBY: What are kidnappers?

TEACHER: They are people who pick up children and keep them till the children's parents give them some money.

CHUCK: I heard about them. Ambulances go through red lights too.

TEACHER: That's true; someone may be very sick and the ambulance has to get them to a hospital in a hurry. If any of the children ever want to go on a trip, they can ask the teachers, and we can plan one. In fact, I thought maybe you would like to go on one today, because I heard the children saying that they would like to go to the bowling alley.

PAUL: I'd like to go to the bells.

CHUCK: Not me—they're scary.

TEACHER: Well, we just went to the bells, but there is another place we haven't seen. There is a beautiful window on the tenth floor which shows little children from all different countries. We can take a vote. You can put up your hand to go to the bowling alley or to go to see the window—but remember, just vote for one.

ELLEN *[to Rosemary]:* Where do you want to go? *(She has moved over close to her.)*

ROSEMARY: To the bowling alley.

[The children voted four to two for the window.]

TEACHER: We'll go to the window then.

ROSEMARY: I wanted to go to the bowling alley.

ELLEN: Me too.

TEACHER: Do you know why we're going to the window?

ROSEMARY: Yes, because the most children want to.

TEACHER: That's right. Rosemary, since you know we can go on trips, why did you and Ellen run out?

ROSEMARY: We didn't want to rest.

TEACHER: That really is a problem, because most children do not like to rest, but why do you think we have to?

PAUL: So we'll get strong.

CHUCK: So our bones will grow.

SHARON: If you're tired.

ROSEMARY: I'm not tired, and I don't like to.

ELLEN: I don't like to.

TEACHER: Well, you know, often people have to do things they don't like to do. Sometimes daddies don't feel like getting up in the morning, but they have to go to work, so they have to get up. Sometimes mothers feel very tired and would like to rest, but they have to keep right on working. And, at school, sometimes we don't feel like cleaning up, but the things have to be put away, so we just have to do it. That's how it is. Everybody has to do things that they don't like to do.

CHUCK: That's right.

TEACHER: So if you don't feel like doing things, we can talk about it. It makes you feel better to talk about the things you don't like. And now it's time for us to go on our trip.

Fives are usually ready for such embryonic town meetings and discussions, but the younger children are less so. Now and then teachers make a stab at it with fours, but the results are seldom worth the effort. Usually everyone gets carried off on ludicrous tangents. A nucleus of one four-year-old group was repeatedly obstreperous going to and from their playground. Because this school was situated in a busy parish house where important activities were in progress, the children were expected to be reasonably quiet in the halls. This is a courtesy which can be acquired. Twos and threes usually followed their teachers in a fairly placid fashion, but these fours had difficulty checking their exuberance. Requests to talk softly, not to run, not to wrestle, and to stay within certain bounds were repeated over and over. The children's desire to play hide-and-seek games while filing through the halls was understandable, but it could not be permitted. However, no amount of explanation or reminding had the hoped-for sobering effect. One morning Mr. Johnson had considerable difficulty rounding up this small herd, some of whom had started running down a long corridor out of sight just as the others reached the classroom door. Ten minutes later, at the milk and cracker table, Mr. Johnson brought up the subject for discussion. Could anyone suggest how to improve the comings and goings to and from the playground? Blank stares at first greeted him.

"Remind us," said someone.

"I have reminded you many times," answered the teacher.

"Speak to us roughly," suggested another.

"I'm afraid I've even done that," he answered with a wry smile.

"Lock them up in the bathroom," suggested an earnest little girl.

"Tie them up with rope so they can't get away."

Once launched on the subject of punishments fours have fruitful minds. "Chop off their heads!" "Put them in jail!" "Throw them out of the window!" etc. etc. It was interesting that the onus was put entirely on the adult. The children apparently failed to realize that they could exercise some restraint themselves. Perhaps the incident goes to show how much young children depend on adults to keep them on the straight path.

Another area in which children need adult guidance and example is in developing a proper regard for materials. It is easy to tell in what homes books are treasured by observing the children's behavior at school. Teachers have a healthy respect for books, all of which they have selected with care and some of which they may have helped to repair. Books are accessible on open shelves in all groups and may be perused at any time. They are perishable, however, and demand considerate treatment. It is wrong to allow books to be trampled underfoot, to be marked up with crayons, or to be stuffed into a doll carriage as freight. Books should serve the purpose for which they are intended.

Puzzle parts are so easily lost that they are best used only on table tops. Scissors, paste, and crayons should also be kept on the table and used for the purposes for which they are intended. It may be fascinating to try out scissors on your neighbor's hair or skirt, but this is not a legitimate occupation. Nor should children be permitted to toss clay balls about the room.

All the things that children long to do have a legitimate basis. They have an urge to climb, to throw, to shout, to run, to jump, to cut, to hammer, to dig, to romp, to wrestle, to fight, to be silly, and to mess about with water, mud, or sand, but they need to be helped to find out where and when to satisfy these urges.

How do teachers enforce these various rules? First of all, they are not discouraged by having to repeat them over and over. They want to make sure the rules are understood. Fortunately, most children do not need lengthy explanations. They are usually quick to recognize the sense behind them and seldom challenge the wisdom of such suggestions. Teachers assume that the children want to live up to them, and that if they fail to do so it is because they have forgotten for the moment. If there is no mistaking the fact that Jonny is deliberately defying the staff, it may be wise to deprive him of the equipment, saying that he obviously is not in a good mood to use it and had better try again another day. A tantrum may develop, but this should not alter the decision. Sometimes it is well to have a showdown. The child discovers that the adult is not to be intimidated and can be counted on to stick to his word. A lot of argument, rationalizing, begging, whining, and other histrionics on the part of children can be discouraged if adults only manage to be consistent. Children who have a reasonable amount of freedom in the way they spend their playtime are usually not averse to accepting normal requests and suggestions from their elders.

If it is not made clear what the limits are, children are sure to waste a lot of time trying to see how far they can go. How can any child settle down to creative work at the easel if he is allowed to experiment all over the surrounding territory and to decorate the radiator and walls? If a child shows a desperate need to express himself by continually going out of bounds, individual therapy may be indicated. Though a considerable amount of therapy goes on unobtrusively by means of the nursery school curriculum, the techniques of the educator and therapist do not exactly coincide. The therapist and the teacher should complement, not duplicate, each other's functions. At school the staff is responsible for the entire group. They cannot let any one child solve his problems at the expense of the others.

Although teachers welcome the active interest of parents, they do not cater to them, nor do they let commercial pressure affect standards. Some years ago, TV programs stimulated a cowboy craze in many classrooms. Children came to school attired in elaborate outfits, with holsters, guns, chaps, boots, and other paraphernalia, which their parents had been badgered into buying. Sometimes competition was rife as to who had the finest costume or the fiercest-looking gun, and these schoolrooms became Wild West scenes with cowboys, sheriffs, and desperadoes charging about on their steeds, shooting off imaginary bullets. Finally, all other interests took second place. Nowadays, characters from outer space, super-heroes, and other reflections of current media favorites dominate the scene, but their effect on group living is precisely the same.

The staff of one large school took a firm stand in this matter. No costume might be worn to school, for a child's activities are limited when he is constantly reminded of the role he has assumed. A large assortment of dress-up clothes was provided in all groups, which could be donned or doffed as the mood dictated. TV-inspired play still persisted but it lost much of its former hectic quality. On one day in the year—at Halloween—the five-year-olds of this school are invited to appear in a favorite costume. If children in the other groups wear a costume or mask this is not frowned upon, but ordinarily there is no genuine interest in this phase of Halloween with children under five, unless it has been stimulated at home. These days, one often sees babes in arms carried around in costume, trick-or-treating with older family members. The infants' eyes are large with a vague excitement, but one wonders what they make of it all. So much stimulation now surrounds Halloween that, for many children, this night has taken on greater glamor and thrill than Christmas or Hannukah. Even at this particular school, Halloween's excitement casts its flickering spell on many of the day's activities.

If children bring guns or other treasures to this school, they are allowed to show them off to their friends, but must then put them away in their lockers until it is time to go home. However, if a child seems to need the comforting presence of a doll or toy to which he is especially attached, this general rule is disregarded. Candies are permitted here only on special occasions when the entire group has an equal share. This prevents surreptitious distribution of sweets to win favor within small cliques. If a child wants to give a piece of candy to a friend it is suggested he do so at the close of school.

Having a chapter devoted to "rules" may give the impression that nursery schools keep a rather large assortment of "thou shalt nots." Actually, a very free, informal spirit prevails. Children find plenty of opportunity to act crazy, to roughhouse, fight, or show off. Most teachers do not clamp down on language which, in polite circles, would be taboo. In an atmosphere of acceptance and understanding, the children soon find that "objectionable" words are not potent.

Confident that they may forge ahead within the prescribed limits, and engaged by the warm support and friendliness of the staff, children feel free to experiment, to acquire skills, and to discover the capabilities within themselves.

Dramatic Play

An active group of four-year-olds in the doll corner is apparently in a hospital. Two patients are stretched out on beds while a busy nurse repeatedly takes their temperatures and pours medicine down their throats. Suddenly there is a cry from Anne, the star performer, who lies prone on the floor. She says she has had an accident. Soon two volunteers arrive with a stretcher to carry her to the hospital. The "thing-wheeler," a little porter's truck, serves as a fine stretcher, only one of its many functions. Anne is dumped rather unceremoniously into a third bed, hastily improvised by pushing two wicker chairs face to face. There she lies so limp and pale that one suspects for a moment that she has really fainted. The four-year-old nurse calls Dr. Johnson on the telephone and begs him to come and give the new patient some penicillin. Dr. Johnson (really plain Mr. Johnson, who up to this moment was unaware that he was anything other than a nursery school teacher) obliges and goes through the motions of giving an injection. Several pairs of eyes watch him with interest. One or two children recoil as if it were all too real and meaningful. Others ask if they may also have an injection.

49

After a while Dr. Johnson says he must go and attend to patients elsewhere and leaves the hospital. The play continues. Visitors arrive bearing gifts, or come to read stories to the sick ones.

Because of its far-reaching influence on the child's physical, emotional, social, and mental growth this type of imaginative play is fostered. The above scene is more than entertaining. It has value from several angles. The good that it does from a physical standpoint should not be overlooked. It may distress some grownups to see children dropping to the ground, apparently shot dead in battle or felled by an atom bomb, but their limbs are getting wonderful practice in relaxation. How good for a child to be able to let himself go utterly limp as he pretends to be dead, wounded, or in a faint! Also, the stretcher bearers are strengthening their back muscles as they carry their patient to her hospital bed.

The value of fantasy play in overcoming fears is well recognized. Disease, accidents, operations, medical treatment, even death, are potential, if not actual, dangers in the child's life. By approaching them on an imaginative level, a certain amount of familiarity and insight may be acquired. Children sometimes manage to gain the necessary pluck to face a trying situation after having first gone over it many times on the level of fantasy. Those who have had a deeply upsetting experience are helped to overcome its effects by giving it release through dramatic play or other forms of expression.

Sally was repeatedly hospitalized during the first four years of her life, and experienced oxygen tents, penicillin injections, and other treatment. As soon as she was home again, her own room promptly became a crowded hospital ward. No doll escaped medication. Temperatures were taken at frequent intervals, injections administered, and oxygen tents rigged up. The play was an obsession for days on end. It served a very useful function, however, in releasing pent-up feelings. Instead of becoming a permanent hypochondriac, this little girl has developed an astonishingly healthy attitude toward ailments.

Everyday domestic incidents also serve as popular material for dramas, especially those which may be a source of friction at home, such as eating, using the toilet, and going to bed at night. Parents are sometimes represented as tender and loving, at other times as harsh disciplinarians who spank and punish their children unmercifully for only slight infringements. Telephone conversations from the doll corner to a grocer or plumber are sometimes highly entertaining. Tommy's father would laugh to see himself portrayed at the breakfast table, with nose buried in the newspaper and sipping his coffee before dashing off to work with a loaded briefcase. Tommy is trying to figure out what it is like to be Daddy, and his best way of doing so is to be Daddy for a while.

The hospital scene has broken up and now Celia, a maternal type, is talking softly to her brood of dolls.

"It's *very* cold outside tonight. You'll have to put your sweater on. Put out your arm. Give me your hand. Honey, I'll come back. I'll just have to dress my *other* baby, honey. We'll go out and get ice cream, and then we'll see Grandma . . . " At this point she dials a phone and says, "Grandmother, will you please come right over? Because our babies love to see you. They love to see you, and they're *so proud* about you. So you come on quick. You're in New York. You come when the babies are asleep. They'll have to get up to do pee-wee, and then you can see them when they have to do pee-wee." She hangs up the receiver and turns to one of her babies: "Honey, you go to sleep." Now she leans over another baby and whispers tenderly, "Nighty-night, honey. Mommy needs her bath, too. Grandmother is coming to take care of you, so don't cry. I'll be here tomorrow. Sh-sh-sh. Here's a cover. I'll stay for a little while, honey, 'cause Grandma is in the house now." She kisses her babies loudly and tucks them in again.

Suddenly Celia ceases to be quiet and protective, and

turns herself into a very naughty cat named Smokey, who goes about scratching people and clawing the equipment. Her playmates laugh uproariously at Smokey's mad antics, but find them hard to handle. Alice, Joan, and Peggy, all dressed in finery, are trying to have a tea party. They wish they could find some way to get rid of her.

"I'm going to give Smokey some poison," says one.

"I'll get the big, bad wolf," volunteers another.

"I'll phone my cousin and he'll put Smokey in jail," offers the third.

Nothing seems to work, however, and the tea party soon breaks up in confusion.

Celia, usually so reliable and gentle, can vent feelings of hostility only under the guise of an animal or other wild creature. She would feel too guilty to do so openly. It is quite permissible for a tiger to bare his teeth, for a cat to scratch and claw, and for a lion to roar and pounce.

Near the ladder box there are three other animals. Billy is a monkey, Alice a crocodile, and Donald a lamb. What an opportunity for Billy to be as silly as he wants! At home he is expected to behave sensibly at all times. Now he can perform all the mad capers he can think of and win admiration to boot. Alice, who saw *Peter Pan* a week ago, is still working off her fears of the terrifying monster with the clock ticking inside. Donald goes over to each staff member in turn, bleating gently. Each one strokes and pets him. This is one way for Donald to get the affection he craves. He would hesitate to ask for it directly.

Though children often ignore the adults while engrossed in fantasy, they sometimes seek to include them. It is not always easy to decide how one should participate in the children's dramatic enterprises. To refuse entirely would be unnatural. If a role is accepted, the adult should be careful to stay in the background. Sometimes, however, adults are unwittingly brought into the limelight and may require considerable poise to see their way through. A grueling episode of this type may be worthy of detailed description. It started early one December, on an indoor day. Miss Brown reports her experiences:

I was sitting on a low chair writing on a note pad when Tony, Alexander, Barbara, and Jane started building hollow blocks around me.

"Ha-ha! We've got you in jail! Miss Brown's in jail!" triumphant voices cried.

"What have I done?" I inquired.

"You stole. You've been stealing," said Alexander.

I'll be glad to give back everything I took," was my offer.

"Oh—no—you have to be in jail."

I remained on my chair and the building finally surrounded me completely.

After a while I inquired: "Can I have something to eat?"

"No—you can't have anything to eat."

Ronald, who had joined the jailers, said in a rather unpleasant tone, "You'll have to eat b.m. and drink pee-pee."

"If I don't eat, I'll die. You have to feed me in jail."

"No—no—we won't."

I made use of my notepad to scribble a message to Mr. Stern.

"Will someone please take this to Mr. Stern? I want him to help me get out of jail."

Tony, with a sly grin, offered to perform this errand. I gave him the note. He promptly crumpled it up and put it in his pocket. Then Barbara snatched it and tore it. I wrote another note and asked if there was anyone who would take the second one to Mr. Stern, someone I could really trust.

"Me," said Barbara, but her glint was too obvious.

Wallace hesitantly came forward and volunteered to be the messenger. Wallace was always polite and considerate. I gave him the slip of paper and he bravely delivered it to Mr. Stern who was in the locker room. Mr. Stern peered around the door and said, "Sorry—I have to go and play the flute for the fives. I can't help you just now." He disappeared.

I asked every once in a while when they were going to let me out of jail, but the invariable answer was, "We're *never* going to let you out!" So I was doomed to sit there.

After a while several children began shooting at me. "Bang—bang—you're dead."

Finally I slumped over and stayed in that position. The children then discussed what to do with me, and it was decided that they would bury me. "Let's bury her in the gym mat."

So the jail was dismantled and I was pulled forward by several hands until I reclined on the mat. They then folded the mat over my body and pounded a bit—though not too violently. Finally I got up and brushed myself off.

Immediately the children went in search of a second victim and pounced on Miss Farrell, a student teacher. She went through the same sequence of events.

After her demise a calmer spirit prevailed, and the children began building a different block structure. It turned into a "house boat" with a pointed prow. The same children who had just been jail keepers were now going on a picnic on the boat. Alexander, who had been most hostile in his actions and language, came up to me and invited me in honeyed tones to come along on the picnic. I accepted and went with him. A seat was awaiting me. Soon I was being served soup from the stove, prepared by the cooks, Barbara and Jane. Also I was deluged with sandwiches. There was a spirit of idyllic contentment as we all enjoyed our trip. Mr. Stern returned at this moment. He takes up the story from here.

Mr. Stern's story:

When I came into the room, Alexander invited me in a pleasant tone to eat dinner in the houseboat. I accepted and got in. Before long, the boat crashed into pieces, and he and Tony started to rebuild it. I went to another part of the room. Suddenly Tony came and pulled my hand.

"Come with me."

"Where?" I asked.

"Oh, you know," said Tony, smiling mischievously and looking somewhat guilty.

"Is it a house?" I inquired.

"Oh, a kind of a house," he replied.

I sat on a chair inside the structure. Tony went gleefully to Alexander. "I tricked him. Now he's in jail." Both laughed and came close, shutting the entrance.

Someone told me that I had taken money. Susan and Jane were dogs and came yipping in a friendly and concerned way. I told them not to be worried and they left, returning now and again in a kind of half-anxious manner. Soon many children came around, helping to close boards around me. Wallace approached and hit me tentatively. I encouraged him with a smile and he went on gleefully smacking me. Barbara also swatted me, laughing somewhat nervously. Ronald told me that I must eat b.m. Other children vetoed this, and explained that I would get nothing at all. Some said I would be shut up for a long time. Dudley said I would get out tomorrow. The play became less concentrated. Many left until Alexander took a flat board and made motions with it in the air.

"I'm cutting you into pieces," he said happily.

I pretended to slump down. The children had said that I could not get out until I was dead, so now I asked if I might be allowed to leave.

"No! We have to bury you."

I was ushered to the mat, where I lay down. By this time, ten or twelve were crowding about, foremost among them Sheila, whom we all considered an uncommonly shy child. She was afraid of men and had consistently avoided me! She was laughing and joined in with animation. First, they all tugged at the mat, curling the ends over like dirt piling on me. Then, since some were pulling harder than others, the mat began to move. They worked together and succeeded in dragging me (on the mat) to the most remote space in the room. Once there, some of them fell on me. Alexander was a dog, and though growling fiercely, he was careful not to hurt me. When Ronald, Barbara, Jane, and the others showed signs of going too far, I asked them to be careful, and they responded, continuing their play with only slightly lessened vigor. I could see no signs of undue tension in any of the children. None of them showed personal feelings or spite. Sheila completely lost her fears during this play. Suddenly a great number began to crowd about. At that moment, Tony finished the game by becoming a protecting dog. He growled and threatened the others, who backed away. He then crawled round and around my body, keeping everyone else off the mat.

What impressed these teachers was that the children tried to make up in one way or another for what they had done. Miss Brown was taken on a pleasure trip and sumptuously fed after her hideous treatment in jail. Mr. Stern was eventually protected by Tony, who had become a gentle dog. Tony was the one who had originally "tricked him into jail."

On the following day, Tony, Barbara, and Jane tried to lure each of the staff members into jail again. Mr. Stern suggested instead that they might dictate to him what they had done the day before in jailing Miss Brown. The children told the following story:

> Miss Brown walked into jail, and we locked her in jail. She wrote a letter to Mr. Stern. The letter got put in Tony's pocket, and he gave it to Barbara and she tore it up. We didn't let Miss Brown have anything to eat. She died, and we shot her with Tony's pistol. We put her in the mat and we rolled her up.
>
> We pulled Miss Farrell into jail. We wouldn't let her have anything to eat. She died. We all shot her. We buried her in the mat.

To give the children a somewhat different conception of what "jail" was like, Mr. Stern told the children an original story about a boy who was sent to jail after stealing repeatedly. This boy was, of course, much older than they. His home life was not a happy one. He had little to play with, and his parents were seldom at home. Looking for something to do, he roamed the streets. He saw a toy he wanted and took it from a store. He did this again and again and nobody noticed it. But one day a detective saw him and warned him not to take things. He was given another chance. But then one day he was in Woolworth's and saw a very beautiful toy he wanted to have.

Hopefully, Alexander suggested at this point in the story: "And he paid, I guess."

"No, he didn't—he took it," said Mr. Stern.

"He's going to jail," said Jane.

He did finally get to jail, but jail—or the boys' prison he was sent to—was very different from what he had imagined it would be. People were kind and helpful. They taught him many things. What he liked best of all was the workshop where he learned to make furniture and other things out of wood. He was very clever with his hands. Finally they decided he could leave prison. And when he left, he was given a job in a factory where they made furniture. Alexander said, "Then he never did any bad things."

"He didn't need to, did he?" said Mr. Stern. "He was earning money so he could buy the things he wanted."

"And then he didn't steal again," concluded Alexander, obviously relieved.

But this did not put an end to the jail play. It continued almost daily for weeks—sometimes reaching an excited pitch. As time went on variations began to occur. One morning Jack and Rob got in with Mr. Stern and shot outward at the crowd. Rob then got out, but Jack stayed inside and protected Mr. Stern in a wild shooting fray during which Mr. Stern had great difficulty in persuading him that they were defeated and had both been shot dead. Finally Jack admitted defeat and both were rolled up in the mat side by side.

A few children did not at first participate, but some of them joined in later and prolonged the game after the others grew bored with it. For lack of victims, two brooms were "jailed" one day.

Despite the teachers' willingness to be "jailed" day after day, it was a game which continued to obsess the group for months. Some children enjoyed being somewhat sadistic. This was particularly true of Ronald who had recommended the unpleasant diet. Once when asked if the prisoner could "have a window to look out at the world," he replied, "Yes—so that if you try to escape we can shoot you." Alexander offered feeding the prisoner "dirty food and garbage," while Dick suggested cooking Mr. Stern. "We're beating you into an egg," he added. Jane said in a rather spiteful tone one day, "We're poison ivy leaves and you'll soon be itching yourself." Take your last breath of air. Bang!" said another. Pouring hot water on the prisoner was another form of torture.

Although careful never to let the children hurt them, the teachers gave them leeway to say and act as they wanted. As long as it was accepted in an impersonal way, there was no danger of stirring up feelings of genuine hostility. Had Miss Brown or Mr. Stern shown annoyance or resentment, the children might have concentrated their general antagonism against them as specific individuals. This could develop into an unhealthy situation, with guilt feelings on both sides. Instead it was kept in the realm of drama, where no one needed to feel personally wounded. Both teachers admitted feeling uncomfortable and somewhat shaky at times, for it is no fun to have a number of "guns" aimed at you and hideous threats hurled in your direction. Fortunately, the children and their teachers remained good friends. Eventually, a few of the children were willing to accept the victim role. On March 13th, Alexander allowed himself to be imprisoned alone, shot, and buried! After that he had a most successful day—did two fine crayon drawings and an excellent painting. Handling the situation in this way had certainly proven right for him. Toward the end of the year the majority of this group became fed up with the whole business of jail play. A few still persisted in it. It was prolonged by those who were on the outskirts of the group and who probably thought it might give them an entering wedge if they acted in this way. But their efforts were rejected—and when the group entered the kindergarten in the fall this form of activity was no longer of interest. It had run its full course.

"Jail play" is a yearly performance in one form or another. It expresses the four-year-old's delight in having the adult at his mercy for a while. Seldom does this need for stripping the adult of his power reach such a peak as it did in this group during the winter just described. The four or five initiators of this play were the most vivid and dynamic members of the group. Their example set the pace for the rest, who were all too ready to tag after these exciting leaders. The reasons for the hostility which the jailers expressed were varied. One came from a home where intellectual standards were too exacting, another's parents worried constantly about financial security, another had to adjust to crowded living conditions and conflicting types of authority, while the fourth had to compete with a dominating older brother.

The following year, jail play in this school's four-year-old group was so mild as to be dull in comparison. Most of it took the form of dictating notes between the adult prisoner and the jailers.

"I love you—I'll help you get out," was the ardent message of one little girl to Mr. Stern.

"I want you to meet my sister some day," dictated another.

"I want you to come to my house sometime for dinner."

No gruesome tortures were even thought of.

As a rule, teachers do not enter into the children's imaginative play to the extent that these were forced to do in the jailing episodes. The staff's main function is to encourage dramatic play by providing the right sort of equipment. Anything which can be put to a thousand uses is suitable material for children's play. Large hollow blocks are one of the best investments, for they have manifold uses. Dolls, portable ladders, saw horses, planks, boards, wooden crates, boxes, car tires, ropes, and pulleys form props for countless dramas.

Nursery school teachers have a reputation for being shameless scavengers. Bits of rope, twine, spools, cork, ribbons, odds and ends of material, used wrapping paper, wall paper, tin cans, old dresses, pocketbooks, vests, sashes, and belts—there is no limit to the stuff happily toted to school. Some of these treasures may be stored away in the closet to await the moment when they may meet an important need.

Children should learn how to be inventive. They are amazing with their ability in this respect. A "thing-wheeler," made of duraluminum, which the average adult would regard simply as a porter's truck, can serve as a bed, a stretcher, Santa Claus' sleigh, a swing when slung over a crossbar, and even as a fish to be caught with a rope line. These are all legitimate, constructive uses.

It is impossible to estimate the extent of social learning which takes place while children are engaged in their imaginative games together. Because children often stay in the same nursery school for two or three years, teachers can record changes and progress. When they were four years old, two boys, Paul and Jerry, had been a source of some concern to the staff because of their unwholesome relationship. Paul was a young dictator who lacked feelings of sympathy for his followers. In fact, it gave him sadistic pleasure to make them cringe in fear. Jerry, overly sensitive and credulous, was the chief sufferer. He was constantly in fear of this bossy classmate but at the same time found his personality irresistible. He suffered agonies of apprehension but continued to associate with his tormentor. Lively cowboy dramas were chief among their free play activities. Jerry invariably got the raw end of the deal and often needed to be rescued by one of the teachers, who stayed close at hand in case matters got too rough for him.

The following year, in the kindergarten, the two boys were still found often in one another's company. One day a group of boys seemed to be involved in some violent scene. Miss Tyler hurried to watch. Two boys were grappling with Jerry, who was kicking and struggling on the ground, resisting their efforts to tie ropes around his ankles and wrists. Miss Tyler had an impulse to break up the game but she decided to wait. Paul stood close by giving orders. It didn't take Miss Tyler many seconds to recognize a rodeo scene in progress. Jerry was the steer, Paul the chief cowboy. Instead of whining for help or looking distressed, however, Jerry was obviously enjoying his role, while Paul was giving commands to his assistants:

"Tie the ropes tight enough so he can't get away, but not tight enough to hurt. We don't want to really hurt him."

Hurrah for Paul, Miss Tyler thought to herself. And she looked with satisfaction at Jerry who was calm and unperturbed during his good performance as a wild steer. She was glad she had not interfered with their game. It had taken many months to establish this healthy respect for each other. During that time, Jerry had been encouraged to rely on himself more and more, while Paul had learned to exercise some restraint and develop qualities of consideration. Now things were well under control and mutual trust prevailed.

Three four-year-olds once asked permission to play in the group's locker room by themselves. This was granted. They drew the curtains and had an enjoyable time being "ghosts" in the darkened area. Two boys, Jimmy and Ray, wanted to be included and kept bothering the others, but were loudly refused entrance. The two boys sat forlornly for a while sucking their thumbs, resentful of their exclusion. The staff made no effort to assist them as they felt it was more important just then to give protection to the three in the locker room. Suddenly Jimmy thought of the ideal face-saver. "Let's be guards!" he suggested. Very officiously they allowed only those with legitimate excuses to go through the door. The next day the two went into the locker room to play "ghosts," making up for the rebuff of the day before.

Sometimes a staff member can be helpful when a child longs to be accepted in a situation from which he is being excluded. The teacher of a group of fours watched the repeated efforts of Sammy, who was yearning to join two little girls in the doll corner. They rejected him every time. Finally he turned in desperation to the teacher. She took him by the hand and went with him.

"Sammy would like to join you," was her comment.

"Oh, but you see our babies are sick," said one of the girls in a sugary tone. "They have chicken pox and he might catch chicken pox from them."

"Perhaps you ought to have a doctor in to see them," the teacher suggested.

This was sufficient hint to Sammy. He promptly found himself a bag and announced his presence.

"May I come in? I'm the doctor. I've come to see your sick babies." This time he was welcomed.

As children grow in knowledge and understanding, their fantasy play becomes more complex. If the kindergarten program is not overly structured but allows the children plenty of opportunity to develop their imaginative play ideas, some extraordinarily lively scenes may develop.

The remarkable dramas children create illustrate all the basic problems of human life. Strife, sickness, loneliness, and death inspire as much dramatic play as do birth, family routines, activities of the larger community, and the adventures of outdoor living. Meeting these situations in fantasy prepares children for the time when they must face them in reality. This kind of self-education is the most effective way through which children can come to understand themselves and others.

"*Show your wings and never fear*" 5

Physical Development

"Mommy, Mommy, come *here!* I want to show you something! I can climb way up to the top of the big jungle gym!" An eager little hand drags Mother across the playground to the jungle gym, and as the demonstration begins an excited voice calls repeatedly, "Watch me! Watch me!"

Sheila's mother does watch, and as she watches her vision suddenly becomes blurred with tears at sight of the radiant expression on her daughter's face. Can this really be Sheila? What a change has come over her!

The staff also watches Sheila with a sense of satisfaction. This feat was not mastered in one day. Far from it, for it is already the middle of May and she has been at school since October first. They remember the opening days of school when Sheila had just turned four. It was her first experience in a group. Because of her extreme shyness, her mother stayed at school for some weeks until it was possible to make the break. Even while her mother was present, Sheila was reluctant to venture forth to examine the play equipment. Her list of fears was legion. She had many nervous little habits, such as dropping her head, biting her nails, fiddling with her skirt, and wiping her pudgy hands repeatedly. Loud noises made her tremble and brought tears. She cringed in the presence of men, avoided all her classmates and was terrified of the rough boys. She apparently had no ideas about how to play and no impulse to try. Only the dolls, crayons, and outdoor sandbox offered a safe haven for her during these initial weeks. What was wrong with Sheila? What had happened to make her so timid? A long talk with her parents helped to explain her difficulties. Sheila was an only child whose mother had had several miscarriages. Anxiety over the one child who had survived caused the parents, especially the mother, to be extremely overprotective. Sheila, sensing the fear which surrounded her, dared not step away from her mother's side. At the recommendation of a psychiatrist she was brought to this particular nursery school.

It is not enough simply to expose a shy child to a group of contemporaries. In the presence of her vigorous, active, aggressive classmates, Sheila might have become even more withdrawn, for a shy child is always an easy prey, the one to be teased and plagued. Group experience might have become intolerable torture to her.

It is an interesting fact that few, if any, problems of childhood can be solved by a frontal attack. We would all laugh at the idea of curing measles by trying to rub off the rash. Yet children's outward behavior is just as symptomatic of underlying difficulties. Continual thumbsucking, for example, may be a symptom of some strain or tension in the child's life. It would be not only futile, but even cruel, to try to stop it by direct methods. By so doing the problem is likely to be aggravated. One should seek for underlying causes and try to work on their solution.

Sheila's greatest need was to gain some confidence in herself through the acquisition of a variety of skills, especially physical skills. The teachers began by leading her along a series of raised boards, placed across sawhorses. When she seemed ready to do this on her own they would withdraw their hands, yet stay by to give her moral support. They encouraged her to jump from a low height until she was sure of this feat. Then, as she gained assurance, a higher box would be arranged for a jumping-off place. The fixed outdoor slide was too steep for her, so a teacher adjusted a board to suit her abilities. One of the many advantages of movable equipment is that it can be adapted to a particular need at a particular moment. As Sheila acquired each new skill, she felt a greater readiness to tackle another. The swing did not seem so frightening now. As the weeks went by a great change began to take place in her personality. Now and then she would venture forth on her own without looking back at the staff members. Her face showed expression and she held her head high. Her body moved with a certain spring and grace; her arms and legs were no longer flabby appendages; fat was being replaced by good, firm muscles. One day she learned to skip. Nothing is so indicative of a joyful attitude toward life as the free, lighthearted skipping of a young child. As she gained courage, she no longer shied away from her peers. Their roughhousing was still too boisterous for her, but she began to look rather longingly at them as if she wished she could join in too. Eventually she did. As Sheila became more skillful and sure-footed, more children began to respect her and accept her in their play.

Physical competence is one of the greatest social assets. Are you good at climbing, jumping, swinging, seesawing, throwing and catching a ball, turning somersaults, boxing, skipping, lifting, lugging, riding a bike, and steering a wagon? Well, then you can play with us. A young child's philosophy is almost as simple as that at times. It isn't very different with teen-agers, for if a girl can dance well, is a fair tennis player and a graceful swimmer, she has a far better chance at popularity than if she lacks these skills. The clumsy, stumbling, fearful individual easily becomes a social outcast. The lot of the cripple is indeed a hard one at this early stage, but if other skills can be mastered to prove his competence in the eyes of his contemporaries, his chance to win friends and to make a place for himself is increased.

If Sheila had been given the opportunity to develop normally, she would not have had so many difficulties to overcome. The skills which she mastered so painstakingly at the age of four could have been acquired many months earlier. The average two-year-old is a glutton for exercise. He has an irrepressible urge to use his muscles. He has so recently conquered upright locomotion that he still revels in the achievement. Most of his activities are variations on this main theme. He is continually on the move—walking, running, jumping, pushing and pulling, struggling upstairs and downstairs, over obstacles and underneath them. He spends ten minutes lugging blocks from one end of the room to the other, only to carry them back once more to their original locality. He puffs and pants, but loves the effort involved. Adults often marvel at this boundless energy and sometimes have moments of terror, for the two-year-old's prowess invariably exceeds his judgment and he often seems on the brink of some fearful mishap. Bumps and bruises are necessary lessons in helping to build wholesome caution. Self-control learned in this way is far better than fear instilled through constant warning of imminent dangers. Children who learn to fend for themselves in a setting suited to their needs soon discover what their capabilities and limitations are. They do not venture far beyond a point of safety.

It happens frequently that a young adventurer scales a new height and then becomes panicky about getting down again. Two-year-old Dicky, who has just managed to pull himself onto the tower gym platform in his classroom, suddenly wails frantically. A teacher is by his side, but she does not lift him down. She assures him he can get down by himself, promises to help him if necessary, and gives him step by step instructions on how to descend. As his feet finally touch solid ground, Dicky sighs and his face lights up with a broad smile. Immediately he clambers up the ladder again, struggles onto the platform, perches there a moment, and then squats and turns over on his stomach in preparation for the precarious downward journey. The teacher watches him. Twenty-three times Dicky goes up and down the tower gym! His round face is pink with the exertion but he beams happily at the world in general. "I can do it myself," is his proud boast. Joy indeed—learning to use one's body with skill.

Acquisition of physical skills is beneficial to anyone. Billy would have less need to talk of his father's miraculous prowess were he to discover some of his own underlying strength and capabilities. For boasting is a symptom that one is not so sure of oneself. The confident individual need not resort to habits of excessive self-praise, tall tales and threats of what he will do to so-and-so when he gets the chance. A good way of dealing with the braggart is to help him gain confidence through competence.

And there is Lawrence who gives up without even trying. "I don't *want* to," is his constant refrain, but what he really means to say is, "I am afraid I won't do it well the first time." He dreads failure and dares not expose himself to ridicule. Instead of learning how to swing, to seesaw, to climb and to throw a ball, he sticks to riding a tricycle, one skill of which he is sure. Lawrence suffers from overly high standards for himself. His case is not uncommon. His parents are idealistic and earnest. Lawrence rarely receives praise. He is often criticized for his own good. In their eagerness to make a fine little boy of their son, the parents demand far too much of him in the way of intellectual advancement and moral conduct. They need to find ways of enjoying him rather than worrying so much about his achievements. At school his teachers can help Lawrence by encouraging him to master one skill at a time. Increased poise and confidence are corollaries.

Adults are often impressed with a precocious child who

commands an exceptional vocabulary. Children judge each other on a very different basis. They are more interested in performance than in words. Language precocity is not always an asset to a young child, especially if it has been achieved at the expense of other aspects of growth. Highly verbal children who have lacked the opportunity for well-rounded development are easily spotted in nursery school. They find themselves ill at ease with their contemporaries, are awkward in the use of their bodies, have limited ideas for play, and attach themselves to grownups with whom they feel more at home. Their apparent precocity is only a thin veneer. They have been denied first-hand experiences. They need an opportunity to explore the worlds of nature and of man with all their muscles and senses, so that the words which slip so smoothly from their tongues may have a basis of real meaning. They should be encouraged to experiment, to test their abilities, to make discoveries of their own instead of standing by as spectators. Their more active classmates are inclined to ignore them. These children, who are often products of homes where booklearning is stressed, are particularly in need of some physical skills. A child who has reached the age of four or five without the ability to climb, tussle, romp, steer a wagon, and handle a ball had a tendency to avoid these skills at the age of two or three when his large muscles were going through their most important growth. But for the sake of his health, posture, well-being and acceptance in the group he needs to learn them now. There should be no further delay, for the longer one waits the more difficult it is to develop good coordination. These early years are the most important.

It is not easy to provide full-bodied activities for young children who grow up in a large city. Cramped apartments offer little chance for climbing and romping. Neighbors object to the noise of normally active children. One reason that TV sets have been welcomed by many parents is that they insure a certain amount of peace and quiet in the home. But the effect on children who sit for hours gaping at the screen can be very bad. Eyestrain, bad posture, lassitude alternating with overstimulation are some of the results teachers observe. Some parents, aware of the child's physical needs, have shown inventiveness by rigging up swings, trapezes, and chinning bars between door jambs. Others have found that a good-sized mattress of foam rubber or other material can serve as a jumping mat or a place on which to turn somersaults and do other acrobatic tricks. Nearby parks offer swings, slides, and jungle gyms as well as natural slopes and rocks. Yet it requires a good deal of effort and planning to give city children the sort of physical experiences they need.

The value which nursery school places on the physical needs of the child accounts for much of the planning of the play space and daily program. Fair weather usually brings groups outdoors. This is true in winter as well as during the other seasons. Snow is no deterrent. On the contrary, children revel in it. Properly clad in snowsuits and high boots they roll in it, wet their faces, dig, throw snowballs, and build igloos. Sometimes there is a strip of ice to slide on. What fun to hear it crackle beneath one's feet! In hot weather, a wading pool, sandbox, or grass and earthplot provide endless delight.

School, as a supplement to the home, gives special emphasis to the pupils' great need for freedom of movement, and offers as many chances as possible to let go wholeheartedly. A spacious level play area is a boon in itself. The children can speed on their tricycles from one end to the other without fear of accident. As they race about one can almost see tensions vanish. Faces glow at the joyful sensation of moving through space. Not only do they revel in this horizontal space, but also in the sky overhead. This blue expanse above is both a joy to the eye and a cure for taut nerves.

Nursery schools usually try to take advantage of good weather whenever it comes. What constitutes "good weather" is often a moot point, however, and the teachers are by no means united in their opinions. One teacher has a strong distaste for wind. Another objects to the dampness in the air. Some dislike the cold. Others suffer from blazing sunshine. There is also the health of individual children to be taken into account. Marcia catches colds easily; Heather is subject to attacks of asthma; Arnold has had an ear infection and should not be exposed to the wind. So a small gathering may assemble indoors under the leadership of one teacher while the majority of the group uses the playground.

It should be added here that the weather is by no means the only criterion on which decisions are made whether children should be in or out. Two-year-olds may be kept in their classroom a good deal at first, for some teachers feel that during the opening weeks of school these newcomers need the sense of security they gain by beginning each day in the same familiar setting. Kindergarten groups sometimes forego a day outdoors, despite fair weather, because they have a special project to carry through. Perhaps they are making cranberry sauce or dipping Christmas candles. When there is a birthday among the older children, small committees sometimes go to their classroom to prepare the tables for the party.

Teachers in all age groups often welcome the opportunity to use the empty room to help individual pupils in one way or another. Sometimes shy children can be encouraged to build with the hollow blocks or to climb the indoor jungle gym, usually monopolized by their more confident and aggressive classmates. Skills can often be mastered more easily in a quiet setting when there is no one to threaten one's safety or to belittle one's first efforts. A budding friendship between two children may be fostered by giving them a free field together indoors. By the same reasoning, an unsatisfactory relationship between two children can be relieved by having them separated for a while.

There is no doubt that a greater sense of unity develops

when a group plays indoors than when it is spread out-doors. So it is a good idea to remain indoors now and then if only for that purpose. Also, it takes practice for children to settle down to indoor play after the tremendous freedom they have found on the playground. In order to forestall a hectic experience on their first rainy days, it is good to let them get used to the classroom ahead of time.

"Indoor days" are seldom as carefree as those which are spent outdoors. There is something about four walls that inevitably creates tension. Even with the most careful planning and provision for climbing, sliding, jumping, lift-ing, lugging, and other large muscle activities in the room it is no easy matter to maintain an atmosphere conducive to quiet, constructive play. With a full attendance the room never seems big enough! After a series of indoor days it is a joy to see clear skies again.

Children yearn for adventure. Although city life holds many hazards, urban children seldom have the chance to be daring and brave. They are hemmed in by pre-cautions—very necessary, of course, with heavy traffic, skyscraper living quarters, and occasional unsavory citi-zens. Perhaps a big jungle gym seems a mild setting for adventure; still it offers considerable challenge to children. While the more agile fours and fives no longer find a thrill in simply climbing to the top, they can usually invent new and more daring tricks to perform. Hanging upside down from a bar, swinging monkeylike along a high rod, or slid-ing down one of the long slanting poles which support the jungle gym are among the possibilities. A narrow two-by-four walking board offers a challenge to budding tightrope walkers; an improvised bannister affords some of the fun usually denied apartment dwellers, and a shaky rope lad-der beckons would-be ship's pilots to scale its heights. Gym mats provided indoors and outdoors encourage jumping from high places, as well as practice in tumbling, somer-saulting, wrestling and boxing.

Though nursery school children use the same play-ground day after day, year after year, they seldom grow weary of it. New ideas and adaptations occur to them all the time. Their originality is well-nigh boundless. Children who tire of going down the slide in a sitting position can try going headfirst. And if they happen to be wearing leather-soled shoes it is quite a test to walk uphill on its slippery surface. Five-year-old tricycle riders like to perform clown-ish antics instead of pedaling sedately along.

The provision of challenging equipment is a major factor in building up and maintaining the children's play inter-ests. What makes a good plaything for children? Probably the chief quality is versatility. Something which can be used in limitless ways will stand the test of time best of all. Also, there is tremendous value in having movable equip-ment, things which the children themselves can lug about and adapt to their plans. Although a jungle gym, slide, swings, and other fixed apparatus are usually regarded as playground essentials, there is more satisfaction in the long run in having a large assortment of sturdy packing boxes, big hollow blocks, sawhorses, planks, barrels, ladders and flexible, smoothly finished boards. By fastening cleats to the bottom of the boards their usefulness is greatly en-hanced. With two cleats in the center and one at each end, the board, combined with one or two sawhorses, can serve as a seesaw, a slide or jumping board. The ladders should be fair-sized but not too cumbersome, and should also be fitted with cleats at both ends to give them a secure hold wherever they are placed. This type of equipment calls forth the use of the whole body, so important for healthy development during these early years. If allowed to experi-ment freely with this type of material children can discover a hundred fascinating variations in their use—far more than even an imaginative adult could visualize. They reas-semble them endlessly, often using them as props for their dramatic enterprises.

Children choose to play on the floor. It is the best place

for them. It is far more beneficial in developing good posture than sitting at tables, which confines limbs and restricts movement. The floor gives solid support. David is frequently seen wallowing on his belly. Just now he is slithering along pretending to be a canoe which has drifted from its moorings. How gracefully he edges along, almost with the suppleness of a snake. Every muscle is under control. No one in the group has finer posture than David, whose parents have allowed him to continue his play on the floor even though the creeping and crawling stage is a thing of the past.

A nursery school director once happened upon a nursemaid who was peering through the glass peek-hole in the classroom door. The nursemaid was grumbling to herself, "Her dress is getting all mussed! Look at her!" The director stopped to look through the other window and spied a dozen forms squirming happily in snake-like contortions around the floor in a rhythm session. Perhaps not so good for Carolyn's dress but how beneficial for her stomach muscles! It is a pity when children worry about soiling their clothes. Fortunately, this is seldom a problem. Most children come to school dressed sensibly for active play and feel free to romp to their heart's content.

The mad shouting and wild display of energy characteristic of children who are finally "let out" of school does not occur among children whose daily curriculum gives opportunity for the release of tensions by means of free play activities. Sitting still is not normal for children. Prolonged physical restraint is inevitably followed by an explosive reaction.

Children need a chance for active participation. Their first impulse is to re-enact any new or vivid experience. Their ideas need to be translated into physical terms. Mental indigestion and nervous tension result when they are expected to absorb too many impressions without a chance to become better acquainted with them through their muscles.

"Oh, dear, what can the matter be?" 6

Conflicts

"How can you stand the little barbarians?" asks a father, half in earnest, as he lingers a few minutes before going to the office. He has been particularly interested in following the antics of Dicky, who prances about the room with an elfish grin on his face as he takes a whack here and there at available heads. Suddenly Dicky grabs Brent around the waist and tussles with him. Brent lashes out furiously and begins to cry.

"He's crying!" Dicky calls out in glee.

He then darts off and accosts Bobby. "Will you box with me, Bobby?"

"No."

"Why not?"

"Just don't want to," mutters Bobby.

Dicky skips over to Ralph and gives him a punch.

"Stop it!" says Ralph, on the verge of tears.

"You used to be so tough, Ralph, but now you're not!" taunts Dicky.

He again resumes his skipping until he spies Susie coming in. She is a respected boxer and he challenges her too. But again his offer is turned down. Dicky continues to

prance about in a triumphant mood. He seems to be saying, "Hurrah! Hurrah! I'm tough! Everybody's afraid to
fight with me!"

The teachers have also been watching Dicky's actions
and regret that there is no time to explain his behavior to
the father, who has had to rush off to work. In the fall
when Dicky entered nursery school he was the picture of
timidity. He used to quail at any sign of aggression on the
part of his classmates, and hid anxiously behind a teacher's
skirts, flatly refusing to stand up for his rights. It took the
teachers many weeks to help Dicky acquire a degree of self-
assurance. As his confidence grew, however, the pendulum
suddenly began to swing to the other extreme and he became the class terror. His teachers recognize his current
conduct as a step toward a day when he will be able to
channel his energies more constructively. Meanwhile he
needs to live through this stage of self-discovery.

"How can you condone fighting?" inquires a visitor. "If I
were in your shoes I would put a prompt stop to it."

This type of comment is made now and then by individuals who long for world peace (as who does not) and feel
that a golden opportunity is lost by not instilling in impres-
sionable youngsters habits of nonaggression. Such adult
conceptions, acquired through years of experience, cannot
be grafted onto the younger generation. It might conceiv-
ably be possible, with the combined efforts of parents and
staff, to put a stop to all outward forms of aggression in a
school program. But it would be folly to conclude that the
resulting atmosphere would be all sweetness and light.
Hostilities, anger, and frustration would be simmering beneath the surface, waiting for some outlet. If the most
straightforward and natural means of retaliation is denied
them, children are inevitably forced to seek more round-
about forms of release. Some of these are a good deal less
ethical then a well-directed blow. Suppressed feelings of
rage and hatred may find expression in all sorts of strange
ways—from imaginary aches and pains, indisposition, and

vomiting attacks to moods of self-pity and vague feelings of guilt which may persist throughout life.

Undue stress on outward conduct is more likely to hinder growth than to foster it, for clamping down on a child's expression of emotions allows him no opportunity to grapple with them or to gain increasing mastery over them. If surface behavior is not related to underlying feelings it is little more than a thin veneer, and unless the control comes from within the child himself there is no assurance whatever that he will not suddenly resort to physical violence under sufficient provocation. Hence adults should be primarily concerned with a child's underlying feelings. An excessive need to hit out at one's fellow creatures often stems from a feeling of rejection. The child who continually fails to measure up to the standards set by either his family or his classmates may express his resentment in this way. His belligerent behavior only adds to his problem. Once the cause is recognized, grownups can help him to discover more constructive ways of winning respect.

Adults sometimes succeed in obtaining lip service from children, who solemnly agree with their elders that it is better to "talk things over." But these children stand on a shaky foundation if language is their only recourse. The child who is good at self-defense wins respect more easily than the one who always rushes behind the teacher's skirts or gets Johnny to fight his battles for him. If young children are discouraged from defending themselves physically, they are inevitably forced into other means of defense or revenge. Applying a kind of double standard for small girls may start them on the road to becoming tattletales, catty gossips, and the perpetrators of sly tricks. And think of the unfair advantage it gives the girls if boys are forbidden to hit them no matter what the provocation! This is no way to build up a pleasant relationship between the sexes. As children grow older, nature sees to it that they become more fully aware of their own sex and their future role in society. Being a tomboy at the age of four or five will not diminish Betty's chance of being feminine in adulthood, but may help her to be straightforward in her dealings instead of resorting to circuitous wiles.

It should not be assumed that all physical encounters between children stem from feelings of hostility. On the contrary, children revel in playful combat. They very much resemble puppies in their desire to wrestle, roll about, and test their strength against one another. It is one of their means of getting acquainted. Children learn best through their muscles and it is often through physical contact rather than by the medium of language that they establish friendships.

Two-year-olds may appear to be unfriendly when they are merely exploring their classmates as they do the other objects in the room. Their techniques may include poking, pushing, biting, hugging, or hair pulling. The fact that a big hug elicits tears often astonishes a young cave man. It takes a long time to learn that other children have feelings and desires much like his own.

To gain entry into a desired circle, a child may often find it necessary to prove his strength. When William entered one four-year-old group in the fall, his great wish was to be Eddy's friend. The previous year Eddy had managed to establish himself as the acknowledged leader. William had none of the physical competence which Eddy displayed. He was tense, somewhat awkward, and unable to defend himself. But he was fortunately endowed with courage and determination, and before a month had gone by he was willing to accept Eddy's challenge to a boxing match. William suffered hard blows without wincing, and though defeated he won admiration for his good sportsmanship. As the weeks progressed the two boys became firm friends. William had plenty of other skills and abilities to offer, but he knew how best to win the friend he craved.

A little girl, Cynthia, was so flattered one day at being invited to box with Charlie, whom she deeply admired, that she was willing to don the gloves and take her chance. She was warned that Charlie might give her some hard blows, but she said she didn't mind and faced the test with courage. Girls can often box as well as boys. Some have an advantage in that they are taller and more developed. A very subdued Chinese girl, who was blocked in speech, won fame because of her astonishing wallops. None of the boys dared take her on after one experience. "I'm not going to fight that whacking lady," announced one of the cautious young males. The confidence which she acquired through this one skill helped in overcoming her speech difficulties.

Children rarely harbor grudges against one another, unless their elders keep harping on past injuries. Peter came home several times with battle scars on his face. His sitter called for him one day and was distressed to see a new lump on his forehead. As they reached home she said to Peter's mother, "That bad boy, Johnny, has hit him again." Peter blazed up angrily, "Don't talk that way about Johnny. He's not a bad boy. He's my friend."

It is also wise for parents not to take their children's complaints about each other too seriously. "Who is Leslie?" asks an anxious mother. "Alice says he's so rough that she's afraid to come to school. Would you be sure to protect her from him?" Her teacher replies that she has noticed that Leslie likes to tease Alice. In fact, he is very much aware of her. As Alice also appears to be talking about Leslie, it may be that his interest is reciprocated.

"Perhaps Alice needs to learn how to cope with Leslie's teasing," adds the teacher. "Yesterday he called her 'scribble-scrabble Alice' and she burst into tears. I suggest you invite him over for a visit some day so that they can get better acquainted."

Alice's mother agrees to try this suggestion and leaves with a somewhat lighter heart. A few days later, Leslie saves the seat beside him at the snack table for Alice. Though he never goes so far as to try to include her among his rowdy cronies, he stops pestering her and Alice no longer regards him with fear.

The aggressive child is usually singled out as a cause for concern, but there may be a far more deep-seated problem in the child who never gets involved in any sort of fracas or faces any issue squarely with his peers. His behavior may be a sign of unhealthy withdrawal which may be very hard to cure, whereas the aggressive child's problems are constantly in the open and can therefore be more easily recognized.

A persistent urge to pick fights may stem from various causes, though a frequent one is lack of confidence and a longing to be accepted in the group. A good example is Philip, who joined a four-year-old group without previous school experience. A small, indecisive child, he was at first completely unable to cope with the other children. Soon he began to center his attentions on Lucy, the tiniest, most delicate-looking child. Her timid, frail appearance gave him courage. He teased her by hugging her about the waist so tightly that she was actually hurt. He pushed her slyly so that she fell from the seesaw, bit her to make her give up a tricycle, and so completely demoralized her that she wept and quailed at his approach. His teachers never accused Philip of having bad intentions. They suggested to both children that what Philip was trying to convey to Lucy was that he wanted her for a friend, that he would like her to play with him. They made it clear to Philip, however, that Lucy did not like it when he hurt her. And to Lucy they pointed out that one reason he teased her so much was that she cried so easily. Philip nodded agreement with these sentiments, and even made use of his teachers' arguments when he felt a bit guilty about what he had done. "I only wanted to love her," he explained with cheerful duplicity as he had just made her cry. During the year the staff gave Lucy some pointers on self-defense. After a time she was brave enough to don the boxing gloves in gentle bouts with trustworthy girl friends. On one momentous morning she resisted Philip's advances with such surprising vigor that he retreated in amazement. This was a turning point in their relationship. They had developed a healthy respect for one another and were on the road to becoming friends.

Lyman was a boy of exceptionally small stature. His classmates referred to him as "the baby." In order to prove he was not, he got involved in numberless frays and frequently had to be rescued from beneath a formidable opponent. He always fought back his tears and valiantly announced, "I'm glad I hit him." The intense urge to prove his worth by means of physical combat declined when Lyman was able to accept himself with his own particular limitations. He soon found more satisfying ways of winning respect, for he was an intelligent and gifted boy. Eventually he could say quite calmly when questioned about his age, "I'm four and a half, but small for my age."

Wherever people live together, disagreements are certain to occur. Small children are no exception. As their paths cross and their interests conflict they are bound to have some clashes. There are innumerable ways in which children meet or fail to meet their social problems. Some make a hasty exit, leaving a clear field for the aggressor. Others rush for aid from grownups or more sturdy classmates. Others simply weep. Some shriek so dramatically that the opponent beats a hasty retreat. Others hang on for dear life to the object under dispute. A few resort to hitting, biting, or hair pulling as an effective mode of attack, or defense. Among somewhat older children bargaining, offers of substitute toys, threats, and promises begin to replace the more primitive physical tactics. Though the staff may be keeping hands off, they never relax their vigilance. They are on the alert for any signs of physical danger and also stand by to prevent unfair dealings. Obviously one cannot allow such behavior as kicking, biting, and scratching to continue unchecked, but there are ways of helping both the attacker and the attacked to find better means of coping with their differences.

It is a good idea to encourage children to take an active part in solving their own problems rather than always relying on the adults to smooth things out. Otherwise they will find themselves unprepared to meet life's simplest threats. If Martha comes to her teachers weeping and complaining that Barbara took her dolls away, their attitude is to encourage Martha to do something about it instead of expecting them to settle the situation for her.

"Go and get it back," they may urge her. They stay by, however, to see what happens. It is of paramount importance that justice prevails in the classroom. Children sense whether teachers are fair in their dealings, and can only feel at ease if they are certain that there is no favoritism or disregard of serious injustice.

Should Nicholas come in tears saying, "Danny hit me," the staff does not say, "Well, hit him back." They do suggest, however, that Nicholas find some way to cope with it himself. Nicholas may be quite satisfied to inform Danny, "That hurt me. I don't like you when you hit me." He may decide, on the other hand, to repay Danny in kind. If he does hit back, the idea was his own and not one recommended by the teacher. This is an important point, for it leaves room for him to cast off this primitive solution as he discovers better social techniques. If the adult has urged him to use the "eye-for-an-eye" method, however, this may seem to him the noblest solution and one which must be carried out at all costs. There is an added danger in telling a child to strike back at an aggressor. If he hasn't the courage to do so, he may feel he has failed in the eyes of the adult. By encouraging him to work out his own solution, he can go as far as he feels able at the moment.

Many children are at first leery of applying physical force because of the disapproval they have sensed at home or in the community. Once they feel confident that both teachers and parents do not disapprove, they can use their fists without misgivings or burden of guilt.

With the older children, especially, a point is made of

coaching them in the use of fair methods of fighting. "Use your fists," "Don't kick," "No scratching or pinching allowed," "Two against one is not fair." The children soon learn these rules and remind each other of them.

The stable adult can watch two children fight without growing panicky about it. It is not a major crisis. In fact, it is astonishing how often an apparent death struggle comes to a sudden conclusion and the two combatants continue their play together as if nothing had come between them. Adults should keep hands off unless one child is no match for the other. However, the weaker child needs to be taught better methods of self-defense.

If tension between two children reaches a venomous pitch and they fly at each other in a blind rage, one must hurry to step in before damage is done. If it is necessary to break up a fight, the teacher may suggest that the two children put on boxing gloves and have an organized match. This suggestion may be rejected, but tensions are cooled off because of the interruption. As long as emotions are under control and the fight is fair, teachers do not interject themselves except as referees.

If organized fights between children are properly refereed and kept within fair limits, there is little danger of hostile feelings developing between the combatants. In fact, the opposite usually occurs. When children select an opponent for a boxing match, they invariably decide on a friend. And it is impressive to note how often the choice is a fair one. The teachers could hardly show better judgment than do the children in pairing themselves off. Great hilarity often accompanies these sparring events. Now and then a child will get a bloody nose or a painful whack, but if these matches are properly supervised, serious damage is not likely to result.

Occasionally injuries inflicted accidentally or intentionally by a classmate do occur at school. Sometimes teachers need to be as concerned about the child who has caused the mishap as the one who is hurt. His feelings of guilt may be a heavy burden. It may help the aggressor if he is allowed to assist in applying medication. If Peter has bitten Margaret, for example, the teacher may take them both to the bathroom and ask Peter to help to treat the wound. Peter will see the result of his action but is also given a chance to do something constructive about it. Although Peter is made to understand that biting hurts and is not acceptable behavior, his teacher will not belabor the point. It is well not to let such an incident be overdramatized, lest it should seem interesting enough to warrant repetition.

Conflict is sometimes necessary in shaping character. Judy, who had always played second fiddle to her friend, Jane, suddenly turned the tables on her and began to challenge her assumed leadership. As they were playing in the doll corner an angry argument could be heard.

"I don't want to be the baby today! I'm the Mommy," announced Judy.

"No, *I'm* the Mommy. You have to be the baby," retorted Jane, stamping her foot.

"I don't want to," parried Judy, whacking her friend angrily. "I won't play with you any more." And to Jane's obvious amazement, Judy stalked away.

This was the beginning of a revolution in the longstanding friendship between these two girls. The teacher who overheard the argument was secretly delighted, for she had been troubled about their relationship in the past. Though free of conflict, the attachment had never been a wholesome one, for Judy had always submitted unquestioningly to Jane's suggestions and commands. For several weeks life between them became stormy and quite disagreeable from the onlooker's point of view. But the turn of events meant growth for both girls. Jane gradually learned to accept suggestions from others while Judy discovered that it was not always necessary to do what she was told. Eventually, a fine relationship was established between them, based on mutual respect.

Eloise and Marjorie, both on bikes, met face to face beneath a bridge made by high ladders. Neither wanted to back out. They bumped their bikes in the middle. Eloise appealed to Mr. De Mott: "Make Marjorie get out."

Mr. De Mott did not seem to hear. Both looked more determined, knocking each other's bikes harder. Suddenly Eloise found a face-saver.

"Marjorie! Push me out with your bike," she suggested.

This solution came as a happy relief to both girls.

Children often welcome a face-saver when in conflict. They hate to give in when they have reached an impasse. They are no different from grownups or nations in this respect. This is a valuable thought for teachers and parents to keep in mind, for tense situations often can be cleared up by suggesting an honorable way out.

None of the incidents recounted above is at all unusual or abnormal. They are fairly typical of the sort of behavior that can be expected at the nursery school age level. Now and then, however, a wave of aggression and hostility may sweep through a particular group and cause a lot of unhappiness. If there seems to be an undue amount of friction, bad language, negativism, and other signs of resentment and fear, it is well for the staff to make a thorough analysis. It is not at all impossible that the teachers themselves are at fault. If they are critical of one another and fundamentally at odds, the children will sense this and respond unconsciously to the emotional tone set by them. Sometimes physical conditions of the play area may cause increased tension. Children need plenty of room in which to move about. Some of them become highstrung if they feel hemmed in too long, and a series of rainy days may coincide with stormy weather in the classroom.

An individual child may come to school in an angry mood and transfer his feelings to his associates. Certain children have especial need to let off tensions accumulated in a difficult home situation. Close contact with their families usually enables teachers to gain some insight into the underlying causes. If they realize that John's father is fretting because he is unemployed or saddled with an uncongenial job, that there is conflict over discipline between Barbara's parents, or that overly high standards of conduct and achievement are demanded of Arthur, they can better understand why these children need to let off steam in the school situation. Just as the business man who has had a hard day at the office may take out his annoyance on his wife, so do children carry their troubles from home into school or from school into the home.

There are, of course, methods of sublimating one's antisocial drives. Pounding with a hammer, bashing one's fist into a heap of clay, tackling a dummy, or delving into a colorful mass of fingerpaints may serve as a useful surrogate and provide the hoped-for release. Yet such tactics do not always satisfy the deep underlying need of a child. He may want to come face to face with the problem that haunts him rather than having it diverted into side channels.

Adults need to have an abiding faith that all children, no matter what their present behavior may be, have a deepseated desire to grow toward maturity. Without this trust, no one can do a truly satisfactory job. The confidence and genuine friendship of both parents and teachers are the child's strongest allies in his struggle to grow up and find better ways of behaving.

"This is the way we wash our hands" 7

Routines

Everyone is familiar with the genius who demonstrates an extraordinary talent in one field but is utterly helpless in all others: the wizard at the keyboard who is incapable of using his hands for any practical tasks, the artist who needs to be waited on hand and foot, or the scientist who lives in a world cut off from his fellow men because of his complete disregard of time, custom, and convention. Although teachers are delighted to see a child utterly absorbed in creative effort or scientific exploration, they know it is not necessary for a gifted person to be irresponsible, antisocial, or inconsiderate of others. Now and then they find among their pupils a young counterpart of the adult described above. Clarence's ability to improvise on the keyboard and his extraordinary skill at beating the drum had placed him in the realm of a genius in the eyes of his parents and others. He constantly won approval among grownups for this one great talent, so it hardly seemed important for him to strive in other areas. At school, however, he gained only mild attention from his classmates, who would have respected him more had he been able to do acrobatics on the jungle gym or had original ideas for block building. When it came to dressing for the outdoors, Clarence was so helpless that he was promptly labeled "a baby" by his critical peers. To Clarence, petty chores seemed beneath his dignity and he was unconcerned about the opinion of his classmates. Three doting adults were only too glad to wait on him at home. By so doing, they had made him unfit to face life's simplest tests. He lagged far behind his classmates in general physical, social, and emotional maturity.

Lester also ranked very high intellectually. He could read fluently at the age of four, but when it was time to get ready for outdoor play he would dump his jacket and leggings into a teacher's hands and demand in loud, insistent wails, "Help me! Help me!" to the utter amazement of his contemporaries, who stared at him open-mouthed and sometimes offered to lend a hand. But he would thrust their proffered aid aside in a rude way. He only wanted help from the teachers. A talk with his mother threw light on his difficulties. Until recently she had catered to his various needs—had dressed him, fed him, and put away his toys in order to give him more time for intellectual pursuits. After observing the competence demonstrated by his classmates, however, she decided that he too should fend for himself. Her change of tactics was so abrupt that he balked violently in the face of her determined campaign. Apparently he interpreted her withdrawal of support as a sign of rejection. Consequently he refused children's offers of aid. All he wanted was the assurance that adults were willing to back him up. He was not quite ready emotionally to do the whole task himself, but with the assurance that the adults at home and in school would see him over the humps, he gradually gained independence.

Peter could talk familiarly about "converters," "commutators," "belts," "couplings," and so forth, and was encouraged by his proud parents in scientific research. Although he was so impressive in mechanical knowledge he did not grow up socially and emotionally. He had no regard what-

ever for other people and ignored all limits set for the public weal. Nothing could be carried out in a matter-of-fact
way. Arrivals and departures, going to the toilet, washing
hands, drinking milk and eating a cracker, taking a rest,
helping to tidy up, removing or putting on wraps, learning
to stay within prescribed boundaries on the playground all
met with various forms of evasion or resistance. A great
amount of time was thus wasted which might better have
been spent in play when it was time to play. The teachers
were firm in insisting that Peter abide by the regulations at
school. Time and time again he was reminded of the limits
of his play area, restrained from destructive acts and un-
provoked hitting. His disorganized conduct was so firmly
established when he entered nursery school that it took
three whole years to replace the old set of habits with more
constructive ones. Peter eventually learned to live in a
group without having to be "different." He is no less gifted
for being more agreeable, cooperative, and self-reliant.

One reason Peter was slow to conform was that it took
time to convince his mother that the routines were important. "I leave it up to him to decide when he's ready for
food or bed. It saves a lot of argument," she stated. Such a
haphazard system might work in a small family unit but
would not make for agreeable living in a larger social
group. Peter's mother may have been brought up in this
laissez-faire manner herself, or she may have been rebel-
ling at too rigid a schedule in her own childhood.

Routines should never be an end in themselves. They
should serve as a sensible framework for the day, planned
to provide a happy balance between activity and rest, with
meals at regular intervals. Individual differences need not
be disregarded, for there can always be room for choice
within the established framework. Most children welcome
an orderly day and find security in knowing what is coming next.

Planners of full-day programs for young children face

particular challenges, for they must see to the needs of their groups across a span of eight hours or more. Some children will be with them only until lunch time, but many will require not only snacks, but a proper meal at noon and an afternoon nap, as well. Maintaining sensitivity to the differing needs of children—and to the day-to-day variations in the needs of each individual—puts heavy demands on the teachers' emotional stability, physical resilience, and educational training. Programs which are predicated on the day-long presence of teachers must also make provision for the needs of adults, with quiet periods away from the children and chances to get together with colleagues for planning, assessment, and professional growth.

A matter-of-fact acceptance of the routines is a healthy attitude. There should be no need for excessive praise, cajolery, threats, bribes, rewards, or punishments to get children to do the things which they ought to be doing as a matter of course. The child who rebels constantly is going to make life miserable for himself and others. Equally unhealthy is the compulsive child who is overly concerned about the meticulous execution of each aspect of the routines, who frets constantly about getting clothes soiled or torn, who has a tantrum if the wrong button is fastened first on his snowsuit, or who cannot eat unless he has a particular spoon, plate, or TV program to watch. Flexibility is a valuable trait for anyone who hopes to survive in our present-day culture. The extreme conformist has as hard a time as the rebel.

Though no two half-day sessions are identical, each situation has its simple routines which form a daily pattern. At some time between ten and eleven o'clock most nursery school groups stop to clean up, have a glass of milk or juice with a cracker, and then rest for twenty minutes. Because the so-called "routines" are determined by the staff members and do not permit great leeway, resistance to authority on the part of children usually finds its focal point at such times. Protests are likely to arise when it is "time to clean up." One way of avoiding too much opposition is to give children fair warning: "In five minutes it will be time to start putting blocks away." "You can do one more painting and then we'll have to clean the easel." Teachers are not insistent that children tidy the things which they have been using. If block builders were always expected to put away all the blocks, there would be a risk of discouraging this worthwhile activity altogether, for this is quite a chore, especially after one has given great care and energy to the work of construction. The real aim is to have each one do some part of the cleaning up. Quite often two or three children may decide that they want to put the hollow blocks away all by themselves. Needless to say, no one objects. If a child complains that he is too tired to do any of the chores which need to be done, his teacher may suggest that he sit on a chair a while. Why allow him to go on playing while the rest are putting the equipment away? Some children will do five times as much work as others, but this is to be expected. No two children are alike. The staff does not indulge in derogatory comparisons nor do they wish to stir up competition to see who can do the most work. They are satisfied if a general spirit of willingness prevails. The final burden for cleaning up rests with them and, depending on the day's circumstances, they may need to do the lion's share of it themselves. Teachers find, however, that children often consider it a privilege to be allowed to clean the easel, wash off table tops, and do many other tasks which adults usually take upon themselves to perform. By letting the children help, staff members not only give them a chance to grow in competence but may be saving their own strength for more important things. Teachers need to learn how to spare themselves. Getting children dressed for the outdoors in winter time is a backbreaking job. It is sensible for grownups to make themselves as comfortable as possible during this tedious process. By sitting on a low chair, for example, one can be within easy reach of everyone. If there is a scarf to be tied, a button to be fastened, a pair of rubbers to be pulled on, or a sweater to be donned, one can lend a hand here and there without growing purple in the face from stooping.

Needless to say, twos and threes require considerably more assistance in dressing than do older children. If a two-year-old lifts his foot at the proper moment instead of collapsing like a bag of meal one can consider that he is doing his part. The active participation of the child is the important thing. How often one sees adults stuffing limp objects into sweaters, leggings, jackets, and boots as if they were nothing more than rag dolls! Some children grow so accustomed to submitting inactively to the dressing process that initiative becomes atrophied. It is more healthy and normal to hear a child of three protesting violently, "I want to do it myself!" Even though it may seem unlikely to the onlooker that he can succeed on his own, this is the moment to let him try. This may require extra time and forbearance on the adult's part, but it is wise to accept his struggling efforts, as far as possible. One day the mother of a three-year-old brought him to school with a bit of egg on his chin and his sweater on inside out. She hastened to inform the teacher, "Robbie dressed and washed himself without any help this morning." She wanted to be sure to protect her son from being deflated and herself from being looked upon as a careless parent.

Although many a four-year-old can dress himself completely, there is often need for help and moral support. If Peggy comes to her teacher looking discouraged, with her arms loaded with garments, it may be psychologically helpful to hand her one at a time and suggest that she put that on. By doing the job step by step it seems easier than being confronted with all the clothes in a bunch. As soon as the children find that grownups are willing to assist in the difficult places, they assume more responsibility for themselves.

Marcia had always been a self-sufficient child who made few demands for adult assistance. Her mother was puzzled and irritated when at the age of five she suddenly went on a sit-down strike. Marcia insisted that she needed help with her snowpants. She and her mother had daily altercations in the locker room. "Take your snowpants off." "I can't! *You* take them off," was the petulant reply. "You know how to do it," argued the mother. But Marcia grew more whiny and insistent. Her mother then often helped her in the end. A new baby brother demanded so much of the mother's time at home that Marcia had begun to feel left out of things. Once it was understood that this regression stemmed from a yearning for attention, the mother found more time to enjoy Marcia's company. Soon the unreasonable demands were a thing of the past.

Not infrequently a child of five reverts to a period of helplessness because he becomes bored with the rather tiresome process of dressing and undressing which held a challenge for him a year or two before. The adult's assistance may be sought even though the physical aspects of the job are no longer an actual hurdle. An impasse may develop if help is refused, and relationships may suffer unnecessarily. At such times more harm may be done by an adamant attitude than by giving a friendly boost.

When it is necessary to insist that children put on an extra pair of leggings or a sweater because of a sudden drop in temperature, those children who do not have extra garments of their own at school may have to borrow from the school's supply. Although most children accept a proffered garment without demur, a few object violently. It is not always easy to understand the reason for a child's strong reluctance to wear a garment that does not belong to him, but it seems somehow to represent disgrace or a loss of face. One morning Lucille arrived with the cuffs of her dungarees soaking wet from having been splashed in a puddle. Her teacher found her a pair of maroon overalls, but at sight of them Lucille hid in her locker, weeping and protesting. It was explained that it would not be safe to play in wet clothing, but Lucille continued to wail. Two of her friends came out to tell her that she was being silly and that she was wasting time when she could be having fun playing. But still she crouched mournfully in her locker. Her teacher left her alone but returned now and then to make renewed efforts. At last she heard a small whisper emerge from Lucille's lips. "I like dungarees better." Fortunately there was a pair of dungarees in the locker belonging to Jane, Lucille's best friend. Jane agreed to lend them, and all was well. Happily Lucille had found a face-saver. A few days later Lucille spilled a glass of milk all over her dress. This time she took hold of her teacher's hand and skipped cheerfully to the locker room. She was even willing to don the maroon overalls which she had spurned on the previous occasion. As she was changing, she laughingly commented: "Isn't it funny, I had to change my clothes twice!" She had grown up quite a bit in those few days.

A similar incident occurred with four-year-old Matthew who came to school on a chilly fall morning dressed in shorts. He was offered a pair of leggings but he refused to wear them. When told that he had to choose between accepting the leggings or playing indoors, he said he wanted to go indoors even though his pals were all outdoors. His resistance baffled his teachers until he was heard to protest unhappily, "My mommy didn't know it was cold weather." He apparently felt it would disgrace her if he wore them, as it was an implied criticism of her judgment. It put him in an awkward position. At the end of the morning the same problem came up again when the group went outdoors. This time, after some initial refusals, he accepted the odious leggings. When his mother called for him she was relieved to see him warmly clad. He then refused to take off the leggings and asked the teacher if he might wear them home and keep them all winter.

The business of toileting looms large in the life of a two-year-old. Little wonder, since so much attention is usually centered on getting him properly trained. But, in addition to this, his bladder cannot hold as large a quantity of liquid as that of a child a year or two older, so he needs to relieve himself more often. The teacher of the twos makes a point of remembering how frequently each of her pupils should be taken to the bathroom. This varies with the individual. She keeps a mental note of each one's rhythm, and tries to act accordingly. The main responsibility rests with her as the children cannot be relied upon to remember, especially when deeply absorbed in play. A few children, however, are so obsessed with the toileting process or so fascinated by the diminutive bowls and washbasins, that they make frequent excursions on their own initiative and use the facilities even though there is no need for it. Twos can act like lightning sometimes, but this is not characteristic of their behavior in the bathroom. There, they are more like the proverbial snail. They have no sense of time or feeling of urgency. There are so many things to examine and explore. Curious eyes peer down the drain or look under the washbasin to discover where the water has gone. The soap has to be tasted. Billy's fingers feel the strange sucking motion of the water as it rushes toward the drain. "It feels like a cushion," is his interesting comment. Marian stops to stare soberly at Bart, who uses the toilet standing up instead of sitting down as she does. No one rushes her on. Each child is allowed to move at his own pace in an unhurried atmosphere. A very large part of the two-year-old's day is of necessity devoted to routine activities. This may seem boring to some adults, but it is not at all dull to the child.

As two-year-olds find security in repetition and familiarity it is wise to let them rest in the same locality each day. This is less necessary for older groups. Most of the threes do not object to shifting their place of rest, though an occasional child may look upon a particular nook or corner as his private property, in which case he is usually allowed to have it. However, it is healthy for children to learn to accept a certain amount of flexibility and not to become too dependent on the details of any routine.

It is astonishing to note the contrast between two four-year-olds, Alice and Violet, as they come in for routines. Alice swiftly doffs her outdoor clothing, hangs each article neatly in her locker, dashes to the bathroom, uses the toilet, flushes it, washes and dries her hands efficiently, and heads for the milk and cracker table where she promptly proceeds to eat. Having finished her snack, she gathers up her rest pad and blanket and spreads these meticulously on the floor of the darkened room next door. She settles down and announces rather smugly, "I'm the first one."

Meanwhile Violet is still in her snowsuit. Having had an important conversation with her pal, Ruth, she has now flopped down on her back in front of her locker. As a teacher approaches her, she raises a leg hopefully. "Help me! Pull my leggings off, please!" The teacher starts the leggings over Violet's heels and urges her to apply some effort. A bit later Violet is still sprawled on the floor—a vague, dreamy expression on her countenance indicating that her thoughts are in another sphere. With some more helping and prodding Violet is finally steered in the direction of the bathroom, where the slow-motion process continues. Most of the children fit somewhere between these two extremes.

Of course, one can expect some resistance to toileting among the twos and threes. Some may have had unpleasant associations in the past, have suffered from too much emphasis on the subject at home, or feel uncertain in the unfamiliar setting. A little girl of two refused for some time to use the school toilet because of having been frightened by an unpredictable toilet at her grandparents' home which flushed when it shouldn't and made sudden banging noises. Until she gathered some confidence, she was allowed to use a pottie chair. After she had time to examine the school toilets and assure herself they were to be trusted, she felt confident to use them.

One four-year-old boy announced each day, "I want privacy," while another simply waited in the locker room until the entire group had vacated the bathroom. This reluctance usually disappears in a few days or weeks, although an occasional child may persist in this attitude for months. If so, this behavior is usually part of a larger pattern of maladjustment. Teachers protect such a child, and are careful not to urge him or to make him more selfconscious. Now and then a child is too tense to be able to urinate at school. As he feels more and more at ease in the group, this difficulty wears off. The teachers note these symptoms of tension but make no comment about them in the child's hearing. This is the kind of problem which needs indirect treatment, never a head-on attack.

It is common for small children to show curiosity about each other's bodies. Two-year-olds stare solemnly and unselfconsciously, but a year or two later an embarrassed note may be added. Little girls are observed peering earnestly at the boys as they urinate. Questions may come up which are answered in a matter-of-fact way. "Yes, that's his penis—boys stand up to urinate." Sometimes teachers see the girls trying out this stance in front of the toilet. Sex differences are soon taken for granted and correct terminology is gradually picked up during this informal bathroom procedure. Furtive whisperings or secret goings-on behind closed doors occur rarely because normal curiosity is being satisfied in a wholesome setting. Children whose curiosity is not fully satisfied may turn ordinary doctor play into experiences that are not entirely wholesome. Sometimes guilt feelings are present and the children choose out-of-the-way corners for these activities. The staff members do not let such experiments go too far. They stay nearby, where their mere presence is a deterrent. If a child is obviously overcurious his mother may be urged to let him visit and help bathe an infant of the opposite sex.

Another time when children can examine each other's anatomies is during hot summer months when outdoor wading pools are in use at some of the more fortunate schools. The surrounding area is then full of little naked bodies changing in and out of bathing suits.

It is quite common for fours and fives to indulge in a certain amount of bathroom language and snickering about bowel movements and other terms dealing with the process of elimination. Young children are very much interested in all bodily functions and it is just as well for adults who have to associate with them to be free of all feelings of embarrassment.

A perfectionist might be irked at the dawdling and nonsense which may accompany the bathroom procedure. Twos take an interminable length of time. Threes are a bit more efficient and boast of their achievements. The fours, however, begin adding horseplay. Their teachers are quite willing to ignore a certain amount of tomfoolery provided the children follow through on what they are supposed to be doing. Children resent, and rightfully so, a lot of unnecessary orders and reminders. These are an insult to their intelligence. It is well for the adult to keep quiet and wait to see whether Tommy remembers by himself to flush the toilet. A child who is irritatingly slow will get plenty of hints to speed it up from his peers. These will carry more weight than repeated urgings from the adult. Fives take pride in performing these rites with dispatch. They are the capable seniors.

After hands are washed and the paper towel disposed of, the children find their way to the lunch table for an informal snack. The older children enjoy taking turns setting the napkins, crackers, and milk or juice glasses in place. In most classrooms children may start eating as soon as they sit down. There is no conversation among the twos. Eating occupies their total attention. Threes begin to show awareness of their neighbors at the table, and some communication takes place. As the fours reach the age of five sociability looms very large. There is much saving of seats for

special friends, wisecracking, mirth and elementary conversation. Generally it is only at parties that everyone re-
frains from eating until the entire group has gathered. Unnecessary strain is avoided by not expecting this every day.

Children may be loath to stop their play to rest, but even
with a break in the day some children go home tired. The
vigor, zest and intensity with which they fling themselves
into their play activities exhaust their energies. Children
cannot judge for themselves when it is time to stop and
take it easy. Obviously a child who is having fun would
prefer to continue playing, and is likely to proclaim loudly
that he does not need to rest. But this is where the adult
needs to take a firm stand. Children are not mature enough
to make such a decision for themselves and so it is better
not to give them a choice. Once children learn that the rest
period is an inevitable part of the day's program, they will
cease to struggle against it and often come to welcome it.
Some children may never be happy about this interruption
in their play, but even they can learn to accept the routine
philosophically.

After having spent fifteen or twenty minutes near a mass
of wiggling bodies chanting to themselves or whispering to
neighbors, an uninitiated observer may be astonished to
hear that this was considered a good rest period by the
teachers. No one aims at having perfect silence. Nor are the
children expected to lie like ramrods. On the contrary,
teachers are interested in having them learn how to relax
their muscles and minds at their own volition. In our
highly geared society, there is no more valuable safeguard
to health and sanity than the ability to relax easily and to
gather renewed strength by means of brief periods of rest.
To keep the body immobile and the voice from uttering a
sound would be no easy matter for the children to achieve,
and furthermore, such a goal would cause tension rather
than producing relaxation. A pleasant hum and a normal

amount of wriggling are reassuring signs. By lifting an arm or leg now and then to see if they flop lazily, adults can further ascertain the value of the rest period.

The rest period often serves as an emotional barometer for the day. It reflects the mood of the group and indicates whether the preceding play period was a satisfying one. Just as adults toss and turn in their beds at night when the day has presented too many unsolved problems, so will the child's experiences affect his ability to rest or sleep. If rest periods go haywire a number of days in a row, teachers find it advisable to put their heads together and do some planning. There are chaotic days. Children chase off and refuse to lie down, they make loud noises, toss their blankets about, scoot around on their bellies, giggle, and hurl threats at the staff members. Teddy, who is being steadied by a firm hand on his back, pours out a stream of dire threats. "We'll throw Mrs. Hermann out of the window, won't we? We really will. I'm going to kill you. My brother has a real gun—a .22 caliber. And some day I'm going to bring it here and shoot you! I'm going to kill Mrs. Edwards and Mrs. Hermann and every teacher in the whole world." Other forms of intimidation are attempted. "If you don't read us a story we won't rest—we'll scream and make lots of noise." Teachers may be pulled up short, realizing that their promise, "I'll tell you a story if you are quiet," is coming back to them in reverse.

Undesirable language, intended to shock, increases during rest period, for it is another way of expressing resentment against authority. "Enema peepee squirts! Dirty snot nose! You're a stinky teacher." These are only mild examples of what may come forth. One rest period was thrown into an uproar when a child started to recite, "Teacher, teacher, I declare—you forgot your underwear." It is not easy to keep a straight face with children. Fortunately, it is not always necessary to keep a straight face, but it is important to maintain poise and not to become upset or ruffled by these threats to one's dignity and authority. If the teacher can remain serene and not show signs of anger or irritation, chances are that these terrorist tactics will eventually be abandoned by the children. A stern manner may increase defiance, while little sermonettes will only be met with clever arguments. Children learn through their muscles. A quiet, restraining hand placed on a child's back will carry far more weight than a thousand words. More important than all else is the teacher's confidence that the children will rest. It is impossible to hide one's feelings from the children. It takes them no time at all to spot any indecision on the part of the adult and they will play it for all it is worth.

There is no foolproof formula on how to get a child to rest. The very best techniques and preparations will fail if the relationship between adult and child is a poor one. A child who continually wants to "get even" with grownups can find plenty of ways of doing so, but where mutual understanding exists many a hurdle can be crossed safely.

Disturbers of the peace are sometimes isolated from the group, but this is not done in a spirit of punishment. "If you feel like talking, you can do it out here. Others would like to rest," is one way to put it. And one might add, "You may come back when you are ready to lie down quietly."

Teachers react differently to different children. Miss Aki may close her eyes to the antics of Brent, who is sowing his oats for the first time. His behavior worries her much less than Alice's boast, "I'm the best child in this class because I'm the best rester." She is not concerned if the children notice that she does not always treat them alike. They are not always treated alike because no two people are alike. The adult needs to be sensitive to each one's needs and to act accordingly.

Persistent nonconformists at school usually fall into two categories: those who have had too many demands made on them at home and those who have not had enough. Undue emphasis on order and cleanliness in the home may burden some children with an exaggerated concern for such details. The fear of getting hands or clothing soiled may actually prevent carefree use of the play materials at school. These children look askance at finger paints, paste, and clay knowing that they are messy, and when outdoors they hesitate to let go in the earth, sand, or snow. If a garment is accidentally ripped while such a child is climbing or sliding, the incident may loom as a major catastrophe. The loss of a mitten or scarf may cause similar distress. A broken cracker or one with an uneven edge may be rejected for its imperfection. If a sheet or blanket is not entirely straight, the finicky child may fuss until it is properly adjusted. Any change in the daily routine may cause an emotional upset. New experiences and strange situations are often a threat to children who have been subjected to too much conformity and regimentation.

Excessive approval for their good performance in routines may encourage some children to strive hard in this realm. To stimulate pride and competition in doing a good job of finishing meals, brushing teeth, and being in bed on time, parents of young children occasionally resort to awarding gold stars. Their offspring, more often than not, develop a self-righteous, holier-than-thou attitude toward their less efficient contemporaries. They take pleasure in being tattletales, and look constantly for imperfections or infringements of rules. "She forgot to flush the toilet," "He's not resting well," "Bobby took two cookies!" "Lester's not helping to clean up."

After spending some time in nursery school, these children discover that their conformity is not lauded to the degree that they had expected. The teachers, though glad for their assistance in putting away the blocks, give more praise for their efforts at construction. The less rigid atmosphere at school may encourage them to try their wings and to rebel against all rules and regulations.

Gentlemanly Willie, who had always complied without question, suddenly turned into a trying young revolutionary. He began to mimic all the "bad" things he had previ-

ously found so shocking, and strove to ally himself with the
"tough guys" who liked to challenge authority. Though a
salutary change, his teachers felt that the parents might
need some warning in case the revolution should spread to
the home. Even with this preparation, life for Willie and
his family became very difficult for a while.

Martha's parents had to face a similar upheaval. Always
compliant, sweet, and gentle, Martha assumed the role of
teacher's helper for her first days at school. On the playground she could not find anything to occupy her. She preferred to stand near a teacher and frequently inquired,
"When will it be time for rest?" Her greatest treat was to be
allowed to go indoors with a teacher to pour milk and set
out the table for midmorning lunch. She did this expertly,
never spilling a drop. She felt competent and secure in
these household tasks, but lacked the normal resources for
play. She was unable to meet her classmates on their level,
being much too prim and proper in her approach. There
was an appealing quality about Martha, however, which
caught the eye of Juliet who happened to be her neighbor
one day at rest time. Juliet, with her mischievous, devil-
may-care spirit, held a fascination for Martha. After this
incongruous pair became close chums a marked change began to be noticed in Martha. From then on her teachers
had to get along without their demure assistant, but what
a delight it was for them to watch the sprightly, saucy little
elf who had blossomed in her stead! Martha was hard to
live with during subsequent weeks, both at school and at
home, but her parents agreed that she was really living for
the first time. Like Willie she found a middle course before
the school year was over.

Whereas some children are held to overly high standards
of conduct, others have been given insufficient opportunity
to make contributions to the comfort and happiness of the
family. Some have been made to feel that they are too little
to be of any use. "You go off and play" is the attitude of

many a mother who possibly finds it easier to do her household tasks alone than having a young helper in her way. But it is very important for a child's self-respect and his mental health to be given an opportunity to do really worthwhile jobs. Dicky, who had lived on a farm until he entered a city school at the age of four, had a serenity which few city children ever show. He had had real experiences in tending the soil, caring for animals, and working simple farm machinery. In school Dicky took it as a matter of course that he should lend a hand in cleaning up at the end of a play period.

It is not easy to find chores that have integrity about them in a modern city, but many families have managed to find a solution to this problem, especially those who have little or no domestic help. A small child can begin to make himself quite useful. He can help to set the table, do his share of cleaning up, and even lend a hand in cooking. A four- or five-year-old should not be expected to dry the dishes every day, but he can do them sometimes. On other days he may be delighted to polish the brass or the furniture, or to shine his own shoes. He will do these tasks with joy and enthusiasm. To pay him for his labors is to remove one of the chief values of such work. He does them as a member of the family—because he loves his family and wants to contribute to the common good. Once the commercial aspect enters in, the finer spirit is practically lost and will be hard ever to recapture. By letting a child share in honest work parents show respect for him as a contributing member of the family.

Conversely, parents who cater too much to their children are not likely to be respected. Children who have grown accustomed to having Mother clean up after them will begin to take it for granted that this is her duty. They will regard her as a useful slave or a personal handmaid. When Angela was told by a teacher that it was time to start putting the blocks away, she replied, "That's your job," and proceeded to find other play materials. This same little girl expected teachers to run errands for her: "Get me my gloves," "Put this drawing in my locker"—all in a tone of command. Her mother was startled to hear this about her daughter but noticed the same behavior at home after her attention was called to it. It is unfair to everyone to be always at a child's beck and call.

One mother with three children had never permitted herself an evening off since the birth of her first child. She dared not trust anyone with them and dreaded leaving them for fear they would miss her. The children doubtless would make a terrible fuss if she ever did decide to go on a spree, but such an experience would be wholesome for the whole family. Parents are also people who need to be allowed to have a good time and to follow their own interests now and then. Unwittingly parents may place an excessive burden on their children's shoulders by constant reminders of the sacrifices they make on the children's behalf. As years go by the debt owed to a "martyr" parent accumulates and the growing child will feel that he can never repay it.

In our present-day culture it is difficult not to overindulge children. So much is available for their entertainment and intellectual growth. The tendency is to rush children into all kinds of advanced experiences. Ballet and music lessons, ice skating, movies, children's concerts, and stage musicals would better be postponed until they are not so overstimulating or frustrating. Future pleasure is often spoiled by being introduced to this rich fare too soon. Watered down versions of fairy tales and children's classics are travesties on the beauties of the originals. The right time for all these things is far beyond these early school years.

Various motives may lead parents into lavishing toys, fancy clothing, food, and entertainment on their offspring. The reasons are not always clear but they are symptomatic of deep-seated problems. The mother who works full time may be trying to compensate for her lack of companionship. Others who do not really love their offspring may cover up their feelings of guilt by such means. Members of minority groups, envisioning future discrimination, may try in this way to give their children a happy start in life. Those who were underprivileged in their own youth may wish to spare their children similar feelings of want. Whatever the motive, the recipients of such material gifts are not made happier by them as long as their basic needs remain unsolved. Unless they feel wanted and accepted as worthwhile members of the family such children go through life fretful and dissatisfied.

There are children who can boast of few possessions or special privileges, yet face each day with joyful anticipation and without making undue demands for themselves. A sense of personal worth gives them this equilibrium. They are not obsessed with a need to win recognition because they have found it within the family. In the process of discovering their own worth they have also become aware of the worth of others. These children share in all important family experiences. They are included in its sorrows as well as its joys and in its responsibilities as well as its amusements. Parents and teachers must provide children with opportunities for honest sharing in the tasks and burdens of the group. The resulting sense of personal worth is the cornerstone of individual happiness.

Creative Arts

During these early school years, children are exposed to a variety of stimulating arts and crafts materials. Teachers want everyone to tackle and enjoy the art media—not just a chosen few who show special talent. These activities encourage experimentation; the end products are of far less consequence than the satisfaction derived through unimpeded manipulation of the materials. The teacher's task is to set the stage in such a way that children will be eager to try, will feel free to develop their own techniques, and will have the fun of discovery for themselves. This is not easy. It necessitates an attitude which encourages the inhibited as well as the uninhibited, the unskilled as well as the skilled.

When anyone is first confronted with a new tool or art medium he is not likely to produce artistic results. This is especially true of children, who have a limited experience. Handling a paint brush, for example, is difficult for a small child. If in his first attempts he succeeds in getting the paint from its jar onto the paper he is doing all that can be expected. A two-year-old, or a beginner at the age of three or four, is quite satisfied to have one jar of paint placed before him. He is not yet ready to experiment with color combinations. The mere problem of wielding the brush absorbs his whole attention. Even at this early stage of the game he can learn how to wipe the brush at the edge of the glass after each dipping in order to minimize drippings. This is a good habit to establish from the start, and helps rather than hampers subsequent attempts at self-expression.

Grownups watch with interest as children discover the magic of a brush. By pressing it firmly a solid line can be produced; by moving it lightly over the page a feathery effect is attained. Straight lines, wavy lines, dots, dashes, fanlike shapes, or airy wisps can all be created by varying the pressure and direction of the brush. As mastery over this tool increases, the addition of one or two colors provides a new challenge. How exciting to discover by oneself that yellow painted over blue makes green. "Look what I did! I made green!" The contrasting effects of colors placed side by side are also an unending source of fascination. To suggest what children should design, or to draw a sample house, cat, or human for them to copy, would limit and deprive them of the opportunity to perform at their own level of development.

Children give the cue as to how much supervision they require in the use of any of the art media. Some children— even at five—require the proximity of an adult. A two-year-old needs someone close at hand all the time he is painting. The surrounding territory, passersby, his own person, anything within reach are in danger of being jabbed with a bit of red or blue. He may need to be reminded over and over again to paint only on the paper. This is not an impossible lesson for him to learn. Similarly, clay may not be tossed across the room or carted about indiscriminately. It may be pounded, twisted, and mutilated to satisfy the most frustrated soul, but it must stay on the table. A smock is worn for all "messy" activities. Rather than hampering creativity, these simple restrictions give children freedom to experiment.

Although the chief satisfaction in finger painting is gaining a feeling of abandon, there are limits even here. Close supervision may be required, especially with the younger children who wallow in this medium without really comprehending its purpose. Fours and fives revel in the experience of creating whorls, swirls, snakes, and junglelike effects by using their palms, fingertips, knuckles, fists, arms, and elbows. Big sweeping motions provide greater release than tiny tentative jabs; if teachers see a child persistently limiting himself to the use of one index finger, they may encourage him to plunge in more deeply. Otherwise, they refrain from offering advice or help.

Each teacher may vary somewhat in the method of presenting this material, even though the general purpose may be the same. The staff of one group noticed that the children spent more time demanding colors than using the materials they had. "I want red! Now gimme blue! Yellow! Yellow! Can I have orange?" These requests became a tiresome refrain. In order to place the emphasis on actively working with the finger paints, these teachers limited the children's choice to two colors. Too many colors mixed together make such a muddy concoction that further temptation to work with it is usually dissipated. Having chosen his one or two colors, however, the child can concentrate on making the most of what he has got. It is sometimes fun to dispense with paper and use a light-colored formica table top. This surface, perhaps two by four feet in size, provides plenty of elbow-room for wallowing to one's heart's desire, and the children feel free to mess about without concern for the finished product. An added advantage is that the table top is just right for two children working simultaneously. Some pairs may keep their territories strictly apart, but others gain a keen delight in overlapping and mingling their colors. The social interplay may detract from the artistic results, but this is all to the good. When the fun wears down, each child may be offered a sponge with which to wipe the surface clean for the next users. This is also a welcome occupation and provides opportunity for real responsibility to be taken by the child. A distinct asset in not providing paper for finger painting is that emphasis on the end product is automatically removed. At times, however, it is fun to take home finished products, to use them as table mats for a party, or to decorate the classroom walls with these often interesting creations.

Parents should be encouraged to do finger painting with their children, for it is one medium in which the average adult rarely puts the child to shame. Both can have an equal amount of fun without placing the younger one at a disadvantage.

A few children look askance at this medium. They are afraid to allow themselves to get messy. It may take weeks, even months, to break down their reserve, which may have been brought about by a parent who is overly zealous about cleanliness. Once they have broken through their restraints, however, these children are likely to go haywire in their wild abandon. A marked change in personality may follow such an experience. A lot can be discovered by watching a child's behavior in a finger painting session. Teachers' impressions of a particular individual may be strengthened or confirmed by his manner of attacking this art medium. They are careful, however, about drawing conclusions from a few samples of his work. It is just one of many channels by means of which adults can gain access to his deeper feelings.

Finger paints or clay are an especial boon when tensions run high. If Charlie arrives with a chip on his shoulder or Susie with a sulk, nothing is more beneficial than the chance to wallow in this pleasant squoosh or to pound and pummel the clay.

Clay is presented in sizable balls, bigger than an adult's

fist. This is done in order to encourage the use of the child's whole hand rather than only his finger tips. As they twist, knead, roll, and pound this malleable material, hand and arm muscles are being strengthened. Some children develop sufficient skill after two or three years to make representations of animals, humans, and other objects, but after these have been duly observed they are broken up and put back into general use. "Dough" made of flour, salt, and water is a variation on clay and offers budding pastry cooks a chance to knead and mold and to display their artistry. When it is time to stop work the bits of dough can be combined into one large mass and stored in the refrigerator for another day. Woodwork products, if well made, sometimes go home with the children. Simple planes, ships, or doll beds can serve a useful purpose in the child's room. Unless adults feel keenly about keeping all these products, the children themselves are not especially concerned. Once they have finished their work they turn to other interests. How often teachers save drawings only to find them left behind in the children's lockers! However, it is still important to keep them in case one child does care.

Manila paper and crayons offer a variety of experiences to young children, provided they are left to their own devices. Adults may see nothing but jagged lines or uncoordinated efforts during the first year or two, but the foundations are being laid for the more deftly executed products which emerge later.

After the fourth birthday there appears to be a noticeable spurt of interest in drawing, and there is always a little "crayoning crowd" which gathers around the table. The noisy chatter which accompanies their work reminds one of a ladies' sewing circle or bridge party. Parents often complain during this year that their children do better art work at home than they do at school. There is a very good explanation for this. At school the main concern of four-year-olds is to make friends, so they cannot give as full attention to their products. Sometimes out of sheer delight in sociability children will deliberately make crazy jumbled drawings, meanwhile laughing hilariously at their own wit. This minor setback in art products is soon balanced by a new stimulus to effort in their desire to impress each other. Four-year-olds do not hesitate to offer criticisms. They sometimes show surprising acumen in judging work, although they can be quite brutal in their attacks. Any immature work is pounced upon as being "scribble-scrabble," yet many children are willing to give praise where it is due. Learning to accept criticism from peers is a very valuable lesson.

In offering criticisms children reflect the opinions which have been expressed in their presence by grownups. Adults need to be careful in giving praise, and need to drop many of their preconceived notions of what is good art. Slickness of execution is a poor substitute for creativity and a willingness to experiment.

A revealing conversation took place one day at the crayon table. Some children were discussing the "scribble-scrabble" drawings of their younger brothers and sisters. Mrs. Robertson said that everyone made scribble-scrabble when they were little. Betty said, in a tone of defiance, "Well, I didn't, because by daddy taught me too soon." Her father found it difficult to accept any immature products and had given her coloring books to fill in so that she would learn to stay neatly within the prescribed boundaries. She had learned her lesson well, but over a period of time there was no progress evident in her work. She continued to draw flowerlike designs which she filled in. Had she been allowed to do her scribble-scrabble, to experiment freely with color combinations, shapes and forms, she might have done far more original work. The boundaries of the coloring books had a restrictive influence and cramped her freedom of self-expression. Now and then one finds a child who has been taught how to draw a specific object. Mary, for example, can draw a conventional house perfectly, but she goes on drawing that same house over and over again because she has not been encouraged to develop her own ideas and techniques.

Plain sheets of paper and good-sized crayons are the best materials to give children for drawing. It may take many months before anything recognizable or pretty will begin to take shape, but during these months the children are developing their hand muscles, are gaining mastery over the materials, and are having fun in making discoveries for themselves. It is sometimes astonishing what a variety of products eventually appears if work is not interfered with. Lovely designs are created. Teachers make a point of admiring these "designs," which have value just as much as clever representations of human figures or other subjects. Crayoning probably offers less chance for emotional release than do some of the other art media, yet children have been found to give expression to their feelings in their drawings. Before they can do so, they need a certain amount of skill in representing what they have in mind.

Children are often reluctant to discuss their drawings or paintings. A direct question, "What is that?" usually elicits an evasive answer, for it puts the young artist on the spot. If the adult is told that it is "nothing," he should not be surprised. On the other hand, he may be treated to a lengthy explanation, fabricated on the spur of the moment. Children quickly sense whether the adults are really interested in their art work. Once they feel at ease they will readily volunteer information about the ideas they are trying to express. A willingness to listen is probably the best way of inviting confidences. Children's unsolicited comments are most revealing.

Harmless domestic scenes may be portrayed, but at other times fears, anxieties, and hostilities come to the surface. Harriet, a lonely child, commented about her drawing, "This is a little girl. She is standing there because no one likes her." Another child's drawing was accompanied by this tale, "It's a little girl lost in the woods. She doesn't know her own way home." A woeful-looking child in another drawing was having the following experience: "It's raining and snowing and this little girl was supposed to be home at 3:00 and she's getting home at 6:00. Look how sad she is." A grim drawing of a train on tracks approaching a girl had this explanation: "A girl ran across the tracks and a train came and she got killed." A meticulous little girl, always concerned about order and neatness, drew a picture which included a girl, a cat, and an open umbrella. Her story was probably a true one: "The girl is mad at the cat because it scratched the umbrella. It was drying. They just came in from the rain." Another child, the oldest of several in her family, drew "a little girl with lots of arms." The child in the picture actually had eight arms—possibly necessary to hold on to all the younger ones.

One picture has the innocent label, "We are eating supper." A close scrutiny, however, reveals some astonishing details. Three figures are shown: Elizabeth Ann, the artist; Jane Ellen, her younger sister; and the mother. Oddly enough, Jane Ellen is outside the framework of the house while Elizabeth Ann and her mother are close together inside. There is a table, but no one is sitting at it. The front door, with a big lock, is placed exactly between the two little girls. One can only surmise the meaning behind this little scene. Meal times were known to be difficult in this household. The children seldom stayed long at the table. But it also seems to point up strong jealousy on the part of Elizabeth Ann toward her sister, who has been conveniently planted outside the house.

Another expressive tale was told by a little boy, Michael, who filled his page with a series of colorful windows. "These are windows. Windows have faces. One window said to himself one day, 'I think I'll break myself to pieces!' So he broke himself with a smash bang and a lickety bang smash. Then the family woke up and heard this lickety bang smash in the night." On the reverse side of this page was a tall ladder with some other shapes. Michael went on to dictate: "One ladder, one day, said to himself, 'I think I'll break my bar so no one can climb me again,' He was a bad ladder; it used to be good but it changed his mind. He smashed his bar, lickety smash, smash, bang! Then a jungle gym came and just watched. When the ladder was all smashed (this was on a snowy day), the jungle gym helped to put him together again and fixed him all up." The author had great need for showing defiance and belligerence. A psychiatrist might find much food for thought in the above stories.

Now and then humor appears. One child's comical drawing portrays "a fat lady with a little bit of food in her tummy." She is indeed enormously fat. In the center of several layers of flesh is a tiny dot to represent the morsel of food. "People standing on their heads," "a funny clown," and "a duck with four legs" are other four-year-old portrayals of wit.

Children's interest in details of the human body is evident in their art work. Whereas some concentrate all their attention on facial details, others represent people with enormous bodies and overgrown limbs, with the head insignificant. The navel, nipples, and sex organs may also be prominent. This probably indicates what part of the anatomy seems to the child most important. Teachers sometimes get an inkling of the child's concept of himself in relation to the other members of his family. In one picture, for example, a little boy appears with his father and baby brother. He himself is colorfully clad, has detailed features and hair on his head. The other two are drawn sketchily, appear to be bald, and have few features.

Some children approach art intellectually. Their meticulous representations of planes, trains, boats, or steam shovels point at a scientific interest rather than feeling for color and design. If their concern for detail seems to produce tension, adults may try to steer them away from such fine work by recommending that they make large swirling movements with their crayons in order to get a feeling of release.

Now and then a child appears at school with a little notebook in which he starts writing a series of ABC's. The stimulus may have come from an older brother or sister. It is not a normal interest of a three- or four-year-old. There are far more important things for him to be doing. By the age of six or seven, printing the alphabet may be learned quickly and painlessly, whereas at a younger age there is likely to be frustration and disappointment, not to mention eyestrain. It is quite common for many pupils to print their own names on their drawings or paintings, and teachers accept these without comment. If they do not label their own work, staff members make a practice of doing so and always add the date. It is useful to know when a certain drawing was made. As they look over a pile of one child's art work, teachers can note the stages of development that have taken place.

Actually, it is hardly necessary to put a child's name on his art products, for his own peculiar style soon becomes so familiar as to be almost a signature. A casual onlooker might think all children's efforts look more or less alike, but the observant adult can discern unmistakable characteristics. There are Judith's inevitable networks of spiderweb design, Carl's meticulous trains and buses, Alice's wavy airy lines, Bob's straight crisscross patterns, Rose's lively peasant women, and Art's mad, stormy masses. Believe it or not, this is even true at the age of two or three. Teachers sometimes test one another in identifying the art products of their young pupils and are frequently right. They might be fooled, however, about the authorship of an art product in a kindergarten group, for during this year the children develop an interest in copying one another's work. This is a stage of development which may disappoint many a parent who had been delighted to see individual expression blossoming so clearly during earlier years. What is happening? Actually, an important lesson is being learned. The ability to note details sufficiently well to be able to make a somewhat accurate duplicate is essential if one is to master the symbols involved in the three R's. Art may undergo a setback at this time, but other progress is taking place.

Knowing each pupil well and watching him as he engages in a number of activities, teachers find that drawings and paintings help to corroborate and strengthen their opinions about him. It is important to see the child at work, to know what kind of a mood he happens to be in while he is painting, and whether he is alone or with a friend. The paintings by themselves do not give a complete story.

A certain number of children hastily cover over their initial efforts at the easel with a thick blotch of paint. Some do this habitually. Are they dissatisfied with their work? Are they ashamed to lay bare their feelings and thoughts before the eyes of onlookers? It is not an easy matter to judge the motive underlying such behavior. One little girl needed only a word of praise from an adult to make her blot out with fierce jabs of her brush whatever lovely thing she had designed.

Not infrequently praise may have the effect of producing extreme jealousy in others. Felice, an unpredictable young lady, was often guilty of tearing or otherwise mutilating art work which she recognized as being superior to her own. She needed to gain self-respect by improving her own skills. Merely reprimanding and scolding her would have been of little avail to see her through her difficulties.

Some children gain considerable release as they apply paint to the easel paper. Wesley, just five, seldom painted, but when he did he would get a sort of jag on and work with feverish excitement. Several pages would be filled one after the other. One day he did a series of "fire" pictures, obviously the result of a recent experience. "The house is on fire! There is smoke from the cellar. See the broken windows! They broke the windows to get in. It's burning the steps!" Wesley was sufficiently skillful to make fairly accurate representations of all these details. The next picture showed an ambulance with windows and wheels. Nearby was "water streaming down from the fire." This was blue in color, but some other water was painted orange and was said to be "rusted." The third picture was "a Europe house burning. I read about it. It really happened."

Another series of his paintings was inspired by a visit to the Natural History Museum. It began with a painting of "toys," including a toy man and a toy horse, both standing on wheels. The second painting showed only one horse, this time a real one, with a tail and "inside bone." A huge "pee-pee" out of all proportion to the animal, dominated the page. "This is where the pee comes out," explained Wesley, "but I didn't see how the baby grows inside. Daddy will take me to the museum to see that. . . . Now I will draw a mother with a baby inside of her." On a new sheet of paper he painted a mother with a baby in her stomach. He carried on a continuous running commentary while painting, and demonstrated with a series of vertical lines near the edge of the paper how the baby's legs grew bigger and bigger inside. He explained that the baby was a girl. "Now I'll paint the daddy." Daddy was placed beside the mother, somewhat taller and wider. The climax came when a baby boy was painted inside the daddy! After this mammoth effort Wesley did a completely different type of painting. This was his only nonrepresentational one. It was sparsely covered with spirals and wavy lines of great freedom, suggesting that his mental tension had finally been worked out.

A project which has proved popular with fours and fives is a group mural. Teachers stretch a roll of brown wrapping paper along the wall at suitable height, and several children work at this simultaneously. The result is a bit higgledy-piggledy, but the children enjoy the great mass of intertwining colors. Now and then two or three work more seriously on a smaller-sized mural. This work gives new impetus when inspiration is at a low ebb. In the fall there is neither sufficient skill nor group feeling among four-year-olds to introduce such an enterprise, but in the spring it may be highly successful.

In the older groups scissors are always available on the open shelf. Some of the three-year-olds enjoy using them too, but are given access to them only occasionally, for although the scissors are blunt-tipped for safety, their use still presents some hazards. With constant practice in cutting out their own drawings, making party mats of their own design, or cutting pictures from magazines, the children's finger muscles gradually become remarkably deft in manipulating this rather complicated tool.

Paste is enjoyed by all the children. Initial efforts are likely to be extremely clumsy, but it is a fascinating medium. It can be so absorbing that an older classroom sometimes resembles the traditional kindergarten as all the chairs are occupied at the same time with earnest cutters and pasters.

As the children choose their own pictures to paste from a heterogeneous assortment, the adult onlooker may sometimes gain insight as to their interests and concerns. Olive, aged four, was observed cutting from magazines with great concentration, though the results were not very precise. Her selection was entirely of one subject: men. About twenty small pictures surrounded her. Mr. Johnson went over and asked what she liked most to cut out. "Oh, these men," she replied. "Which do you like best?" he inquired. She chose them all as favorites. Suddenly Olive was seen dumping an armful of paper into the wastebasket. "Where are all the men?" inquired Mr. Johnson. "I throwed them away because I didn't want them any more. I'm going to paste some ladies on there." This might seem like an insignificant incident except for the fact that Olive's father had recently deserted the family, and she was continually obsessed with this overwhelming personal problem.

As grownups watch the amount of concentration, persistence, willingness to try again, and general steadiness required in block building, they cannot doubt its tremendous value in character growth. The children find it a most satisfying activity, and take pride in the way their structures take shape as they add one block here and another there. Now and then a pupil refuses to use the blocks but begs adults to build for him. "You show me," is his refrain. Teachers suspect, and usually find their suspicions verified, that Daddy has been too eager to demonstrate the proper techniques of building. It is fun to share these activities, but the parent should let the child set the pace. His own discoveries are of greater value to the child than suggestions made by the more experienced adult. Furthermore, he may become discouraged if his immature efforts are continually corrected or improved upon. The fault may also lie in the use of advanced construction sets, which are provided with books of illustrations that the children struggle in vain to copy. Parents may have to come to the rescue, and again, the result is lack of confidence. Unit blocks, on the other hand, allow unlimited experimentation. Children's structures are likely to be quite unconventional, showing few of the characteristics of normal architecture. Buildings sprawl haphazardly and towers teeter precariously on a thin foundation. Teachers would hesitate to interfere in their experimentation. There is a certain charm and freshness in the child's approach. Furthermore, he discovers soon enough that a tower topples if not provided with a solid underpinning. Basic principles of balance are recognized in due time. Besides appropriate materials, sufficient encouragement, space, and time are required to stimulate and promote this type of play.

Block structures often reflect places of interest to which a group has been taken. While some exciting visits lie within easy walking distance, more distant safaris may be made possible in a fleet of cars driven by parents who can spare a morning or afternoon. A fire station, the zoo, a marina, or a pizza parlor will be reconstructed with reasonable accuracy by four-and five-year-olds, on their return to school. Their thoughtfully planned block buildings may become the focus of related dramatic play for several days in a row, while they are given further validation in drawings and dictated stories.

Some block structures are a delight to the eye. Now and then, when possible, children are permitted to place a sign on a structure requesting the person who cleans the room not to disturb it. A sign may read, "Please do not touch our station. John and Eddie." This stimulates further interest in block building and sometimes carries play over from one day to the next. Teachers often protect children as they work, or suggest safe spots for them to get started in order to minimize interference. Generally, a rule is established that no one should knock down another's block structure. "Knock your own down, if you want," is an alternative suggestion. It is surprising how much respect children soon begin to show not only for their own products but for the work of others, too.

The cleaning-up process may dampen enthusiasm. Where no issue is made of it, willing hands often lend support. Five-year-old Mimi found real satisfaction in this chore one day. "I'm putting the blocks away," she announced. "You know, it's fun doing this! It's just as if you're *making* something. I'm even cleaning up this mess next to the nest. You know what? I *love* to do this. It makes me feel as if I were making a nice, pretty building. Did you think I was getting tired of doing this?"

Making collages is another interesting form of constructive work. Children love to be set free with an assortment of odds and ends, such as small scraps of wood, spools, dowel sticks, cork, shells, beads, lace, sequins, buttons, pine cones, bits of material, pipe cleaners, etc., together with some glue or cement. The idea is to assemble these in any way desired. After the collage has stood around for a while and been properly admired, it can be soaked apart so that the separate parts may be reassembled on another occasion.

Many schools keep handy in their bathrooms a basketful of water play toys—strainers, funnels, beer cans, bits of cork, and other articles. Water play has considerable therapeutic value for highstrung individuals. There is something infinitely soothing about pouring water back and forth. Also, while this play goes on interesting discoveries are made and commented upon. Some things float, others sink. Air is really something. You can see it rise to the surface in great bubbles out of a tin can.

Now and then busy little laundresses bring their doll clothes and dishes to be washed, and do a creditable job. The use of water is a valuable part of the program. Outdoors in warm weather there is no more fascinating occupation than going about with a tin can containing water and a paint brush. Practically every piece of equipment, the walls, and fences receive a thorough going-over with this make-believe paint.

Carpentry is an area in which good habits of workmanship should be stressed. First of all, good tools are essential. Their proper use and care are part of the value of this experience. This is one of the favorite activities with girls as well as boys.

Some twos are ready to handle a hammer. All the equipment needed at this age is a piece of soft wood, a well-balanced hammer, and some large-headed roofing nails. The children are content simply to pound away. They have no end product in mind. Later, the saw can be mastered also. Again, the process of dividing a piece of wood by one's own strenuous efforts is sufficiently thrilling without having to produce anything with the sawed-off pieces. During initial stages the mastery of the tools is the main thing.

By the time children are four, many of them are eager to

make definite objects: airplanes, boats, doll beds, chairs, rocketships, etc. Their enthusiasm at the start, however, is not always matched with sufficient patience to see the product through to the end. Some initial planning is advisable. Fours soon weary unless given moral support and help. Left to their own devices they are likely to dash off with a half-completed airplane, held together vaguely with one nail. Teachers find that the constant guidance of an adult is necessary in seeing any four-year-old's carpentry efforts through to some sort of satisfying completion.

Fives enjoy additional tools. They are interested in measuring with a ruler, in drawing straight lines, and making accurate square corners. Many of them are also capable of handling a brace and bit. Their interest may be sustained long enough to carry over to the following day, and they take pride in giving their final product a thorough treatment with sandpaper to ensure a lovely satiny finish. Unless kindergarten children are held to certain standards of good workmanship, involving some planning and sustained effort, they will begin to flounder around aimlessly and eventually lose interest.

With almost no direct instruction, children gradually acquire astonishing manual dexterity, as well as constructive ideas of their own. The type of planning, support, and stimulus provided by the adults with whom they associate does make a difference, however, in the extent to which they can proceed in their creative efforts. It is wise to limit the number of art media provided at one time, and to vary them from day to day. Fortunate is the child who has found in parent or teacher an ally in inventiveness, one who takes delight in experimentation and who can envision the play possibilities of many things not usually recognized as toys for children. The provision of proper tools and assorted work materials is the adult's primary responsibility, but to these basic ingredients should be added the spice of enthusiasm. The varied skills which children acquire play a vital part in building self-esteem and confi-

Music

John, just four-and-a-half, stops on his way to the easel. "When are we going to have 'ribbons'?" he asks, "I want to be bears."

Margot prances over to Miss Allen. "Don't I look pretty in my costume? I want to be a lobster in rhythms. Tie my sash. When can we dance?"

On an indoor morning, the chances are that if Miss Allen senses enough interest among the children, a session of rhythms around the piano will start just before or just after routine time. When the equipment is being put away and the children feel that their free play time is about ended, most of them are ready to devote their attention to the first group activity of the morning. In fact, so eager are they to clear the floor for action that putting away the large hollow blocks seems a mere trifle.

The subject matter of these dances is varied. Already, bears and lobsters have been suggested, and as soon as the children crowd around the piano, other demands follow: "Mountains! Cockroaches! Let's be lions! No—mine! I asked first." Simply to set things in motion, since she has heard enough ideas to fill several hours, Miss Allen starts a jumping song or a march. No sooner have the first notes begun than several pairs of feet are working in reasonably good rhythm, while two or three children mount the climbing box to look down on the proceedings. The participants are grinning from ear to ear, throwing their bodies into the spirit of the song. They recognize "See How I'm Jumping" and "See, Here Comes the Big Procession." After a short time, Miss Allen plays a loud glissando down the keyboard, and the group slides with the notes down to the floor.

Now the problem is to make the most of the children's imaginations. One can imagine bedlam following a request for lions or gunboats, but children can discover a host of other things that lions can do besides roaring, or that gunboats can do besides shooting off their artillery. "Lions sleep," someone suggests. "I went to the zoo with my daddy and we saw a lion sleeping." "They hunt for food," comes from tough Billy. "They creep up and then they jump at it." "A lion lives in a cave sometimes." So the ideas are pieced together to make a logical story, to give an imaginative but accurate picture of lion life, and to form a kind of crescendo and decrescendo of action. Perhaps they decide to begin with the lion asleep in his lair, waking to prowl stealthily in pursuit of another animal. After a sudden leap, they crunch their prey avidly, roar with tremendous vigor, and at length return to their cave to sleep. Needless to say, Miss Allen is sometimes hard put to it to pick up their ideas and translate them into appropriate music. It is important to stay in the mood of the action and to sustain a steady, rhythmic pattern. Melody is secondary, and even harmonic relationships go by the board. The children have no difficulty whatever in adapting themselves to the spirit of the dance. They most often choose to be things that they have seen, and their portrayals of these familiar sights are surprisingly accurate.

Some ideas are called out that sound crazy or impossible. How to dance "curtains" or "a table" might tax the ingenuity of an adult. For the children there is no such thing as an impossibility in rhythms. Curtains turn out to be a simple matter. First, you go downtown—you are a big fat lady, so you waddle—and buy the material at the department store. Then you take the bus home. There is no division of roles in these stories; the entire group plays each part as it comes along. You are the fat lady, the bus, the store clerk, and later on, the lady's daughter. Everybody knows how to cut and sew, so with cutting-and-sewing music from the piano to keep fingers moving together, the curtains ("They are blue curtains," says Margot, "with lace on the edges.") are soon finished and hung in the window. "And when the little girl comes home," Miss Allen is informed, "she is so happy that she jumps for joy." Tables turn out to be equally simple. There is hammering and sawing and planing, and the job is ended. "No! We have to paint them now." So while the piano furnishes sloshing music, paint is applied. Some of it is put onto invisible tables in the air; some is applied generously to tables transformed by imagination from hollow blocks and the woodwork along the walls.

Miss Norris stands by the ladder box, watching and taking an occasional note. When Clyde began to wrestle in the middle of the lion's stealthy prowl, she reminded him that the lion was alone and trying to be as quiet as possible. Otherwise, she has not entered the dance since the opening march. Now, while the carpenters are putting the last touches to their tables, she invites Christopher to come down from his perch on the box and join his pals. He has been kicking his foot in perfect time to the music since it began, but has simply not had enough courage to enter the game. Miss Norris' friendly word does the trick. Almost without realizing it, since he has been so much in the mood of the music already, he slips to the floor nearby and coats his table with bright green (pretend) paint.

It is not so easy to bring "individualists" into the group. Walter is a good example. A tough and wiry boy, he talked in cowboy lingo all day. The girls cowered in fear when he stormed by on his way to capture the bad sheriff. His ready fists and superior manner had won him a group of admiring, if subservient, cronies. For two weeks, he sat on the top of the block pile, his friends about him, and scoffed while the others danced. "They're stupid," he sneered. "That's not what a pony looks like." But he could not be induced to come down to demonstrate. One day the group was in the midst of a cockroach dance. Cockroaches were items of real interest to these city children. Hearing a click on the piano, which represented the snap of a light switch, they swarmed out into the dark room in search of crumbs. Feelers quivering and legs scuttling from place to place, they looked like real insects. Walter and his gang sat in their accustomed spot, very much interested, but keeping up a pretense of derision. On their heads were fire helmets, cut from manila paper. From her place at the piano, Miss Allen could see their supercilious expressions beneath the paper flaps. Then, an idea! Jangling a few notes to suggest the ring of a telephone, she held an excited conversation with the fire department. Her house was crawling with roaches, and no one seemed to have anything to kill them with. Did Walter and his men own exterminators? They did, and they would be right down. After much screeching of sirens, the gang descended with "spray guns." Fairly leaping in time to the music, they pumped clouds of suffocating fumes on the roaches, who cooperatively curled up in death spasms. Their job done, the fire department returned noisily to their perch. But the step had been taken. After that, it was never so hard again to interest them in some of the more vigorous dramas. Cowboys lassoing and branding cattle caught their imaginations, and they often asked for a loping accompaniment while they sang "Home, Home on the Range," astride invisible ponies.

Provided that she is not ignorant of and easily embarrassed by some subjects, the rhythms leader can make much of ideas related to nature, sex, or death. Drawing on the fund of her own childhood experiences with caterpillars, tadpoles, and plant seeds, she can contribute a few accurate but simply expressed facts that introduce new information at the same time that they create added interest. The eternal cycles of egg-to-tadpole-to-frog or egg-to-caterpillar-to-cocoon-to-moth excite in children a unique kind of wonder about the world around them.

A birth-to-death dance helped some children in the same group to get anxieties out of their systems. Judith started it all with a simple request: "I want to be a seed that turns into a baby." For a moment Miss Allen was nonplussed. Just how much about birth did Judith know? Where did she want the dance to start? "It should start in the mother's tummy," Judith said. Miss Allen turned to the piano and played a series of single notes while she described the smallness of the seed. The children hunched themselves into tight spheres and waited. Now soft, atonal chords accompanied her description of the warmth and darkness inside the mother. In a short time eyes and arms and legs had appeared; the seeds were beginning to look like babies. Monotonous patterns in the music emphasized the slowness of the process. It seemed like a long time to them, though by the clock they had taken shortly more than a minute to develop into a child ready to be born. The mother, now big with the child inside her, felt its kick. Finally, with a glissando that swept down the keyboard, the children slipped easily into the world. Satisfied that she had given enough, Miss Allen turned the rest of the dance over to the group. They thought of their own baby brothers and sisters and suggested that the child would start to scream. Rhythmic wails were pacified by a bottle. They chewed objects, crawled about the floor and made infantile sounds. "Now he is two," said John. "He can start to walk," Margot suggested, "and he can run." When the baby had grown to be their age, four-and-a-half, how many things he could do— jump, swing, skip, turn somersaults! "Then he goes to school and studies arithmetic," said John again, suiting his actions to his words. And after school, they decided, came college, with more studying of harder arithmetic and a violent basketball game. After college, what? No one had any idea. When Miss Allen suggested that their parents had married, the entire group started a strange, slow dance. Most of the girls sought other girls, and the boys chose their regular pals; each couple drifted about in a close embrace. And next came old age. Some of them hobbled on canes; one said that their hair should fall out. Miss Allen mentioned that sometimes teeth came out too. "But how should the dance end?" she asked. "They die," came the response. Limply, the aged folk crumpled to the floor, stretched out, and lay motionless. The dance was over.

The following day, two parents came to greet the staff. Mrs. Braun confessed that she had always felt awkward about discussing sex; she had wondered what she would do when Karen asked about babies. "And yesterday, Karen came home and told me about the baby, and how it grew in the mother's tummy! I can't thank you enough. You've made my job a lot simpler." A second mother, troubled about death herself, had worried about exposing her child to a concept that seemed rather terrifying. "At lunch yesterday," she told Miss Allen, "Bobbie said, 'Mother, today we danced dead people, and it was so beautiful.'" While it would be easy to overemphasize the importance of this dance, it had introduced the idea of death in an untroubled, uncomplicated way, and had given accurate, if simple, information about the process of birth.

In all these sessions the children learn to create as a unit. They find that it pays to cooperate. Teachers invite those who appear restless or uninterested to find other activities; the children themselves often take care of momentary problems, hushing up a disturbing chatterer or forcing a fighter out of their midst. They delight in choral speech, which depends on group participation. In a dance based on the Christmas story they had learned in songs, one group shouted, "No room here! No room here!" with tremendous vigor, in a rhythmic chant that fairly shook the walls. Similarly, as the gingerbread man, they called, "You can't catch me!" in a derisive chorus that became metronomic with repetition.

From a purely physical standpoint, rhythms have much to contribute. The ability to synchronize body movements with music is not easily won. At the first of the year, it is common to see children unable to jump evenly; their feet do not hit the floor at the same time, and they seem unaware that the piano is setting a steady pace. By the end of the year, the group jumps pretty much as a whole, feet bouncing in time and together. Most of the actions called for demand large, sweeping motions that relax while they exercise. Rolling, crawling, and stretching do much for good posture. Vigorous activities should be spaced between slower ones; it is easy for adults to forget how exhausting many of these activities can be. A successful rhythm period ends with a feeling of completion. Muscular tension eased away, the group breaks up feeling released and happy.

Care must be taken lest enthusiasts force music into undue prominence. One can be warned by the example of Miss Curtis, who supplied her children with a never-ending flow of melody. She greeted them with a musical, "Good morning, boys and girls," and warbled, "Now it is time to fold up our blankets." One morning little Katie called to her from the swings, "Give me a push, Miss Curtis." As she walked over to comply, she was startled to hear Katie add, "And you needn't sing about it, either." The receptive adult, who knows when to make suggestions and when to stay in the background, will be rewarded with greater responsiveness from her children.

There is always music in the classroom. At almost any minute, some scrap of song or some rhythmic pattern can be heard above the other noises of play. Even derisive calls like, "Karen is a cry-baby" or "Bill is a stinker," typical of four-year-old groups, must be recognized as musical experiences. Chants often spring up spontaneously, usually based on the musical refrain, *sol*-mi-la-*sol*-mi. One group sings: "We built a bigger," while their rivals at blocks wait for a lull to shout back: "Ours is the biggest."

Among two-year-olds and young threes, one is often conscious of musical hums coming from various parts of the room. These barely audible melodies crooned by a youngster busy at work grow surer in pitch and fuller in word content as he becomes older. Such unself-conscious improvisations are usually over before they can be taken down. Often they are created atop a climbing frame or inside a packing box, from where only a scrap of unconventional but beautiful melody rewards one's listening.

Those who think of the youngest groups simply as a mixture of cuteness, wet pants, and blissful ignorance may be surprised to learn that many of them already have a rather large repertoire of songs. Davy asks his teacher to sing "The Surrey with the Fringe on Top"; at play with blocks, he hums his version of the latest rock hit. Radios and records are no strangers to this little fellow. Mother tunes in to a program of music while she irons; a singing commercial interrupts Daddy's news. Of course, his parents have provided records for him, or better yet, have sung with him. He brings to school as many as a dozen nursery rhymes, which he is soon singing in company with his young friends.

At the age of two or three repetition is magical. "Jingle Bells" is none the less exciting for the thirtieth time than it was when it was new. Its total familiarity gives the child something to hold onto, something he recognizes as home ground. Long-time favorites do not become monotonous to the group, for so many new experiences take place around them all. Some children who recognize "Jack and Jill" and "Are You Sleeping" at the first of the year stay silently on the fringe of singing groups until three months at school have given them enough confidence to add their voices to the rest. Suddenly, as they participate, the old song takes on a new feeling. Simple actions are added to some familiar tunes; appropriate motions for "Rock-a-bye-Baby" and "Little Jack Horner" lend freshness to these favorites.

Socially, too, much is going on in connection with music. A room full of individual and independent boys and girls will react in various ways the first time the teacher sings. A small interested group will form around her. Others stop their activities for a time and listen, faces alight or attentive or wondering for a moment. Then blocks or dolls claim them again. Robert, in the far corner by the window, appears to hear nothing at all, but his foot is tapping involuntarily in time to the music. The few young individualists who get together around the teacher's place on the floor, or who follow as she sings, "See, Here Comes the Big Procession," soon become aware of other equally determined singers and marchers.

Throughout the early years a teacher's voice remains her most successful musical instrument. Her hands are free to initiate motion, and she is able to move about without restriction. On occasion, groups are happy to sing with her at the piano. And she may find that the definite chords of the piano add impetus to the rhythms of marches and horse trots. For the most part, though, the comfortably familiar sound of her own voice, however untutored it may seem to adult hearers, is her greatest asset. She can change its tone easily, from the gentle quality she uses at rest time to the more alert and definite way she sings for simple rhythms like jumping or walking. Unfamiliar sounds may be frightening to the two-year-old. He does not react with the curiosity of his five-year-old brother, but often wilts into a fearful uncertainty. Even his own teacher may not find it successful to play her violin at school.

From the youngest group on through the fives, a continual experimentation in sound goes on. Twos love to shake bells or pound on drums. But as curiosity about their environment expands they begin to improvise their own ways of creating sound. Two aluminum pot tops make an admirable crash if you slam them together just so. Iron rings banged against swing poles jangle the stoutest nerves. Blocks can be slapped against one another, or stones can be clunked into a tin can. How different all these noises are!

The piano stands ready for the children's use, as well as for sessions of songs or dances with the teachers. One day, five four-year-olds squeezed onto the piano bench. Van Loon's songbook was open in front of them, and they leafed through it, looking at each picture in hopes of finding one that illustrated a familiar song. Suddenly they came to the page devoted to "Here We Go Round the Mulberry Bush." The picture showed a circle of people dancing about a round, green bush. "Ring Around the Rosy!" went up the shout: "Let's sing that!" All five had a wonderful time, singing with lusty voices in perfect rhythm. Five pairs of hands struck the keys in time to the music as the song went on. When the song ended ("Ashes! Ashes! All fall down!") the final word was underscored with a particularly loud crash. In love with their own music-making, the five went on, repeating the ditty innumerable times.

This freedom to experiment at the keyboard brings many a soloist to the piano, as well. Sometimes one enterprising child organizes a rhythms session, imitating as well as she can the kind of unconventional patterns she has heard her teachers use, while willing friends go through appropriate motions on the floor beside the piano. More often, the children sit down alone to sing without self-consciousness songs of their own making, accompanying these melodies with carefully fingered figures on the keys. Or the piano may sound forth in solo passages, with one finger or one hand or two hands put to use. These moments of solitary improvisation are full of strange and beautiful sound, unrestricted by formal instruction.

The piano is also opened up for inspection by eager four- and five-year-olds. With the removal of the front board, another aspect of this instrument comes to the children's attention. Its amazing mechanism calls forth excited comment. A teacher stands nearby to see that no one goes at the interior with rough hands or destructive intent. The touch of pudgy fingers on a key brings a shout from excited on-lookers as the felted hammer hits the strings. The more they discover about the piano and its intricacies, the greater is the respect they show it. Later, when they sit down to sing to themselves, they have some awareness of the complexity of the instrument at their fingertips.

Although children create songs full of uncertain rhythm, they respond best to songs that have a definite pulse. Like their improvised melodies, the songs they pick up most easily are of limited range and have only small intervals between notes. If the adults around them are eager to introduce more difficult songs, a few children taken off as a separate group may pick them up quickly. The bulk of the class moves at a slower tempo. Needless to say, it is important that the subject matter and word choice should be appropriate to the age level. This is an area where the teacher must choose wisely. Of course, a few songs that might not otherwise be included are used because they seem to be part of our heritage, and others are accepted now and again because the children request them. Similar forethought must attend the selection of records. The teacher's choice is going to influence the taste of her group.

Sometimes parents are able to bring new musical experiences to the children. Perhaps one father is a member of the local symphony orchestra; another may be a piano teacher or an accordion-player. Danny's mother is a well-known singer. More than likely, they will be glad to be pressed into service. Before he enters the group, the parent-of-the-day needs a briefing as to what is expected of him. To begin with, he should be warned not to "perform." No four-year-old is going to sit passively and listen through an air of Gluck or "On Wings of Song." Even the fives would weary before the end. They want to take part in the music themselves; they will learn more by doing something actively than by hearing a lecture about it. It is better to start by showing the case and how it is opened, and then to demonstrate the instrument itself. If it must be put together before it can be played, can the separate pieces make sounds of their own? Yes. The longest part of the flute can be blown like a fog horn, and the section with the mouthpiece used alone to wail like a fire siren. The children insist on making a study of each piece before hearing the whole. They discover that for all the funny noises one can make with each section alone, nothing really like music is possible until the instrument is joined together properly. On the violin, they hear the difference between pizzicato tones and those that are made with the bow. They find that the Autoharp can be played with the thumb, but that it is necessary to use the pick for clearer notes. They must hear the highest and the lowest notes the instrument is capable of producing. They ask what each part is made of. Did the bow hairs really come from a horse? Can Mr. Potter make his own oboe reeds? What is the sharp thing on the bottom of the cello Bella's father is playing?

Before long they have heard enough. Perhaps John Thompson's father is demonstrating his viola today. The children have already become acquainted with Miss Carter's violin, and they want a turn to try this new instrument themselves. This is a serious business. John asks to be first, but he is not so sure he wants to risk failure in front of his pals. He walks slowly to the viola and holds the bow according to Mr. Thompson's instructions. Everyone is attentive as he draws it hesitantly across the strings. His efforts are madly applauded. There is no doubt in anyone's mind that it was a perfect imitation of a snore. Margot's turn is next. She strides bravely to the viola and makes a successful, if violent, jab at the strings. Robert refuses to use the bow and contents himself with plucking one string. After a while they have all attempted to draw a sound from it. Now they ask to hear Mr. Thompson play a song. He chooses "London Bridge," and the children call out the title with delight as soon as they recognize it. The session may turn into a song fest or a barn dance, but no one's feelings are hurt. The viola has been enjoyed, and perhaps it can be brought back again. The interest and enthusiasm evident in these demonstrations are sufficient reward for the busiest of visiting parents. Similar experiences are possible with all the instruments one can name. More saliva than tone goes across the flute's mouthpiece, but the children are not discouraged. They can play a trill on the keys while Mr. Andrews does the lipwork for them. Miss Daniel's guitar and Miss Field's Autoharp are especially satisfying, for anyone can strum them in steady rhythm.

If the school is housed in a church, or if nearby there is a church with an obliging organist, it may be considered worthwhile to pay a visit to the nave and see how the organ is played. This experience became an annual event among the older nursery school groups in a large New York church. The children would arrive en masse, skipping eagerly up the steps usually closed off to the congregation. The organist described how the manuals worked and allowed some of the children to make sounds as he changed registrations. When David touched a key it sounded like Mr. Andrews' flute. A switch of a button and the same note was a trumpet blared by Paula's pudgy thumb. Ada's spindly leg barely reached to the lowest pedal, but the noise she created was as loud as thunder. The organist told them of a pipe that was big enough to surround six men, and he showed them where it was hidden behind a screen of cloth and stone. He played their favorite songs, using the rich and varied tone colors at his command to show the organ's versatility. His demonstration lasted but a short time. The children trooped out unaware that this enthusiastic friend was one of the world's foremost virtuosos.

Fortunate is the teacher who can make even a modest contribution in the field of music. If songs and rhythms sessions are given less emphasis at school than simple nature studies, no doubt one reason is the difference in training necessary to present them adequately, even at the nursery school level. It is easy enough to read up on tadpoles and cocoons, but to play a song on any musical instrument requires hours of practice. Many teachers who lack skill at the piano or feel apologetic about their singing voices allow music to slip into a kind of Never-Never Land. Others try to fill the gap by calling in an expert. The specialist, for all his capabilities, cannot achieve results comparable to those attained by an imaginative teacher in her own classroom. This is particularly true among two- and three-year-old children, who are noted for their conservative response to strangers. The guest is lucky to be met with wide-eyed and silent amazement. More frequently his endeavors are rewarded with tears and nervous whimpers. Even in older groups, he is handicapped by having to visit at a prearranged time, thus making it impossible to provide musical experiences when the need arises spontaneously within the group. Nor can he hope to secure a sense of unity with the children that can match the close relationship they have established with their regular teachers. The awareness of group interests and sensitivity to individual needs, gained by the staff through daily contacts, cannot help him to the same extent that it serves them. For these reasons it is important to develop resources that lie within the permanent staff, even if it means dusting off that neglected guitar or setting aside time for lessons on the piano. Teachers who have never played an instrument before find drums or an Autoharp relatively easy to use. After only a little practice, they can be introduced effectively at school. Music specialists, in discussions with the school staff, will have other helpful suggestions which the teachers themselves can utilize in their classrooms.

Whatever private agony teachers may suffer in their efforts to stimulate music at school, they will feel amply rewarded after an exhilarating song session or a particularly creative dance. Music is unique in its capacity for providing simultaneous physical and emotional release, and deserves a fair chance to exercise these benefits.

Language

Miss Tyler has settled herself near the doll corner with her note pad and pencil. She is surrounded by alert five-year-olds in a whirl of busy play. It would be worthwhile to watch Hazel, she thinks. Most of the notes in Hazel's file deal with her exaggerated fears. It may be wise to follow her while she is absorbed in quiet work. Miss Tyler writes Hazel's name and the date at the top of the page. Suddenly she overhears Elise, speaking in a matter-of-fact tone as she pretends to iron a dress in the doll corner:

"My mommy and daddy are going to die."

There is a sudden chorus of oh's and ah's from Elise's companions. Miss Tyler notices that Hazel is listening, a tense look in her eyes. It is only a second or two before the others have accepted the comment as a remark having to do with some remote time. Margaret, bending over a doll she has just tucked into bed, adds another bit of related information.

"My pussycat's going to die."

Ada nods sagely and comes forth with the statement, "Everybody dies."

None of these children seems anxious about it. They continue quietly with their domestic play.

Not so Hazel. She rushes from her chair by the crayon table and screams at the little family in the doll corner: "Stop saying that! Stop saying that! People *don't* die!"

At once, the subject assumes new proportions. Tony defends his lady friends with the stout assertion, "Yes, they do! Everybody dies."

Hazel has completely lost control of herself now. She weeps and stamps in fear. Miss Tyler comes up and puts her hand reassuringly on her shoulder. Tony looks to his teacher for reinforcement.

"When people get old, they die, don't they?" he asks.

His question redoubles Hazel's frenzy. "Stop saying that," she wails again and again.

Miss Tyler speaks to her in a quiet voice, suggesting that if she doesn't want to listen she may go to another part of the room. Children may say what they want to at school. Mrs. Irving, the assistant teacher, goes off with Hazel and soon has her calmed down enough to return to her work at the crayon table. Miss Tyler stays long enough to agree with the opinion of the group in the doll corner. Then she takes up her note pad again and writes about Hazel's exaggerated response to the subject of death, unaware that the issue is soon to confront her group again, this time in an immediate, tragic form.

For several days now, Tommy Mason has been absent from school. Katie, who lives across the street from him, brings regular reports about his health.

"His mother says he has swollen glands," she announces clearly.

Miss Tyler thinks perhaps a letter from his friends would cheer him up. During one of their regular discussions she makes this suggestion to her group. It is taken up with great enthusiasm. Each child promises to contribute a picture, or a story, or a sentence to the letter. Before the end of a week, a large envelope is bulging with colorful drawings and witty comments for Tommy's delectation. On Thursday, Miss Tyler uses their discussion period to display the various enclosures to the class.

"I guess we can address the envelope today," she says. "And I can put it in the mailbox this evening."

Sarah interrupts, "Please wait until tomorrow. I want to draw him a funny clown. That will make Tommy laugh."

Miss Tyler recalls Sarah's quiet affection for Tommy. She remembers that just two weeks ago Sarah had taken him into the doll corner to be the father in her house. "And when I grow up, I will *really* marry him," she had said, turning to her teacher with a happy smile.

"Yes, we can wait," Miss Tyler says. "We'll send the things to him tomorrow."

No one in the group, not Sarah or Katie, or even Miss Tyler, suspects what is taking place at that very minute in the hospital. Worried because Tommy's swollen glands did not respond to ordinary treatment, the doctor had insisted on a thorough check-up. In a matter of hours, the reason was evident. Tommy had leukemia. While the group is agreeing to wait until tomorrow, Tommy's parents are watching over his bed. He dies at suppertime.

The following day, Miss Tyler finds a note tacked to her bulletin board.

"Tommy Mason died yesterday of leukemia," she reads.

How strange that all the hope and worry of his parents, all the achievements of his active days at school, should come to an end in this brief message! Miss Tyler sits down and thinks for a long time. The envelope and its cheery enclosures come before her mind's eye. The children will have to be told why it is no longer necessary to send them off. It is fortunate that Sarah had asked to postpone the mailing. Now that Tommy is dead, their belated arrival at his home could only bring added grief. Miss Tyler thinks of other group discussions in the past: one about rocks, another about nests and eggs. "But today's meeting will be different," she fears. "How can I begin?"

The children troop in. Some go to play at once with the large blocks. Five girls and their trusty defender, Tony, meet in the doll corner. There is a small group at the crayon table, Sarah among them, laboring over the clown she had promised to draw.

"That's for Tommy," she tells her neighbors.

"He's coming to my birthday party," says Amy, not to be outdone.

A few minutes later, Miss Tyler asks the children to put their things in order and come together for a discussion. They surround her eagerly, ready to contribute ideas to any subject that may be suggested.

She looks at them for a minute and then begins. Somehow the words come without effort.

"Do you remember last week when some of you were talking about old people dying?"

Some of the heads nod wisely. Elise pipes up in a clear voice: "Last summer, my grandma was very, very sick, and she died." Her tone shows little emotion. She is only being helpful, adding what she knows to the statement thrown out by Miss Tyler.

Katie follows this with another matter-of-fact statement: "My cat died."

Hazel has betrayed her nervousness only by plucking at her skirt.

Perhaps it would have been better to talk to her alone, Miss Tyler thinks, but it is too late now.

Hazel speaks up rather loudly. She cannot accept the finality of death. "Some people get *sick*," she insists.

Tony has taken some time to consider what he should add. Miss Tyler privately calls him the sage of her class. Seeing his hand waving for recognition, she asks him to speak up.

"Sometimes," he says slowly, "when babies are just born, they die."

This is the time, Miss Tyler thinks. He has given me the perfect cue.

Aloud she says, "That's true, Tony. Sometimes children get very, very sick and don't get better. Remember, Tommy has been very sick—and in the hospital. Yesterday, he died."

For several seconds there is total silence in the room. The children look at her and do not speak, each one thinking his own thoughts and wondering at what she has said.

Finally Katie speaks.

"Is it true?" she asks slowly. He lives across the street from me, she thinks. Is it true that we will not walk to school together any more?

Miss Tyler nods her head. "Yes," she says.

There is another moment of silence, broken this time by Katie's nervous giggle. "I'm going to the country this week end," she says abruptly. No more about Tommy, she thinks to herself. I won't think about it any more.

Tony does not notice her interruption. He speaks pensively. "It's like I said: sometimes babies die."

Hazel twists at her skirt and declares loudly: "I had a old aunt who was very sick, but she didn't die." With a smile of relief she turns to watch the other children.

Martin raises his hand, though no one else has made any attempt to hold the floor.

"It's very nice to die, because you go to Heaven," he says. "Heaven is pretty."

Bill interrupts.

"Why couldn't Tommy get better?" he wants to know.

Miss Tyler explains that the doctors did not know the right kind of medicine to give Tommy. In response to other questions, she adds that doctors do not have cures for every disease, but that they are working hard all the time to discover new medicines.

Suddenly her eyes light on Ellen, who has recently returned from the hospital after a tonsillectomy. She thinks at once of Bill, who is going to have his tonsils out in another week or two.

"Children usually get better very fast," she says. "For

instance, when Ellen went to the hospital, it was all very simple, because doctors know how to take out tonsils."

Bill smiles in relief. "I'm going to have my tonsils out at Easter," he announces.

There is another short pause when no one speaks. Then Margaret speaks for them all.

"I know Tommy was very sad to die," she says seriously, "because he loved to come to school so much."

What else is there to say? Miss Tyler suggests that it is a good time to go outdoors for some fresh air. The group files out to the locker room. Only Sarah is left in her chair. She is thinking of the boy who used to play with her in the doll corner. Perhaps she remembers saying, "When I grow up, I will *really* marry him." Whatever her thoughts, she has said nothing. Now she sits and absent-mindedly fumbles with her shoelaces. A word from Miss Tyler does not arouse her. Miss Tyler goes into the locker room and brings out Sarah's wraps. She helps her into the sweater and buttons the jacket, though Sarah usually insists on doing it all by herself. Together they go to the hall and follow the rest of the group outdoors.

Life at school is often touched by experiences which, like this one, defy labels. Chubby little Carol pours out her unhappiness to her teacher at rest time.

"My daddy used to be so nice, but now he isn't anymore," she says in a soft voice. "He doesn't love us any more. He made my mommy cry."

Her tragic story goes on, painting in simple but graphic pictures the situation of marital strife that troubles her so at home. Her teacher listens and says little. How lucky it is that Carol can talk about it! How much better than bottling it all up inside!

The earnest and intelligent responses that met Miss Tyler's announcement about Tommy could not have been expected from younger children. Nor could Carol have explained her father's desertion with such wisdom and clarity a year or so ago. Five years of observation and experiment and living were needed as background for these meaningful comments.

Miss Tyler has had occasion to look into past records for information about Tony, her "sage." She has no way of remembering him as he was when he was in the youngest group. He had not started to wear glasses then, and his eyes had a somewhat owlish appearance. Gestures and monosyllables were his stock in trade, and despite the simple ways in which he framed requests there was no mistaking his intentions. He pulled his teacher's smock and announced, "wee-wee," in a clear voice. Without delay his message was interpreted by the teacher at his side, and he was escorted to the bathroom. At this time, he was more involved with finding out his own status in a new and wonderful world than in discussing abstractions like birth and death.

"This *my* basin?" he would ask as he washed his hands. "That *my* towel?" Then for further reassurance, he might say aloud, nodding wisely, "That's Tony's towel. *I* Tony!"

The sage of the kindergarten said "wa-wa" when he meant "water" and "aks" instead of "ask." Taken through the nave of a large church, his only comment was, "Pretty window." And as if to fasten such a long word in his mind, he repeated in a kind of rhythmic croon:

> "Window! Window!
> Pretty Window!"

Hearing his teachers or his parents use some unfamiliar word, Tony parroted them, relishing the novel sound as he formed it again and again. Thus his vocabulary began to grow.

By the time Tony reached his third birthday, he was well aware that he could assert his own will with a firm or impish, "No!" instead of following wherever grownups led. At home, another favorite word was "why." His mother confessed at the time that on occasion she could have throttled him cheerfully, for no matter what she said, he was sure to follow it up with a question. Part of it, to be sure, was her fault. Without realizing it, she had fallen into a typical adult mannerism: that of speaking to her child only in terms of interrogation. "Isn't it a lovely day?" somehow always came out instead of the simple statement, "It's a lovely day." "We had fun in the park, didn't we?" "Let's eat now—O.K.?" "Don't you think it's time for bed?" Small wonder that Tony responded in kind, asking question after question until she was dizzy.

Before worrying about choice replies, she would have done well to ask *herself* the question, "Does Tony really want an answer?" His teachers often found him standing beside his locker, asking, "Is this my locker? Does this say 'Tony'?" though he knew very well it was his own. He was merely giving them an opening for a pleased response of, "You found it by yourself, didn't you?" (And notice how their answer ends—with that eternal question mark!)

But some of his queries undoubtedly sprang from honest curiosity, a wish to become better acquainted with his expanding world. Patient replies set him on the road to wider understanding. His vocabulary grew rapidly. His parents were justifiably proud of his achievements with words.

"Dat song is so delightful," he said as he sat by the radio one afternoon. "Faburt (favorite) one in my life!" At school, his teachers were equally satisfied with the wonderful sounds he invented as he moved his hands rhythmically across the fingerpaint table:

"swish-swash, swish-swash,
mish-mosh, mish-mosh."

Like most older threes and young fours, Tony began to regale receptive adults with simple stories about himself— episodes that happened at home or on the way to school. Most of these were told briefly, and the only character that assumed much prominence at all was the narrator himself.

At school, however, teachers still got most of their notes on his language by hanging over the blocks or standing close to the doll corner. They stood by the swings and listened to the lovely poetry Tony created as he sent himself higher and higher into the air. They watched him as he prepared to jump from the climbing box. His arms were out-stretched like wings.

"One for the bird out in the yonder sky," he sang out, "One for the bird that jumps in the flaming water!"

Happy play is usually accompanied by some form of speech: dramatic exchanges or orders to friends, comments to the world in general, mutterings to oneself, vague hums, or rhythmic sounds that unconsciously keep time to the motion of the child's body as he works. It is obvious that when the occupation is one that can be done with complete freedom and zest, language appears too, as a natural and joyful corollary.

Tony's friends were advancing, too, and notes on them all were full of delightful quotes. During rhythms, Nancy watched as her friends danced like various creatures of the sea. She pulled Miss Phillips' sleeve and remarked, "The jellyfish look as though they are crying like weeping wil-lows." Buxom little Olga's comment at the end of a partic-ularly quiet rest period just before winter vacation was: "I was so quiet I could hear the Christmas tree speaking." Keith looked out of the window and observed only a few patches of white left as the snow melted on a warm day. "All the world has nearly gone back to brown," he said. Teachers heard descriptions of parts of the body that had gone asleep: "My shoe is full of air—my foot feels like 7 Up." "It feels like needles." Sometimes they were surprised by the accuracy of the children's statements. How many adults would be as perceptive as little Sarah, who said of herself, "When I feel unhappy I have a cold, but when I feel happy, I don't have one." One might not expect a young four to speak with Elsa's matter-of-fact aplomb. She was invited by Terry to be the mother in his house. "Yes, and I'll be pregnant, too," she said by way of comment. "I'll have a big tummy."

Five-year-old Angelo asked his teacher to write down his version of something he had heard about winter. "It'll be a poem," he said:

> "Winter, winter
> Where do we get winter?
> The world carries winter on its back.
> Winter always comes,
> But I don't know the fact.
> I know the world carries winter on its back.
> Then winter goes away
> And spring peeks through the crack."

But children, so wise and so poetic at times, have equally strong urges to be crazy with their language—to jump above all hurdles and create pure nonsense for their own delight. Whoever knows the highly word-conscious four-year-old will also know "Mr. Cuckoopoo," "Hooble-Dooble," "Aak-aak-pack" and a limitless number of other amazing sounds. Adults are greeted with "Hi, Mr. Poo-pa-paw. Hi, Mrs. Drumstick Chicken! Hi, Mrs. Kaleido-scope!" Rhymes are magic, and occasion many a giggle at this time. "Choosing Shoes" by Ffrida Wolfe fits into this pattern happily, and teachers may fill notebooks with simi-lar spirited verse which can be read on many an occasion throughout the year. Even some of Edward Lear is appre-ciated by older fours and fives. They recognize a kindred soul in the author of this mad doggerel. The rhythm of such poetry, along with the satisfying sound of its rhyme, is irresistible to their ears. Great mirth attends the telling of lowbrow jingles picked up from an older brother or sister:

> "I see London, I see France.
> I see teacher's underpants."

or

> "Baby, baby, suck your thumb,
> Wash it off with bubble gum."

Adults should be quick to enter the mood of these sessions, and may even want to add their own creations:

> "Roger, Roger, I suppose
> You have lost your eyes and nose."

Such happy moments do much to encourage children's awareness of sounds in language. The whole day is full of funny talk.

With this interest in words to help them, teachers find that many little defects in speech disappear naturally, without the use of self-conscious corrections and disciplines. Katie said, 'Puss me," at the first of the year, and was occasionally taken to task for this lapse by her cronies, who told her rather severely, "You mean *push*." When Katie was in a frivolous mood, her teachers tried to introduce words that included the "sh" sound: "How is Mrs. Shoe-shop today?" Before the end of May, Katie was calling them "Mrs. Shim-Sham" and "Mr. Ship-shape" without a trace of difficulty. One must remember not to expect these habits to change overnight. Many of them straighten out of their own accord only after a year or two. Their remedy is sometimes as simple as merely repeating the difficult sound when natural situations arise, until the child hears it accurately.

More often, delayed speech or stuttering or stammering results from fears and emotional tensions. Only an oblique method of attack will have success here. Drawing attention to the language problem itself will only increase anxiety. It is wiser to find out the underlying causes and to relieve them. Does Judith feel that her mother doesn't really want her to grow up? Perhaps her immature-sounding speech is a source of pleasure to her parents. They repeat her baby-talk with little winks of happiness. No wonder Judith still says "bow-wow" instead of "dog," and "Me want a dwink," when her peers are able to frame their requests more clearly. Does Harold go through an entire day at school without speaking more than a word or two? Perhaps when he is helped to face the jealousy he harbors toward his older brother, his language difficulties will ease away. Overly high intellectual demands block Ralph's speech. So many factors may be involved! The important thing is to give this child confidence in himself and to foster satisfactory relationships with the people around him. Learning to climb the jungle gym, winning a friend at school, or getting along more comfortably at home may have dramatic effect on a child who halts between words or who is silent much of the time.

Of course, some stammering is to be expected between the ages of three and six. Suddenly, there is so much to say. So many things happen that demand comment! But the child is faced with a gap between vocabulary and matters of interest. In an effort to express himself, he may be forced to halt to find the proper word. If adults are willing to devote wholehearted attention to the things a child says, little by little he will begin to feel more leisurely about his conversation. Knowing that he will be heard out, he no longer needs to feel pressed for time. While he is working to shape new ideas, it is best if grownups can curb their urge to prompt him or to correct his errors. Sometimes this business of talking is a serious matter. One can lighten the burden simply by devoting enough time to ease the child's tension and enough interest to encourage his efforts.

The importance of the adult's role in the stimulation of children's speech cannot be overstressed. Parents might be amazed to hear the accurate imitations of them that are noted in the doll corner at school. Dolores' mother is an opera singer, given to sudden emotional outbursts, and a great lover of hyperbole. She admits this readily, if somewhat ruefully. Notes on Dolores are full of quotations like these: "Oh, my poor broken heart! They have taken my rope again." "I have no strength, and I have no breath. I'm all out of breath." "Miss Quayle, life is so difficult. Oh, I can't stand it. I just can't. It will kill me. It will kill me." Where does Dolores pick up such dramatic language? Believe it or not, her mother had no idea when asked that question by one of the teachers. It came as a shock to her that what she said at home in moments of fatigue or excitement was so extreme.

Still another problem had to be faced by Michael's parents. When he was but an infant, they decided that they would not fall into the errors their parents had made. Disciplined sternly all through their own childhoods, this couple resolved never to try similar treatment on Michael. "We will be permissive and teach him to reason things out sensibly," they thought. Consequently, they set no limits, never addressed him harshly, and attempted to mask their feelings of annoyance at the mischievous things he did. Each time he committed some misdeed, he was taken gently aside and given reasons why such behavior should not be repeated. This plan backfired. Unable to decide what his limits were, Michael deliberately transgressed in a pathetic effort to discover just how far he could go. The lectures he was given had but one effect: he quickly learned to beat his parents at their own game. He became, even at the age of three, a master of rationalization. Naturally he brought this skill with him to school, confident that it would work there, too. Teachers saw him knock down a girl's block structure. As they came closer, Michael would smile blandly and assure them, "I'm helping her. I'm fixing it for her." If one of the staff suggested an activity, Michael inevitably refused, protecting himself with arguments like, 'I've decided painting isn't such a good idea," or "I'm too tired to play. I didn't sleep well last night." When adults ignored his protests and insisted on his dressing to go outside, Michael shouted, "Stop it! Leave me alone! That's *not* the way to treat a person! You're not my boss." If a teacher put a restraining hand on his back during rest, Michael whined and complained, "That's my sensitive spot," Yet what a relief it was to him when grownups at school showed him the places beyond which he could not go! His rationalizations ceased by the end of the year, since he realized that they were not effective at school.

Teachers, on their part, are taken aback to learn that much of what they say goes home verbatim, while their speech mannerisms are parroted at the breakfast table, to the amusement of a whole family. Staff members are forced to keep in mind the importance of their example. Their grammar should be acceptable and their words well chosen. Sloppy English like "It's time to lay down" and "They gave it to Hugh and I" should be corrected. A pleasant, well-modulated voice will help them create a calm atmosphere. Shrill or booming tones only step up noise and confusion, while a tentative voice makes no impression at all. One should speak clearly and to the point, so that children will be able to devote their brief attention span to what is being said.

Older brothers and sisters, the radio, and television are all contributors to children's vocabularies. The four- and five-year-old who dances about saying, "Me strong man. Me eat big wolf," is probably not retarded. He is under the spell of an old "cowboy and Indian" movie he saw on television. That rather self-conscious boy in the book corner, waving his arms like a madman, saw a gentleman conducting a large symphony orchestra last week on public TV. Teddy's talk shows the influence of his older brother: "Do you know what team I'm for? The Yankees! The Yankees are going to win the pennant." Sometimes he tricks teachers with jokes his brother played on him: "Miss Miller, do you want to hear a riddle?" Miss Miller says she does.

"I can jump higher than the Empire State Building!"

Miss Miller expresses surprise. After a perfectly ordinary jump, Teddy explains, "The Empire State Building can't jump!"

In this era of excitement and stimulation, it is surprising to find some children badly in need of first-hand information. Strangely enough, such children are likely to come from bookish homes. They hear about many things— perhaps too many—but have little chance to compare the word with its actual counterpart. Ricky's father brought up the subject of death and explained it long before Ricky had shown the slightest need for such detailed knowledge. The idea of being dead haunted Ricky's mind. One day at school he said to a friend, "Will you always be my friend? Always play with me? And when you're dead will you let me look at you?" His ambitious father had also labored to teach him other bits of information which had no relation at all to Ricky's everyday life. In his efforts to express this advanced knowledge, he stammered painfully until he remembered the exact phrases which his father had drilled into him.

"I know what fire does to water, er—ah—I know. . . . Ah—um, I know what water does to fire. It is lots of little firemen. It has chemicals in it that put fire out."

In the midst of an interesting circus story, Ricky, with furrowed brow, gasped excitedly, "You, you know, ah, you know, ah, er, ah, you—ah, I know what tusks are, what they, ah, are, ah, made of. I know what tusks are made of. They're made of matted hair!" His head was full of such undigested tidbits. He needed time to absorb his impressions and work out relationships in his own mind. Ricky's father reported that his son was interested in acquiring information and kept pestering him for more. A far more likely explanation was that Ricky had discovered this to be a good way of gaining his father's approval and attention. Similarly, a four-year-old who claims to be interested in *Alice in Wonderland*, Grimm's *Fairy Tales*, *Dr. Dolittle*, or *Swiss Family Robinson* has sensed his parents' fondness for this particular literature.

The child who holds his own in the group by merit of his abilities with clay or tricycles or blocks is building on a surer foundation than the child who tries to succeed with language alone. A large vocabulary means so little among preschool children that a "silent partner" may well be one of the most popular in his group. Maria came into her class unable to speak a word of English. She set out at once to learn how to climb the jungle gym, and soon became an expert on the tricycles and the swings. She created lovely designs at the easel and crayon table. Before she could say twenty-five words, Maria had become one of the inner sanctum of the little girls' clique, and was welcomed by the boys as well. Of course, her social success might not have continued had she neglected to improve her English. At first, a vocabulary was not necessary to smooth her way with peers, but it was nevertheless important for subsequent growth.

Young children with extensive vocabularies, who hold forth at length about fields of advanced knowledge, have doubtless achieved these intellectual heights at great expense. Perhaps Ellen has found that Daddy looks pleased when she asks questions about his car. He perks up even more when she remembers some of the words he has mentioned: carburetor, transmission, and battery. Daddy was not very much interested in watching her do a trick on her new tricycle yesterday. Ellen will not trouble with that today. She knows a better way to gain his approval now. Such perception is the rule among children. They soon find out the spots where they can gain most recognition from the adults they are striving so hard to please. Little by little, Ellen will replace her interest in the new tricycle with a set of mechanical terms whose magic sounds make Daddy's face light up. Her vocabulary does not indicate a real interest in the workings of his car. It does not indicate mental precocity. What it does show is the extent to which a little child can go to make Daddy know she is there.

The child who sits next to his teacher and gives forth with long harangues is another to watch with care. It is likely that he engages adults in conversation simply because he is not getting along with his contemporaries. Perhaps he is surrounded by grownups at home, and has little occasion to meet with peers outside of school hours. Whatever the reason, it is wise to shift the emphasis from talking to doing more active things together. Tossing a ball back and forth may be a good start. Suggesting, "I'll stand by the packing box and watch you jump," may work. Other children will soon be about if the activity looks interesting, and the "lone wolf" may gradually be absorbed into the group.

In taking down a child's comments, teachers are forced to be subjective to a certain degree. A note stating: "Frank said, 'Susan is a bear'," would give no idea, three months later, whether his feeling about it had been matter-of-fact, amused, or fearful. Tone, strength, and pitch of voice are important elements, for children's attitudes are expressed to a great extent through them. Feelings and moods are also made clear by a twinkle in the eye, a downward pout of the lip, or a furrowed brow. Nervous gestures and involuntary twitches suggest tension. Adults must be alert to these signs and observant of changes. Sometimes these accompaniments to speech are more eloquent than what is being said.

Occasionally expressions of hostility seem to dominate a youngster's vocabulary. Timothy, for example, took delight in inventing epithets which he hoped would shock his teachers.

"Shut up, you snot river," he screamed. "I could kill you, you pee-pee mess. I'll stick a fork in your fanny."

Instead of looking horrified, which would have given him more incentive than ever to continue this kind of talk, his teachers made no comment about it at all. They took as many opportunities as they could to enjoy pleasant moments with him. Now and again he volunteered to dictate stories. More vile language was spilled out but the staff accepted it all. When he had established satisfactory relationships with them, this behavior subsided and lost its former intensity.

Bill, on the other hand, seared his playmates with sarcasm. When Ellen remarked that the dayliner she was building would be "bigger than the whole world," Bill sneered at her and gave her this adult-like squelch: "That's how stupid girls are. If it was bigger than the whole world, it wouldn't be able to get *in* the world. You're just stupid." One day, a male classmate came to school wearing bright red nail polish on all his fingers. Bill's comment, "Look how silly you look with your red finger nails. *I'm a boy.* Only silly girls wear that!" merely widened the gulf between him and his peers. Teachers did not often remind him that his inconsiderate language was alienating potential friends. They did their best to encourage him to develop skills. Boxing was added to his list of accomplishments. By the time spring came around, Bill was a star acrobat on the jungle gym and his need for verbal aggression had all but disappeared.

Bragging and the telling of tall tales are typical of this age and are seldom matters of great concern. Excessive boasting, of course, indicates uncertainty within. Richard hated to have anyone else brag about exploits or possessions, and he often made up a big enough tale so that no one could top it. Someone who came out with a bit of interesting news was likely to be deflated with, "My daddy knows about everything." When he jumped and made somersaults, Richard boaster, "I could even do that when I was a baby." He once went so far as to say he had had his tonsils out thirteen times already! Another boy once had a whole city block in an uproar by a plausible description of his sister's death from polio. These children were not taken to task at school for being liars. If they told their teachers a particularly amazing tale, they were likely to be told, "That's a good one to put in our book." It was written down and included among other made-up stories. It is often hard for young children to distinguish between what is real and what isn't. It may be a good idea to ask for a made-up story and follow the telling with a request for a true one, thus bringing the boundary lines into clearer perspective.

The vague distinction between fact and fancy affects the choice of reading matter at school. Most fairy tales are avoided since they cause much confusion and often inspire fear. The nursery school years are the age at which nightmares begin to occur. Ghosts, goblins, witches, wild animals, robbers, and kidnappers people the dark. These creatures can be very real, indeed, to a young child, and adults should not add to his burden by filling his mind with stories about cruel people who can perform harmful magic on others. Later, when he is better able to understand makebelieve, he is more prepared to enjoy fairy tales and profit by them. Even the teachers were amazed by the credulity of one four-year-old group who watched Mr. McArthur assemble a scarecrow. One child contributed a crudely drawn mask for its face; another brought over a vest and a straw hat from the doll corner. All of them saw these items loosely attached to a broom. This haphazard figure was then draped over a chair. It sat solemnly throughout their rest period, and the children referred to it as "Miss Thompson, the mad teacher." At the close of rest Mr. McArthur spoke for the scarecrow, telling the children it was time to get up. "She didn't *really* talk, did she?" someone asked in an uncertain tone. Some of the other children had an anxious look, and they circled around the figure suspiciously. Though they had seen "Miss Thompson" created, they were still not sure how real she was.

Five-year-old Frances went to visit her grandmother, who lived in the city. Outside her grandmother's apartment window could be seen a garden belonging to a wealthy art collector. A number of statues, draped in protective covers, stood here and there among flower plots and shrubs. Frances looked at them with mistrust. "I don't like them," she said. "They're ugly." Before she went to bed at night, she insisted that the windows be closed. "I'm afraid they might come alive," she explained, "and climb into the window."

Children can be expected to talk mostly about themselves. No one needs to worry if his child sounds a bit egotistical. It is natural at this age—perhaps at any age. "I'm boss of this school." "See what I can do!" "Mine's better than yours." "I have a good idea about the parade. *I'll* be the leader." It is quite possible to find a half dozen children of four or over working together on a common structure, even agreeing that it is a big ferryboat they are building. But when the word "captain" is mentioned, a great clamor arises: "I'm the captain!" "No—I am." "I said it first." In the end there are as many captains as builders, each on his own high perch, steering the boat in a different direction from the rest.

A year or so later it is not so difficult to think in terms of "we" rather than "I," but at four this is an advanced concept. When David was four years old, he preferred to build alone. "Let me make my *own* house," he insisted, driving would-be helpers away. By the end of March, he accepted the assistance of others, but when the structure was finished, he would call teachers over to "see *my* house. *I* built it." A year later, when he was a member of the oldest group, this note was taken on David's behavior during rest period:

Had built a tall tower of blocks with the help of Andrew and Tommy. While he rested on the other side of the wall, someone in the active group accidentally knocked down a small structure. Hearing the crash, David asked anxiously, "Is our tower still up?" Told it was not their building that had fallen, David said in relief, "Well, you know, we worked hard on it."

The passing of his fifth year had brought about a great change in David's social outlook. Other changes, too, are visible among kindergartners. Their richer vocabularies, wider scope, and heightened perception equip them for more advanced work than was possible in former years. The swift upsurge of speech from the limited monosyllables noted among two-year-olds reaches a peak in the vital interest in ideas and words and sounds typical of fours and fives.

"*I'll Tell You a Story*" 11

Original Stories

Mr. Johnson's four-year-old group was together again after the Christmas holidays. Staff and children alike found it hard to fit back into the patterns that had been established before vacation time. During the first part of one morning, the group had elected to sit on the floor near the piano and listen to *Stories That Sing* by Ethel Crowninshield. The book is a fine collection of stories written and illustrated by children. The appeal of the simple narratives and drawings close to their own standards makes it a favorite with fours and fives. Part of each tale is a short song; they are all in easy range, and children pick them up quickly. Later this particular morning, it was Mr. Johnson's job to supervise quiet play for some of the children while others rested in the next room. His group seemed in no mood to sit happily through another session of stories, so he proposed something new: "You remember the *Stories That Sing* we sang this morning by the piano?" Their reply was a lusty affirmative. "Well, I thought you might like to try writing some stories of your own," he continued, "like the ones those children put into their book. You've heard stories all year. How would you like to tell one?"

In some excitement, two girls ran out to get Mr. Johnson some paper and pencil. He sat down at the book table with ten eager faces in a circle around him. Their eyes looked at his pencil, as though the ideas would flow to them from it. A minute passed. Everyone looked a bit foolish.

"How should we begin?" Mr. Johnson asked tentatively. "Would you like it to be about people, or animals, or things?"

"Animals!" They were all agreed on that.

"But what kind of animals?" he persisted.

"I think it should be about a bear," said Kate. She looked very serious about the whole idea.

"What should the bear do?"

Then Kate came out with the first sentence of this group's first story: "There was a bear that walked a little ways."

That sentence, in a way, set the tone for all the stories that followed. It was childlike: simple, surprising, fresh in expression. And once the first sentence had been spoken and the words set down on paper by Mr. Johnson, other ideas came. Now he had to ask them to go more slowly, taking turns, so that he could write it all out. It became a kind of ritual for the group to repeat each child's sentence as it was given, but slowly, syllable by syllable, while the adult put it on paper. One at a time, the children contributed their ideas to the story, until they agreed that enough had been said. Two of them sat quietly throughout the whole procedure. Though they followed the story with interest, they shook their heads when asked if they wanted a turn to say something. The group's first effort was a pleasant tale that ended with several friendly animals having "a picnic of an egg and a sandwich and salad and an apple, and milk, and nothing else."

When the second group got up from their rest, they were invited by the others to sit down and listen while the story was read aloud. Everyone agreed that it was a good story, and several children volunteered to make pictures to illustrate it. To the end of the year, their enthusiasm for dictated story sessions ran high. It became obvious that this group of storytellers had many anxieties and much pent-up hostility, and that they were, besides, highly verbal. That combination resulted in colorful and significant tales. The staff thus found another useful means of gaining insight into children's problems. Like paints and clay and other creative materials, storytelling provides a way of giving utterance to anxieties and to emotions which are hard to express. Since words are its tools, it is of value only among children whose vocabularies are serviceable for easy communication. As they wait for an adult to set down the sentences they have dictated, they have ample opportunity to notice relationships between spoken and written words, and to appreciate the importance of being able to keep permanent records in writing. In this sense, storytelling sessions serve as a valuable "reading readiness" device. Though the time spent together this way fulfills these important functions, it is an enjoyable time as well. Children look upon storytelling as a pleasant recreation and welcome chances to contribute to their group's book.

Another story dictated by this group had to do with children who were sick. It was a realistic account of what happens in the hospital, and was based on their own experiences. Like many others, it seemed to present a way for these children to face their fears, to talk about them, and by so doing, to see them in better proportions. This particular story was often dramatized. After a teacher had read it aloud, the children lay on the floor, took imaginary medicine, bandaged one another, and recovered as the story was repeated slowly. In the process of acting it out, they became familiar with an experience that had been worrisome because of its vagueness. Various other sessions during the year were devoted to tales about ambulances, sickness, and death. Besides death, the experiences that seemed to cause the children most fear, judging by the frequency of repetition in their book, were fires, getting lost, and being involved in accidents.

It was not long before the staff was asked to take down individual stories; some children had so much to say that they were no longer willing to share the time with their friends. Unbelievable violence was found in these narratives. A doctor was thrown off the roof; a baby was burned in its crib; bears, foxes, and wolves were kicked to death by horses so that children could eat them; a baboon tore out the face of a little girl. Time after time teachers were treated to similar gruesome tales. The staff never turned a hair while this terror was spilled out. In such an atmosphere children feel free to say what they want. Their contributions are accepted in a spirit of genuine interest.

Stories of fear are likely to gain tremendous emotional impact as they are invented. Which of her teachers will forget the expression on the face of Irene, a habitually silent little Chinese girl, as she fairly screamed out the tale of the girl who was stolen by a giant? Or the relief when Irene had a kindly deer rescue the girl and say,

"Little girl, come back to the house." He put her on his back and took her home, and she knocked on the door. "Mommy! Mommy! Mommy!" And the mother was home. The mother went out and when she came back the little girl was in the back yard playing with the ducks. She went to the house and stayed there forever.

But Irene did not stop there. With mounting excitement, she told how the giant took away their home while they were seeing the movies; how after finding a new house, the father went out to get groceries and the mother went alone to the movies, while the girl was attacked by a baboon and the giant lived in their old house forever.

Barbara, frightened of almost everything, told of a dog that was explorded [*sic*] by a car because he didn't look each way. He didn't look any way. He just lay down on the street and then a car came along and ran over him when the car was going down the hill. He just crept up onto the sidewalk and lay in a hole, and a gun shot him and he was dead—and a corpse. Men came and took him to the doctor, but he couldn't fix him up, so they went to every place that they thought they could fix him up, but they couldn't, so they put him in the seminary.

Full of death as these stories are, it is interesting to note how often characters are resurrected, sometimes to live happily ever after, but more often to face new tortures. Children seem loath to accept the permanency of death; many of them confuse it with sickness or other serious physical difficulties. "The doctor who died grew up again and got better." "He got on an electric chair and he killed himself and grew up again." Thread and a bit of magic resuscitated a monkey that had been eaten by an alligator, cut by a glass window, shot with a fire hose, and stamped on by the fireman! Four children definitely settled the fate of one wicked tiger, however:

He went to another zoo and he did such bad things he got killed. Blood ran all over the place. His eyes got bleedy all around them and he died; then all the bleed went over the zoo. They threw him away into a garbage can, then from the garbage can they threw him into the river. Then they made a hole and put some flowers on top. And then they buried him in the dirt.

Of course, children use these animal characters as blinds. Wild beasts can be expected to do things that children are forbidden to try. Just as polite Alice turns herself into a cat in dramatic play so that she may be excused for clawing her teachers, genteel Lee may describe in a story all the things he would like to do; but the evildoer is ostensibly a tiger, so Lee needs to feel no guilt. Behind these masks the children express jealousy of their brothers or sisters, anger against their parents, hostility toward the world in gen-

eral. When tough little Johnny overheard his mother tell a
teacher about a fire she had seen the night before, and how
she had awakened his older brother to see it, Johnny initi-
ated a fire story in which the people who had seen the fire
were killed. He could not understand why he had been
excluded from an experience of such interest; his brother
always seemed to be the lucky one. What easier thing than
to kill both his unfair mother and his indulged older
brother? Since it was all a story, no harm was done, and the
unhappy feeling was relieved. However, he and his friends
were careful, as they concluded the tale, to save the dog
and cat who lived nearby, as well as the other innocent
bystanders.

Karen, morose and generally silent, unbent long enough
to tell a story of a duck that was punished for trivial reasons:

The duck ran under the chair, and a woman came along and
got mad. And the woman took all the water out of the pool so
the duck couldn't swim and she threw the water away. Then
the duck's father came. He spanked the little duck because he
was naughty—because he ran under the chair. And the little
duck ran away and lived in another house. And the father
doesn't know where he lives, either.

A visit in the home shed further light on Karen's glumness.
Her father, a stern disciplinarian, often whipped his children for minor misdeeds. With the unpleasant ability of
the woman in the story, who knew just what would make a
duck most unhappy, he treated his children to sarcasm and
deprivations. Karen was distrustful of all adults and in this
story expressed her bewilderment and resentment.

Ducks are favorites when a gentle animal character is
desired. By contrast, a dragonfly, simply by virtue of its
name, may be used as one of the most ferocious of beasts.
When a real one is pointed out to them, children often find
it difficult to accept the fragile insect as the bearer of such a
fierce-sounding name. One story-book dragonfly jumped

over the world killing people and eating "the whole school in one gulp. . . . He even ate rubbers and boots and paper and crayons and even lockers and clothes and pocket books!" That pretty well took care of the young author's nursery school. Yet, at the end, the dragonfly "learned these things from his own baby: that he shouldn't eat people up, and he shouldn't jump over trees and schools, and he shouldn't eat boots up." During the telling of this story, the original aggressive tone gradually gave way to the final, more amenable mood—an achievement in itself.

Both as an illustration of violence of mood and as a dramatic example of how these sessions can result in a feeling of release, Peter's story of "the lion in the church tower" deserves to be quoted in full. Peter's parents were refined Europeans, concerned with the outward forms of courtesy. They were baffled by his desire to throw his weight about and did their utmost to instill him with their own quiet gentility. At school, he was at first a reserved child, polite toward adults and passive with his peers. For a four-year-old, he was hopelessly awkward in all physical activity. As the year progressed he began to play sly tricks which later turned into hearty attacks on the teachers. This story was written at the height of his spree, when he was gaining notoriety in the group to make up for the respect he could never earn until he had developed some physical skills. Though it purports to be about a church in France, the minute details are all features of his specific church nursery school.

A lion broke a window and also he broke all the windows of a tower in a big church in France. He came up by the stair. He came down by the elevator. And he ate up the elevator man. Then he went outside and ate up all the passengers on the avenue where the church was. And then he went up again by the stair and he ate up four teachers on the thirteenth floor of that church. Those teachers were Miss Barnouw, Mrs. Braasch, Mrs. Taylor, and Mr. Swan. He ate them up. He ate up all the children. Then the lion tore off the handle from the window.

Then he broke off two such bars next to the window. Then he damaged the radiator into such little pieces [*demonstrated with fingers*]. Then he broke a table. Then he damaged the glass on the clock. Then he damaged the windows on the door. Then he came up to the fifteenth floor and he broke the windows and the table and the chairs and the glass on the clock. Then he ate up all the parents at the parents' meeting. And then he went down to the fifth floor, and there he broke the window and tore off the handle and the bars and damaged the table and the chairs and windows in the doors. And he ate up all the children on the fifth floor. Then he went to the ninth floor and there he broke the windows and damaged the radiator and chairs and windows of doors and the glass of the clock. He broke the books and tore them and threw the paper in the waste paper basket, and then he did something more—he tore off all the books from the shelf. Then he tore them to pieces and threw them in the waste paper basket. Then he tore off two earrings from both ears of somebody. Then he tweaked them. Then he spanked them and then he gobbled that person all up. Then he damaged the waste paper basket. Then the shelves where the books are. Then he tore off the dress from a person. He tore off a handle from a door and a door lock. He went into a house. He broke the windows and tore everything into pieces. Then he damaged the radiators and broke up the closets. Then he damaged the toys of a child. Then he broke the dresser and tore the clothes apart. He broke the dresser and the windows of all the apartment. Then he damaged the furniture and the beds, the bookshelf, and the bookcase. He tore the books apart. He broke a belt from a father, a ferry from a child. He gobbled the child up. Then he damaged two bars of the window. Then he broke all the doors and the piano. Then he drank the milk and broke the cracker to pieces. Then he broke the tools of the father and the tool cabinet. Then he ate up the mother and the father and the child and the whole house. Finally he damaged the tea kettle.

All the people were eaten up. He went into the woods to find a fairy and the fairy was his wife. And she gave him everything to eat that he wanted.

The story was told with fiendish glee. Everyone laughed

heartily during the telling. Jack and Mildred wanted the lion to be punished for all his dreadful misdeeds, but Peter refused to accept any such suggestion. "No! No!" he insisted. "Nothing happened to him." Immediately afterward he climbed to the top of the big outdoor jungle gym for the first time! Other achievements of physical prowess followed quickly.

Some groups seem particularly full of hostility and anxiety, and the greater number of their tales will reflect their needs. Not all children's stories are such gory ones. Many are notable for their humor and charm. As always, imagination colors the familiar facts. Take the fantasy of the "friendly tiger" who shook hands with visitors to the zoo. He

pushed open the zoo door and walked away into an apartment house. Nobody started to live there, so he knew it was his own home. He had money so he could buy food and papers, so he could go to work and make money. He worked in an office all the time. It made people surprised when they saw a tiger in the office. They said, "Hello!" and kissed the tiger and hugged him and gave him meat and a peanut. He loved hamburger. He never got back to the zoo. He didn't like it there because all the animals talked too much and the zoo keeper came too often. Two friendly tigers came to live with him. The tiger that got the house first did the cooking, the second tiger washed the laundry, and the third tiger worked in a barber shop and cleaned the house when he came home. The tiger was so happy he bought himself a pair of skates, socks and shoes, some clothes, and a million cans of dog food.

The name of one group's favorite, "The Elephant and Mr. Poo-Poo-Pum," sent the children into roars of laughter; it bordered on bathroom talk, but somehow managed to escape being questionable.

. . . When the elephant ate Mr. Poo-poo-pum up, he was still alive. And when he was inside, he tickled the elephant. The elephant said, "Stop it, Mr. Poo-poo-pum!" And Mr. Poo-poo-pum didn't say anything at all. He just kept on tickling. And then the elephant coughed Mr. Poo-poo-pum up. And then he was still in the cage, but the cage was locked. Then Mr. Elephant ate Mr. Poo-poo-pum up, and then he was really dead for his whole life. And then another person who was very nice—and that was the keeper—said to the elephant, "Did you eat anybody up?" And the elephant told a lie. He said, "No-o-o." They saw him eat the person up so they said, "Elephant! Don't do that any more! You're telling a lie!" Then a lady came and pulled the dead man out of his trunk—Mr. Poo-poo-pum!

In the next example, Robert exercised his sense of humor in a tale about a mouse who

ran under the table while the maid wasn't looking . . . The maid saw the mouse and he ran away, and the poor maid was mad. [*After going to the country and eating some cheese, he returns in a little red car.*] When the maid saw him, she laughed so hard that she plopped on the floor. Then she put him in a cage. She fed him sugar and apples. [*Once again he escapes, this time to the city.*] There he found some butter. He took it home and attached it on to the cheese. The maid jumped with delight and fell plop on the floor again.

Not only do children make use of a lively vocabulary, but they show real awareness of sound in their choice of words as well. In writing a description of trains, a group of boys decided that they "chug along the track," then "go 'toot' and the conductor shouts 'All aboard!' and the train goes 'sh-sh-sh'. . . . The people go 'clop-clop' off the station. . . . trains go 'ding-ding' so that other trains won't run into them." This interest in sound often results in rhymes.

> If your name is Billy,
> You must be silly.
>
> If your name is Ricky,
> You must be a picky.
>
> If you're a dolly,
> Your name is Polly. . . .

> They jumped
> Into a skunk.
> The skunk gave them a bad smell
> And put them in a hotel.
> The hotel
> Was smelly.
> Oh, well!

As with all activities, a few limits are necessary. These restrictions are made as need for them arises. The reason for taking turns is obvious to the children, since they realize that only one sentence at a time can be taken down, and that the teacher can hear nothing if everyone speaks at once. It is best not to urge them to dictate stories, though teachers may sometimes remind them that they can do so if they wish. If the request for writing stories comes from the children, sessions are rarely sterile. When it seems that no one has any real ideas, or that they are using dictation simply as a means to kill time, other activities can be suggested.

There should be no limit placed on subject matter, provided it is original. Ordinarily, bathroom talk is acceptable if it is in reasonable doses or if it has some direct bearing on the plot, as in the story of "the man who ate some doodie," or the one in which a man couldn't get out of a snapping turtle's stomach "unless the turtle made big doo-doo."

Children sense their teachers' interest in originality and understand why they are not encouraged to retell the adventures of Cinderella or Spiderman or the like. Their own stories are the ones that are sought for at school. In manipulating characters he has invented, the child is not influenced by actions they may have played before in someone else's story. He is free to move them at will, to make them say and do what his own feelings suggest. Thus to some degree, their actions reflect and release his inner concerns. Only an original story, told in an atmosphere of acceptance and respect, can accomplish these results.

When Robert, the boy who had written about the mouse and the maid, was seven, his sister was a member of the four-year-old group in his old classroom. She reported to her mother that her teacher had read Robert's story aloud and had it in a book that was kept at school. She was impressed by this proof that children's stories had real value. But to Robert, it was past believing that his tale still was being read, though other kinds of equipment were replaced yearly. "They even paint the blocks over each year," he said.

It is true that these books are prized at school. The children never tire of hearing their own stories reread, and an occasional telling of stories written in preceding years seldom fails to find a listener. To teachers they bring back the children themselves. Stories are in many ways the most concrete legacy children can leave behind. Every page contains some reminder of a noteworthy personal feeling or experience which, though described by a child of four or five, gives glimpses of universal truths. Each tale is highly personal, and its words bring to mind Karen with her great mournful eyes, or tough little John putting on record how much it hurt not to have been awakened to see the fire. Peter left the city several years ago and is now getting along well in grade school, but the lion he loosed still roams the church tower. In a sense, his growl may be heard wherever young children play, for every child brings his own particular lion with him to school. Some are only playful cubs; others, like the one Peter rid himself of, are full-grown and on the rampage. Biographies of many of these beasts appear in dictated story books. Since they present many faces, children give them various names: "a wicked witch," "a wolf," "the mean mother," "the dragonfly." Basically they are all relatives of that unhappy lion who "ate up the mother and the father and the child and the whole house" and "finally damaged the teakettle." Grownups give them less imaginative labels: hostility, fear, resentment, uncertainty, frustration. Whatever the label, each time they are recognized and talked about and called by name, some of their violence is tamed.

If the lion's roar still echoes in school rooms around the country, so, too, does the shout of delight with which Peter greeted the top of the outdoor jungle gym. This happy sound is reinforced by other voices that speak from pages of children's books—voices which on occasion threaten to drown out the lion altogether—for Peter is only one of many children who, through such stories, have found freedom to make surprising progress after unleashing their lions.

12

Nature

Jeremy rushes into the room. He has forgotten to stop at his locker to remove his jacket and cap. He holds a glass jar in one hand, and waves it excitedly at Miss Brown.

"I brought a cockroach for the mantis!" he says.

Miss Brown looks into the jar. Racing around the bottom is an immense roach. It is a good thing that the lid is screwed on tightly, or the roach might get out. Jeremy's mother appears at the door. She is the brave soul who caught this creature. "I saw it run across the hall last night just as I was getting ready to put Jeremy to bed," she explains. "Really, I thought it was a mouse, it was so huge. When Jeremy saw what it was he begged me to catch it. I admit I didn't want to step on it. It gave me the shivers to think of it. So I ran and got a jar while Jeremy watched to see where it went. We chased it all over the hall, and finally got it when it started to climb up the wall. I just put the jar over him, and he fell in. I feel like a big game hunter!"

A crowd of children has formed, and Miss Brown shows the cockroach to them. It must be admitted that this fellow is rather handsome. His glossy brown back with its stream-lined contours and his elegant feelers give him real distinction. But one can also appreciate Mrs. Scott's revulsion at finding him in her tidy apartment. The exterminator had been there only a week ago! Miss Brown continues to show off the roach to late-comers.

"Jeremy," she says, "I'll keep your cockroach here at the table while you take your wraps off. When you get back, we'll put him in with the mantis."

Jeremy rushes off and is back within a minute, his jacket and cap now hanging in his locker. Mr. Andrews lifts down the big glass case that houses the praying mantis. As soon as it is set on the table, a great scramble for ringside seats begins. There is much pushing for good locations, many cries of "I can't see." Finally everyone is settled, and an expectant silence falls over the audience. Twelve four-year-olds and two parents hang over the glass case and watch as Mr. Andrews unscrews the lid of the jar, lifts up the top of the case, and drops the cockroach in. The roach rushes about with tremendous energy.

"Why, he's bigger than the mantis," gasps Judy.

"Sh-sh-sh," comes from the other watchers. They want no interruptions.

The mantis is aware that something is with her in the cage. Her long green body rises slightly on sticklike legs. Her small triangular head pivots from side to side. The round gray eyes stare beadily into every corner. She does not move. Her horny arms are drawn up in the prayerful attitude that gave her her name, but they have the latent strength of a powerful spring, coiled and ready to snap. By this time, the other occupant of the cage has ceased his frenzied race. He, too, is watchful, his antennae probing sensitively ahead of him. Perhaps he is conscious of danger. Now, very slowly, he begins an exploration of his prison. He moves closer and closer to the ever-hungry mantis. At the same moment, all the spectators see the eyes of the mantis turn unmistakably in his direction. "It sees him!"

calls out a breathless voice. She has indeed spotted her visitor, and despite his size has already marked him as a victim. Rising higher on her spindly legs, the mantis begins a weird dance, shifting her body gently from side to side and edging almost imperceptibly toward the roach. He is still moving forward, almost as if drawn to the vicious arms by a magnet. Now the sharp little face juts closer to the roach. The green body tightens. Then like a bolt of lightning the powerful arms shoot out. A violent struggle follows. But the mantis has not grasped her immense luncheon firmly enough. He escapes, leaving only a leg is her grip, and hobbles off to the opposite corner. His leg is waved happily in the air, then crunched with delicate relish by his slender assailant.

A murmur comes up from the onlookers.

"It didn't get him," says an unhappy voice.

"Does the cockroach hurt?" asks another.

"I don't think so," says Mr. Andrews. "They don't feel the way we do."

"Oh, look," Jeremy breaks in, "My cockroach is coming back again!"

The preliminaries are enacted as before. The murderous arms dart out again, but this time they seize the roach firmly, and the fight is on. The great size and weight of her intended victim upsets her balance, and the mantis is soon on the floor upside down, her legs clawing the air. But clasped in an unbroken hold is the roach, whose shorter legs are also scrambling for a footing. Somehow the mantis rights herself. The embrace is folded tighter, and her head comes down for a gruesome kiss. The tiny mandibles find an unprotected spot in the roach's armor. A bite opens it wider, and the greenish snout is soon buried in the roach's neck. A feeble struggle goes on for a while longer, but the mantis continues unhurriedly sucking out her diet. An hour later, with only a few people nearby to see, the empty carcass drops to the floor, and this elegant pet busies herself cleaning her soiled hands.

"Horrible!" says a visiting teacher. "Miss Brown, you are showing your children the most repulsive side of nature. In my school we use cocoons and seeds to show how life unfolds. Why must you put these fearful experiences in front of young children? The other day I taught my four-year-olds a song that goes this way:

> The birds are safe in the air,
> The fish are safe in the sea.
> If God in His Heaven takes care of all these.
> He will take care of me.

I think it makes for a better attitude."

Miss Brown does not agree. She feels it is wrong to teach that "fish are safe in the sea." Nothing could be further from the truth. All around them, inquisitive children observe small creatures living on smaller ones, and large ones in turn preying on them. They could not respect a philosophy that tries to cover up these facts. There is real danger in fostering a concept of God as an all-protecting Creator who looks out for the well-being of each of His creatures, for as children become increasingly aware of the dog-eat-dog existence that prevails in Nature, they may be unable to view it as part of a great plan and see it instead as a disillusioning proof of God's indifference. Later rejection of religion may result from early training which puts all the responsibility for safety and happiness on God.

The hazards of a dangerous existence are wonderfully balanced, however, with devices for protection and advancement. Instinct, special coloring, adaptability, and swiftness are some of the means by which living things are preserved. The turtles in the garden, the chameleon and the cactus on the nature table demonstrate them daily at school. The mantis herself, with her leaf-green color, is a fine example of the advantage of blending into one's habitat. While it serves to protect her, it also enables her to catch unsuspecting passers-by. Fortunately, the spectacle of watching her at breakfast does not affect a child as it may an adult. Jeremy brings to this experience none of the emotional feelings that make grownups shiver and turn away. He observes with greater detachment than is possible for them. He can toss a worm in front of the mantis and wonder nothing more than that she could consume something twice her length.

A number of people were actively involved in this instance of getting acquainted with the insect world. Early in the school year Miss Brown had visited Billy's home and during the course of the chat was shown his newest pets: two adult mantises, one of which had flown into their apartment window. Miss Brown was so enthusiastic about them that Billy's mother promised to bring them to school so that the group could see them. Unfortunately, by the next day, one of these pleasant creatures had turned cannibal and eaten the other up. Only the victor arrived, her abdomen still puffy from this tremendous repast. Along with the mantis, Billy brought a worm, and the class watched with interest as the insect slowly consumed its first luncheon at school. Subsequently, other children brought this pet a varied diet—flies, moths, caterpillars, more worms—and their parents often lingered to see the fate of these offerings. "Fuzzy bear" caterpillars were always spurned by this otherwise greedy friend. Katie's mother brought in Fabre's wonderful book *Social Life in the Insect World,* and the staff pored over it. To everyone's delight, the mantis laid eggs in a remarkable white case at the top of her cage, just as it said she would in the book. She died about a week later, mourned by many. Parents and children and staff together had learned much through this voracious visitor. After such an experience, how could anyone fail to appreciate the value of a praying mantis in keeping down insect destruction of gardens or vegetable plots?

A terrarium, too, can be at the same time a source of pleasure and of information. Four-year-olds may help set one up, though it is doubtful that they have any clear idea of what the final result is going to be. First, they clean out the terrarium with sponges and towels. Next they search for pebbles, and when enough have been collected, they scatter them over the bottom of the tank. Bits of a flower pot crushed with a hammer are added and mixed with the pebbles. A two-inch layer of sand is spread on top of the rough bits at the bottom. Several children can take turns with small shovels, carefully spilling in their share of sand. Others may sift earth through sieves, heap it above the sand and mold it into interesting contours. Next, they help their teachers set in mosses, toadstools, rattlesnake plantain, partridge berry, ferns, and other woodland plants, perhaps leaving space for a small glass dish which will serve as a pool. The rich green leaf colors, varied with the red of partridge berries and the paler shades of toadstools, look like a little section of wet woods brought into the classroom. The pool, ringed about by mossy stones and shaded by ferns, is an ideal home for toads and small frogs. These contented creatures will sit, partly concealed by foliage, near the water and wait for something to eat. Needless to say, children and adults alike become avid hunters for small insects and grubs, offering these morsels daily to the frogs and the toads, or to the salamanders that live somewhere in the fragrant crevices of the terrarium.

Adele reports accurately at home the entire process of setting up the terrarium at her school. She concludes her description with the statement, "The teachers read what to do out of a paper." Quite aside from the fact that she is learning one of the values of knowing how to read, she is also voicing something that teachers try to make amply clear: they do not know all the answers. They admit that they do not know about the bug Sylvia has caught or the flower Vincent found in the country.

"I'll have to look that up in a book," is a typical comment; "I can't tell you what it is."

Nor should adults attempt to give complete scientific data in response to children's questions. There is great danger in giving much information. Interest is killed if many dry facts are forced in where a simple explanation is all that is needed. In these early years, the most important duty is to keep alive the spark of interest, the core of wonder that springs up so often within everyday experiences. The excitement of just seeing the frog is enough for a time. Five-year-olds are ready to spot differences between him and his cousin, the toad, but it is wise not to bring these details in much earlier. It is easy for grownups to forget how wonderful things are! A falling leaf, a cloud passing overhead, an ant on the sidewalk, trifles to the sophisticated adult, are sources of wonder to the child. Each one provides him with something new to discover, a fresh experience. He does not need to be told that the leaf budded in the spring, or that the cloud is a mass of minute particles of water. If he senses that the adult shares his excitement and feels a similar curiosity, that is enough.

Parents and teachers of city children must capitalize on the aspects of nature that do occur in the environment. Grocery stores provide ways of becoming acquainted with living plants. Peas and beans saved from cooking will grow indoors. Seeds of oranges and grapefruit, brought to the city from great distances, sprout satisfactorily, while onions and potatoes can hardly wait to send out leaves. One can learn something about geology from displays in jewelers' windows. Sidewalks reveal differences between sandstone and granite; some of them dazzle the eye with flakes of mica, like the shining stones children unearth occasionally in the park. Mysterious clouds of vapor escaping from the laundry or a manhole help in discussions about weather and cloud formations. Though few city children have ever peered into a pig-sty, a hippopotamus groveling in his mud is a familiar sight to these zoo-going youngsters.

Johnny and his eight-year-old sister once went to the country and visited an apple orchard. When apples hanging on the boughs were pointed out to them, they asked incredulously, "Apples don't *really* grow on trees, do they?" Of course they had heard about it, and even seen pictures of it in books, but somehow it had never before come to them as fact. Now they know that apples they see in the fruit-stand bins did not originate there. Seeing is believing.

Unfortunately, one cannot feel confident that Johnny's playmates have equal understanding. Their teachers must concentrate on areas which can be followed through in the city. The box turtles Miss Murphy's nephew rescued from certain death on a busy highway still live in the garden at her school. Every spring they make a miraculous reappearance, plodding about where the children can see them, only to bury themselves again when the weather turns cold. These children know the feel of their rough skin and remember the peculiar shape of the protecting upper and lower shells. They have watched the box turtles draw in their heads and complete the effectiveness of their armor by clamping shut a door that seals off the area into which their heads were pulled. Watching for the return of these stolid friends each May reinforces other experiences they have in the spring: buds bursting on bushes and trees on the playground, birds nesting in the garden, grass turning green. They begin to be confident about the seasons; they can see an order in things. A related feeling comes to other groups, who moisten cocoons all winter and await the emergence of moths, or who follow the growth of a tadpole until he becomes a frog. These processes can be counted on.

A park or garden plot provides shelter for birds through every season. Warblers stop by on their annual migrations. Chickadees, juncos, and blue jays may be winter visitors. Now and again, one is treated to a glimpse of a hermit thrush or a brown thrasher. Catbirds betray their presence with their distinctive calls. One spring, robins nested in the garden adjoining a city school. The mother robin was visible through a thin network of leaves and twigs. Teachers lifted their children high enough for a good view and cautioned them not to disturb the mother or her babies, if the eggs hatched. In a matter of days, both adult birds were constantly in flight, struggling to keep up with the insistent demands of their offspring. Children could see the scrawny young—all mouths—their heads bobbing on pipe-cleaner necks. After a time, feathers began to cover their prickly nakedness, but they still kept up a din of infantile screams for food. Many a worm and insect fell into their gaping mouths. One day, the nest was empty. The birds had gone. At the end of the summer, a kindly gentleman approached the school's director and informed her that a robin's nest was in a low tree in the garden. "I've known about it since spring," he told her, "but I didn't say anything for fear the children would hear about it. I knew it wouldn't be safe with them around."

Perhaps there is a rabbit hutch at school, or a bird cage, or a small cage for white rats or hamsters. Some older groups will take turns cleaning the cage regularly and providing a steady diet, but even the youngest child will want to bring occasional tidbits from home. At almost any minute during the day, children will be clustered around to peek in or to offer their animal friend a piece of food.

Growing near one school playground is a long pumpkin vine. Its yellow-orange flowers have just begun to close. Maybe there will be pumpkins on it this fall! The children planted several seeds there, seeds which came from a pumpkin used last year to make a jack-o'-lantern at Halloween. The children who hollowed out that pumpkin, separating the pith and the seeds from the hard outer shell, know a good deal about it. They have smelled it and felt it and watched seedlings grow in glass jars. They recognize it as real, as something that lives. Like themselves, it starts with a seed. They contrast it with cardboard jack-o'-lanterns, which have no seeds, which are not alive. This awareness of the separation between living and inanimate objects is an important concept, but it is not thrust upon the children. They are shown as much as is possible in a

concrete way; very few words are used; in a straightforward response to the situation at hand.

While the two-year-old cannot talk as fluently as his
older brothers and sisters, his senses are wide awake, alert
to new smells and new sounds and new sights. So many
things are first-time experiences for him. One sees him
crawling after minute insects or sitting motionless as he
watches a worm. With what wonder does he approach a
flower to snuff up its mysterious fragrance. Will it be pun-
gent or sweet? Will he find it pleasant or will he want to
avoid it the next time? And what is that tiny thing crawling
on the stem? He sees clouds racing behind a church tower.
Suddenly it appears that the whole structure is slowly top-
pling over. He cries and points to the sky. "That's all right.
The church isn't falling down," his teacher says. "The
clouds just make it look that way." How can they? And
what is a cloud?

The two-year-old is a true sensualist. He revels in the
snow, rolling in it, eating it, feeling its different textures
with his hand. The sandbox and the wading pool offer
other sensations. One is gritty but soft, moist some days
and dry on others. The other is cool and velvety against his
skin, but it stings like the sand when it gets into his eyes. He
sees many things. Too many for him to assimilate. He asks
the simplest questions, hard for him to shape into words,
but he wonders about the rest.

As he grows older, he continues to observe. Three-and
four-year-olds see the infinite variety of creation. Leaves
have different shapes; some seeds float down softly while
others, like nuts, clunk to the floor if you drop them; every
sea shell has its own pattern. Their learning is spotty, and
little of it can be put into words, but it is going on all the
time. Something happens suddenly among the five-year-
olds. Questions begin to come to the surface, questions that
must be answered accurately, if simply. "Is Hildy's mother
fat, or does she have a baby in there?" "What does a snake

eat?" "Do robins have teeth?" "How do they eat?" "Where do eggs come from?" A scientific interest is budding and must be kept alive. The two-year-old held a snake fearlessly in his hands, watching it in fascination. Now that he is five, other considerations temper his interest. "Will it bite?" "Is it poison?" "My mother doesn't like snakes."

A magnifying glass opens up new worlds. He sees his own skin, irregular and patterned. He finds holes in a perfect piece of cloth, scales on the side of a fish, countless eyes on an insect, instead of only two. He is ready to sustain steady interest in the exhibits spread out on his nature table. Rocks, seeds, leaves, cocoons, and nests cover it, and almost every day another child brings something new. One five-year-old startled everyone near him at a restaurant by snatching an oyster shell from the plate of the grownup next to him. Called to account for his action, he explained that it was for his science table at school.

Toward the end of spring, gardens and parks teem with insect life. Shiny creatures scuttle out of sight or burst into the air with a great buzz of wings as one approaches. Anne is surprised by a monarch butterfly that lights for a moment on her hand. Even indoors, while she rests, she is reminded of the garden. Through the windows drones an insect serenade.

A safari is planned in the kindergarten. Eager hunters, armed with plastic jars and sharp eyes, creep about the park intent on bagging big game. Peter holds aloft the butterfly net. He has been given a few instructions about how to use it so as not to injure his quarry, and he feels very important as he surveys the terrain. He is determined to capture something exciting, since he will not have another turn with the net until the rest of the group have had their chances, too. Suddenly there is a shout from David: "A dragonfly! Look! Get him, Peter!" Sure enough, a large dragonfly has settled on a tree trunk. He sits there, quite motionless, as if aware of the beautiful sight his wings make in the sunlight. Peter stalks toward the tree. His friends hop up and down in excitement and try their best not to make any noise. Anne emits little nervous squeaks. The net is poised above the dragonfly now, and as yet the creature has given no sign of alarm. The net descends, and at the same moment, the dragonfly buzzes off with lightning speed. There is a moan of disappointment. Someone blames Peter for having scared the dragonfly by stepping too close. Others point at Anne and maintain that she was the culprit. Their teacher reminds them of the dragonfly's amazing eyes, which enable him to see better than humans can. No doubt he saw the net as it started down, and thanks to his ability to take off swiftly, made his escape. Her explanation is cut short by Ellen's announcement that she has seen a butterfly on the far side of the garden. Everyone races off, and the hunt continues.

Before the school year is over, this group has a commendable list of captures to its credit: crickets, grasshoppers, locusts, praying mantises, dragonflies, crane flies, honeybees, bumblebees, blue mud-dauber wasps, leaf hoppers, Japanese beetles, ladybird beetles, innumerable ants, and several kinds of caterpillars, butterflies, and moths. After careful observation, including close scrutiny with a magnifying glass, these creatures meet various fates. Some are fed to the frogs or a mantis; others are released to continue their useful work; caterpillars are plied with their favorite leaves until they make cocoons or chrysalises.

David and Anne have changed their attitudes toward insects considerably since their first days at school. Quite understandably, their immediate impulse upon seeing a "bug" had been to stamp on it, since they were acquainted only with roaches, mosquitoes, and flies—all of which are undesirable visitors from one point of view. Now Anne's greatest treasure is a mantis egg case she found in the country, and David has become an avid insect collector. Both of them look carefully before they swat or squash, and an unwary roach in their apartment is more likely to complete his destiny in the stomach of a toad than in the incinerator. Drawing pictures at the easel is a successful technique in explaining some of nature's mysteries to older children. A few strokes of the crayon suggest a cross section of a pool. Eggs are clustered around a reed stem. In the second picture, the eggs have disappeared, and tadpoles cover the page like a cloud of commas. The children are shown a close-up of one of these creatures, so that they see where his eyes are and notice the shape of the mouth. Successive pictures bring the tadpoles further along the road to toadhood. The legs appear; the mouth widens; the tail shrinks; a tongue becomes prominent. Finally they are given a view of the end of the cycle: an adult toad, bloated and warty, with his sticky tongue on its way to catch a fly. A running commentary fills in the gaps between pictures and allows for questions to be answered as they come along. This method is friendlier and more direct than reading such facts from a book. Its effectiveness is proved by the way the information crops up now and again later in the year. A hundred other subjects can be presented this way: the hibernation of animals in the fall, the life cycle of moths and butterflies, the growth of a seed into a flowering plant, the development of a child inside its mother's body.

Not all of children's discoveries about nature take place around living organisms. Shells, the occupants of which are long since dead, mysterious bones brought back from excursions in the country, leaves that have been dried and pressed, defunct beetles—all stimulate the child's curiosity about his world.

Five-year-old Kathryn, visiting in her aunt's home, showed great interest in a collection of sea shells, dried sea horses, and bits of coral. Nearby, she came upon a colorful butterfly and a large silk moth, both mounted in glass cases. Her aunt explained that the shells had once housed living creatures, and that the moth and butterfly, too, had once been alive. For a time Kathryn admired these exhibits in silence. Then she said, "You like to keep dead things, don't you?"

Many "dead things" are still beautiful, and provide more than mere pleasure to the eye. A dead bee can be scrutinized without fear of its sting. A dried pipefish can be touched and studied without need of salt-water aquarium or glass-bottomed boat.

The deadness of things is a difficult concept for children to accept. They can scarcely imagine that death is permanent, and the possibility of their own dying seems remote—even incredible. They search for the causes of death, look for antidotes. Fact and fantasy, fear and wonderment are intermingled when this subject comes to their attention.

Five three-year-olds boys, all nearing their fourth birthday, are at play near a sandbox. Angelo notices the body of a pigeon, half buried in a drift of sand. He picks it up and holds it for a minute. "Here's a dead bird," he announces to anyone who may hear. No one pays attention to his comment, so he repeats it in a slightly louder tone: "Here's a dead bird."

Philip comes over, looks at the bird with a frown, considers for a moment, then says with decision, "I think it got too cold." He begins to walk away.

Angelo lets the bird drop to the ground. "You can't catch a bird or a pigeon," he comments to Philip's back.

Philip returns for another look. He still wonders how the bird had come to die. By this time, Angelo has walked off, and Philip calls to him urgently, "I want to tell you something." Almost stammering, he continues, "Someone put it in the sand." Finding this second explanation for its demise more to his satisfaction, he ambles off toward the tricycles.

Next Matthew comes up. After looking down at the bird, he asks his teacher, "Can you touch it?"

"If you want to," she replies.

Matthew squats and gently opens one of the stiff claws. "Can you step on it?" he asks. Receiving no reply from the teacher, he places the toe of one shoe on the bird's wing and holds the rest of his foot over the body, without touching it. After a minute, he asks, "Can you paint it?" He has just finished working with a brush and a can full of water "paint."

Again his teacher replies, "If you want to."

Seeing Matthew bring his painting equipment over, Philip comes back again. With mannish finality, he pronounces his final word on the cause of the pigeon's death: "Someone shot it." Finding a paint brush, he kneels to share Matthew's water can. "Let's paint its mouth," he says. He pries the bill open, and together, in silence, they paint the bird with water.

"Poor little bird," Matthew croons as he works. "It's all dead. Poor little old bird." Noticing his teacher standing nearby, he explains, "We're painting the bird so he'll be new again and fly off. Maybe he'll fly again." He looks up at his teacher for confirmation.

"Do you think so?" she asks.

"Maybe he flied backwards," Matthew says, trying to puzzle things out. "*All* birds that fly by the city from here don't fall down. They fly faster. He's all worn out. He's getting ready to fly again when he dries out. He's getting ready to fly again." By the time Matthew finishes, Philip has lost interest and wanders off in search of something new. Now Bradley comes up for the first time, squats alongside Matthew, and touches the bird. "Is he dead?" Bradley asks.

"Yes." Matthew puts on a final touch of "paint."

Bradley is always ready for an argument. He looks at the bird and says, "He's not dead."

"He's dead." Matthew is sure of this.

But Bradley means to have his way. "*He's not dead,*" he states dogmatically. Picking the bird up, he starts for a water drain, down which he has already thrown a rubber ball and all the water he could find in various "paint" cans. "I want to throw it down the drain."

Matthew's emphatic "No!" carries enough weight to discourage Bradley, who drops the bird and runs off.

During all this time, the fifth child, Allen, has continued to play in the adjacent sandbox, showing no interest either in the bird or in the conversation.

Some typical reactions are to be observed in this scene: Matthew knows with his intellect that the bird is dead, yet hopes that by painting it he may restore it to life; Angelo is totally matter-of-fact; blustering Bradley uses the bird as an excuse to provoke argument; Allen ignores the issue entirely; Philip is mainly interested in the reason for the pigeon's demise.

A month later, Philip's curiosity about this subject is just as keen as ever. He is advising Dorothy to tell her mother about something that happened at school. "My mommy died, so I can't tell her," Dorothy tells him. "I'll tell my daddy. . . . My mommy died, so they buried her."

Philip comes out with his old question: "Do you know *why* she died?"

"The doctor couldn't fix her," is Dorothy's sensible reply, "so they buried her."

Philip has thought of another explanation. "Do you know why people die? They get too *old*." He draws out the word "old" so that it conveys a sense of long time.

His friend, Everett, has seen skeletons at the museum and contributes this grisly suggestion: "They take their skin off."

But Philip is going to stick to his latest theory, perhaps one he was told at home. "They get too old," he states, "and they die."

The observant child sees death all around him, and unless his curiosity is checked by fear-inspiring evasions or detailed scientific explanations or by final-sounding assertions like, "God takes things to Heaven when they die," he will continue to investigate this mystery. A pleasant story about a little girl and her father might not seem a likely springboard into the subject of death, but it started the following discussion among the same group of children involved in the foregoing illustrations. They were seated in their classroom for a story. All of them were feeling high and excited after a party, where for all the hilarity there had been some welcome evidence of group feeling. One of them asked to have *A Day with Daddy* read aloud. Miss Gray picked up the book and was soon in the midst of its uncomplicated narrative.

MISS GRAY [*reading*]: This is George. He's my dog. He really belongs to me. He likes it when I give him candy. [*Breaking off and speaking directly to the children.*] Did you know that there is candy for dogs?

LOTTE: Yes. I've seen it in the grocery store.

JANE: We used to give it to our dog before he died.

PHILIP [*back at the same question*]: Do you know why he died?

JANE: He got old.

PHILIP: *How* did he die?

JANE: It just happens.

LOTTE: It's like going to sleep. [*She closes her eyes and sighs, demonstrating the explanation her parents have given her.*]

JANE: And you never come back.

JOHN: And then you're in Heaven.

LOTTE [*standing by Jane's assertion*]: And you never come back.

JOHN: Some woman in the beauty shop said a person in Heaven came back again.

MISS GRAY: Do you think so?

JOHN: No.

PHILIP: Some bad man in my neighborhood went in a store and stabbed a man, and he died.

JANE [*unconsciously turning Philip's question back at him*]: How did he die?

PHILIP: He was stabbed.

JANE: How? [*She is not familiar with the word "stabbed."*]

PHILIP: With his knife.

JANE: [*hesitantly*]: Cut?

LOTTE [*taking refuge in her parents' comforting suggestion*]: It's just like going to sleep, and that's all.

WENDY AND BRADLEY [*in unison*]: Philip, will *we* die?

PHILIP: Yes.

WALTER [*who remembers his aquarium at home*]: Even fish die.

BRADLEY [*looking directly at Miss Gray*]: Will we die?

MISS GRAY: Yes. All people die.

WENDY AND BRADLEY [*again*]: *Will* we die?

SEVERAL CHILDREN [*shouting*]: Yes!

WENDY [*bursts into tears, protesting*]: I don't want to.

CHILDREN [*poking fun at Wendy*]: Cry-baby, cry-baby!

MISS GRAY: It's all right to cry when you feel like it.

[*At this point, one of the boys, who has been rocking backward in his chair, suddenly topples over and crashes upside-down to the floor. In the ensuing din, Wendy becomes composed.*]

WALTER [*having found a vulnerable spot in Wendy, now teases her with the chant*]: You're going to die.

WENDY [*bursting into fresh tears*]: I don't want to die.

MISS GRAY: It's all right to feel the way Wendy does. It's something we don't tease people about.

WENDY [*still tearful*]: I want to get on my bed.

MISS GRAY [*lifting Wendy to her lap*]: We'll finish the story first, and then rest.

LOTTE [*to Wendy, reassuringly*]: You're not going to die.

JANE: You'll *never* die.

Miss Gray made no further comment, but started to read. Wendy's tears stopped and she made several comments about the story. As she settled on her bed at rest, she looked over at Jane and, with a broad grin on her face, said, "No one's going to die except Bradley." Bradley was at that time her pet peeve. Having resolved the problem this way, she rested quietly and did not bring up the subject again that day.

It is rare to find a group of threes and young fours so highly verbal about this concern, though it is likely that similar questions, unvoiced, perplex most children of this age. A number of factors brought out the latent interest of this particular group. Prime among them was the death of Dorothy's mother, which was freely discussed among Dorothy and her friends. Accidental happenings, such as the discovery of the dead pigeon, fanned the spark.

Wendy's mother, upon hearing of the outburst of tears at school, told Miss Gray that this had been typical of Wendy's reactions to the subject during recent weeks. It had all started on Washington's Birthday, when Wendy asked who Washington was and where he was. Told that he was dead, Wendy wanted to know what being dead meant. Her mother explained that it meant not being oneself any more, not breathing, not being alive. Since then, Wendy had brought up the subject several times, crying each time they discussed it. Her mother let her cry and did not pursue the topic unless Wendy asked about it again. Wendy seemed to feel that death lay at the end of growth. Consequently she often said, "I'm going to be a little girl all day today," or "I'm going to stay a baby and never grow up." Her parents were careful not to liken death to sleep, as they felt it might disturb her further. She was apt to wake up with nightmares a short time after falling asleep.

Philip, who sought for the causes of death, was probably the one child in the group, besides Dorothy, who accepted the finality of death. He was a sensitive and intelligent child. These qualities were appreciated by his peers, and it is interesting to note that they turned first to him for an answer to the question, "Will *we* die?"

Death, like birth and growth and decay, is a natural part of life. No doubt it is as thorny an issue to children as it is for adults, but given a chance to observe nature in many aspects, they will see how death falls in with all the rest and fulfills its own important functions. It is not an all-absorbing topic, since children soon exhaust their interest in anything and dash off to explore other fields. On a pleasant day, one will see them in parks and playgrounds, running barefoot and reveling in the cool grass. Some industrious boys with shovels may be digging in hopes of reaching China or locating the devil ("He is *too* down there! My mommy told me so!"). A two-year-old will be poking a curious finger at an ant, while the threes run against the wind, laughing when they feel its force pushing back.

Adults are the children's fellow explorers, investigating and rediscovering the world about them. Everyone profits from a close acquaintance with nature. Those who appreciate the wonders of existence, and find their place in the eternal cycles of life and death, are rewarded with healthy serenity that stays with them through the years.

"Open the gates as high as the sky." 13

Kindergarten's Wider World

It is a fine day in October. School has been in session for several weeks, and children in all the groups have begun to fit themselves into the order of a typical morning. Miss Brown and Mr. Andrews are busy keeping track of their new group of fours. Miss Brown stoops to tie Betty's shoelace. Mr. Andrews is writing notes on William in an effort to get acquainted with this rather puzzling child. Suddenly a cheery shout interrupts their labors. They are being paged by five or six old pals from last year's group. Yes, there is Robert, grinning crazily, just as he always did. Next to him stands Andrew, looking rather gawky and thin. He must have grown an inch or two over the summer! And there is Cynthia, waving and shouting with much more fervor than she ever summoned last June. Ellen and Mary, together as usual, have stopped in the midst of a ball game to rush to the gate with the others. That sixth child, on closer inspection, turns out to be an absolute stranger who has joined the shouting out of pure sociability. Miss Brown and Mr. Andrews wave back at them and shout hello. The children continue to watch from their side of the playground, too conscious of their advanced status to rush over and hug their last year's teachers. It is not long before they return to their games, reassured by the knowledge that they have been remembered, but glad to be old enough to qualify as kindergartners.

Almost as if by magic, these children have developed a capacity for concentration and sustained group effort that was quite foreign to them before. Socially, too, they are making strides. Last year, they occasionally delighted in labeling a playmate's drawing "scribble-scrabble," pulling faces of disgust at it, and racing off after they had reduced their victim to tears. This year the teacher can help them make constructive uses of a similar occurrence. Irene has just completed a work of art at the easel. It shows a man in front of a house. The man wears a hat. The house boasts a chimney, a door, and two windows. Irene has had a bit of trouble controlling her brushes, so the over-all impression is somewhat messy. The man's eyes are a bit outside his face, and the chimney protrudes at a rather odd angle from a wavy roof. Drips of excess paint hang like icicles from every horizontal line. Nelly, very sure of her own abilities as a painter, casts a scornful look at Irene's masterpiece.

"It's stinky," she announces in a superior tone.

Irene stares at her with dismay. "No, it isn't," she says slowly. "It's a very nice picture."

Her critic leers at her and repeats her verdict: "Stinky."

The teacher sits beside them quietly and suggests that they might talk about it a little. Several other children move closer, curious and eager.

"We're discussing Irene's painting," Miss Hoagland tells them. "Nelly says it's stinky. Irene says it is a nice picture. What do you think?"

"It *is* stinky," agrees Teddy. "It's too drippy."

Sylvia adds that the colors are poorly chosen. "Nobody has purple eyes," she says.

David's quibble is with the roof. "A roof should be straight," he asserts.

Miss Hoagland turns to Irene. Poor thing! She looks rather crushed.

"What did you like about it, Irene?" she asks.

Irene hesitates. "I like the door," she says at last. "It's nice and straight."

"I think the man is very funny," says Joan with a twinkle. "His mouth is so smiley. I think it's cute."

Teddy has now found a point in its favor, too. "The smoke is good," he says.

Steven is the oldest member of this group. He steps up confidently and makes his pronouncement: "Some things are nice, and some things aren't nice. It isn't stinky, but it's not so great."

Somewhat relieved, Irene says that she will wipe her brush off next time. Nelly agrees that if it hadn't been drippy it would not have been stinky. Both go on with their own work. Miss Hoagland, who had not found it necessary to comment more than twice during the discussion, writes a note about it for future reference.

These children often surprise their parents by sudden interest in signs and books and newspapers.

"What does that say?" is a frequent question on bus rides and trips through town in the family car. Excited mothers spell out NO SMOKING or ONE WAY STREET. Fathers decipher the headlines of this morning's paper. Billy, now five and a half, begs to be taught to read. Miss Hoagland is asked, "Is Billy ready for formal instruction?" Her answer involves many factors, and explaining it in full may take half the morning. She suggests that an evening visit might be more suitable. She would rather meet both parents at home, so that the three of them can arrive at a satisfactory conclusion together. A date is set, and Miss Hoagland rings their bell half an hour after Billy has gone to bed. They are soon in the midst of their discussion.

"We think we should confess to playing a rather dirty trick on you, Miss Hoagland," Mr. Schule says with a grin. "We know you people at the school don't believe in teaching children to read this soon, so we thought we'd better stock up on some ammunition of our own. Remember last Wednesday? Billy didn't come to school that morning. He wasn't sick. My wife took him over to the University for a test."

"I feel terrible for not telling you," Mrs. Schule exclaims. "It makes it sound like such a conspiracy."

Miss Hoagland smiles. "I'd be very interested to know what they found," she says. "Sometimes those tests can be quite helpful. We don't use them at our school for a number of reasons, but that doesn't mean we hold it against anybody who does."

"Well, I understand that children can't profit by reading classes until they have a mental age of six and a half," Mr. Schule says, looking at Miss Hoagland for approval.

She nods, "Go ahead."

"Billy's tests show that he has the intelligence of a *seven*-year-old. Maybe a little over. What do you say to that?" Mr. Schule has set off his bombshell and now relaxes in his easy chair.

"I hope that doesn't put you on the spot," says Mrs. Schule gently.

"I hope it won't," says Miss Hoagland, wondering just where to begin. "We have all noticed how interested he is in signs and books. I certainly don't blame you for checking the validity of your own reactions by having Billy tested."

Mrs. Schule relaxes a bit in her chair. At least she doesn't need to feel on the defensive any more.

"We certainly make no effort to squelch his curiosity about such things at school," Miss Hoagland continues. "Because we recognize his intelligence, too, we also tell him what he wants to know about words in books and letters about the room. The other day, he made a round of the lockers, looking at each name-tape and asking whose name was printed on it. He already recognizes Barbara's and Bobby's, because they start with B, like his own."

The Schules nod proudly. Miss Hoagland is a pretty fine woman, after all.

"He has been dictating stories since he was in the four-year-old group. Now his stories show greater detail and a broader range of interests than they did last year. Yesterday he dictated one about a strike."

"We were listening to the news on the radio one morning last week," Mrs. Schule says, "and Billy was so interested in knowing why the buses weren't going to run. I had to tell him quite a bit about it."

"Well, it's all in his story," says Miss Hoagland. "I'll show it to you tomorrow at school. You may have a copy if you like. But to go on, the experience of waiting for me to get the words of his stories on paper is a good one for Billy. He is more than ever conscious of the importance of written words. Occasionally he asks what word I am writing. He's beginning to recognize the need for words as a way to keep facts where we can return to them again and again. Of course, we have regular story times, too. He was fascinated when I had to use the index in one of our collections of stories yesterday. The way books are set up begins to make real sense to him. And during the day he occasionally takes a book off the shelf and leafs through it. I must say, he is very careful of our books. We try to impress that on all the children."

"Billy has finally started to treat his own things with a little respect," Mrs. Schule adds. "For a long time, the house used to be cluttered with broken toys and torn pages. Nowadays he never is rough on his books."

"He knows their usefulness," Miss Hoagland says. "He is growing up. But at the same time, even a bright youngster like Billy needs to have a good idea of the meaning of the words he is going to learn to read. There is no point in troubling him with deciphering a word like 'robin,' for instance, until he knows what a robin is. Not by hearing about one, but by seeing one, or by getting acquainted with its nest or its eggs. We have a robin's nest on our nature table: that's what made me use that example. But really, we feel that this year is especially important as a time when many things are added to the children's fund of information. That helps build a rich vocabulary, and a rich vocabulary is essential as a background for reading."

"Yes, I follow you," says Mr. Schule, straightening himself again in his chair. "I suppose that if a word doesn't call anything to mind when you hear about it, it would be an awful snag if you ran across it when you were learning to read."

"Precisely." Miss Hoagland is relieved to see that he has followed her argument. "That is why most schools recommend delay rather than haste in starting reading instruction. Before a child can be expected to understand a very wide range of literature, he must have had firsthand contact with a great many things."

"If he were sitting over books all day, I guess he wouldn't have time for other things," muses Mrs. Schule. "He's awfully happy with his little gang right now. Maybe that's more important for the time being."

"I quite agree," says Miss Hoagland. "And besides getting along with his friends, there are other things he still can learn at school. He will need a month or two more before he can pump himself up in the swings. He hasn't quite felt the rhythm of it yet. And his drawings show us that his grip on crayons is still a bit awkward. It is wise to master that before he is expected to use a pencil for printing. A lot of these little things should be well behind him before he can meet new challenges with confidence."

For a moment there is silence. Miss Hoagland wonders just how much of her argument has found receptive ears.

"Go on," Mr. Schule says at length. "I'm afraid you are beginning to convince me."

"Well, I'd only like to add another point or two before I

finish," Miss Hoagland says. "It's true that some children seem to absorb reading almost by osmosis. Two of our four-year-olds this year are already fluent readers, and they gained that skill without formal instruction. Fortunately, they enjoy many other activities at school. We think Billy still needs more time to widen his interests and consolidate his gains. He's becoming more self-reliant every day, and that's important when we consider a child's readiness for First Grade."

"What do you recommend we do?" Mr. Schule asks.

"Go ahead just as you have been doing," counsels Miss Hoagland. "As long as you don't force it, I think his interest in reading is bound to continue. When he has grown up a little in other areas, he will be ready to make rapid progress with words. His vocabulary is already large, and that is the first step. He is pretty stable at school and holds his own well with children of his own age. That's more important than I can say. When those hurdles have been passed, he is more likely to feel ready to concentrate on close work like reading or writing. As far as reading is concerned, I feel that our job is to give him an attitude of interest, rather than pressure to learn."

It is sometimes hard to demonstrate to parents the many unobtrusive ways by which readiness for reading is encouraged. Even among twos and threes, the beginnings are visible to an observant adult. These children are not forced to sit through an entire story. If they listen with full attention for two minutes and then leave, the experience has still been a wholesome one. Habits of inattention are built as soon as pressure is brought to bear on children to stay longer than the duration of their interest. Stories are chosen that are definitely linked with the young child's experience; objects and ideas mentioned in them are already familiar parts of his own world. The plots should have orderly structure, should embrace but one short episode.

Language must be vivid and specific. Stories are selected primarily for use as literary experiences rather than for direct instruction or the teaching of homilies.

After they have heard the same stories over and over again, these youngsters will begin to chime in. They have memorized parts, and maybe the whole of the story. They pretend to read books to each other, following the pictures and thus staying remarkably close to the sense of the written material. Watching their teachers during story hours, they find out which is the front of the book and which is the end. Many discover similarities in format when they compare pages of their favorite stories. As they grow older, they strike out into less familiar territory. Language becomes an adventure. Everyone has fun with rhymes and nonsense and made-up stories. Teachers are careful to speak clearly, so that the ears of their pupils may learn to discriminate between similar words, like "map" and "mat." Teachers also encourage children to tell about interesting experiences. Creative materials are set out, and these same experiences may be expressed more concretely with paints, clay, crayons, or blocks. Sometimes children ask to have parts of their paintings or drawings labeled.

"Write, 'This is a mommy,' " Sheila directs her teacher. "Does that word say 'mommy'?"

"I want you to write my name on this," says Roger, "so my daddy will know I drawed it."

"Let me tell you the story of my picture," is Hilda's request; "You write it on the back . . . Now read it to me . . . That's just what I said—every word!"

By the time they leave the kindergarten, these children recognize reading, not so much as an end in itself, but as a tool for extracting facts and ideas and beauty from the lore contained in books. They see writing, not as a difficult skill to master, but as a means of sharing facts and keeping ideas in a permanent form.

Five kindergartners were responsible for that painted sign in the center of the grass plot. Its lettering is only slightly askew: PLEASE KEEP OFF. Jerry and David used crayons to print the sign that perches at the top of their block structure. It says PLEASE DON'T DAMAGE THE FERRY. Of course, teachers had to help them out with a slow recitation of the letters involved, but the incentive came from the children. These five- and six-year-olds are by now able to recognize the words HOT and COLD on the faucets in their bathroom. They know the Alphabet Song and can print any of the letters after a fashion. Teachers are aware of this interest in writing, but do not overemphasize its place in the program. Ellen, for instance, would be forever bending over a sheet of paper, printing tiny letters across the page, if her teachers did not urge her to enter more full-bodied activity. John's painting, which today is filled with hieroglyphics that somewhat resemble J's and N's, is given recognition, but the wonderfully free design which he painted immediately after is hung on the wall. It is noted that when Rachel prints, the result is mirror writing, a not uncommon occurrence among young children. Her eyes are not ready for close work. For a long time it will be harmful for her to start reading.

Last year, only one or two members of this group asked for colored paper and paste to make fancy little cards for Valentine's Day. Now, everyone is eager to create something of beauty to take home. Susan asks Miss Hoagland to spell out, "I love you, Mommy," while she struggles painstakingly with the letters. A different message is writing on her twin brother's work of art. His reads, "Jamie made this."

Margot does not know how to write any letter except M. Her teacher obligingly prints the rest of Margot's name. Before her Valentine goes home, though, Margot has copied the other letters on a piece of drawing paper.

Suzie and Kathleen, sitting together at the end of the crayon table, were the most creative artists in their group last year. Each day, something entirely new was the result of their labors. Suzie used to specialize in colorful designs,

Kathleen in lively human figures. But today, what does one see? Identical pictures! It is hard to tell who is the originator, who the copyist.

"Yesterday I copied Suzie," Kathleen says brightly, "and today Suzie is copying me."

Miss Hoagland has watched this happening year after year. Five-year-old groups put a good deal of faith in conformity. They begin to feel happier if they move together. But besides being a trait typical of kindergartners, this desire to copy is a positive help toward preparing these youngsters to write. The ability to duplicate must be well developed before they can make accurate facsimiles of letters printed on the board by their teacher in grade school.

It may seem like a long jump from the block pile to the writing desk, but nevertheless, the two are definitely connected. Muscles that have learned to coordinate by frequent contact with unit blocks, clay, paint brushes, hammers, and scissors are ready for pencils and pens. And Dicky's scribbles at the crayon table are important for still another reason. As he watches his odd marks form on the blank page, he is becoming receptive to the fact that the alphabet's more meaningful symbols, too, are put down in much the same way.

In one school, threes must use an elevator to reach their floor. This is an awkward time. Everyone is so close together. Louise bites experimentally on Roger's finger. Roger howls his protest. Bill pokes Cecily's back and is repaid in kind. But with the sound of the teacher's voice, a kind of spell falls over these wriggling creatures. What has she said? A number. The word, "One." At once, all eyes are focused on the numbers above the elevator door. Each number glows for a moment as the car passes the corresponding floor. The teacher counts: "One . . . two . . . three. . . ." A number of piping voices swell the chorus. This is a magic ritual, a formula repeated without fail every day. The voices chant to "six." The door opens, and the children swarm into their room. It is doubtful that these numbers mean much to such young children, outside of the wonderful mumbo-jumbo they have learned to listen for each day. "One" and "two" present more concrete images than any of the higher ones. Jamie can hold one block in his right hand and another in his left, and he knows that the first is "one" and the other is "two." More than that he cannot really understand.

Four-year-old Ellen sits among a jumble of blocks. She notices Irene beside her, working with but a few. Suddenly Ellen's face clouds over.

"Irene!" she shouts in an outraged tone. "I have only one—two—three—four—five—six—seven—eight—*nine*," she counts accurately, "and you have one—two—three—four! That is lots more than I have. Give me some." Ellen's positive tone and the wonderful sound of numbers befog Irene's mind. Without question, she gives up two of her blocks.

Irene and Ellen, like their other playmates, become increasingly number-conscious. During the story hour, they interrupt the reading of "Make Way for Ducklings" so that they can count Mrs. Mallard's eggs. When the ducklings have emerged, each child insists on having a separate turn to point at the eight little ducks. Teachers twiddle their thumbs while ten or eleven eager mathematicians check the accuracy of the illustration.

As they sit outdoors, waiting for the whole group to collect before going to their classrooms, four-year-olds correct each other's arithmetic.

"Now there are three boys and five girls."

"That makes seven."

"It does not!"

"It does so. . . . one, two, three, four, five, six, seven, eight. Oh, it makes eight."

"I said you were wrong."

Ellen helps set out crackers for the midmorning snack. Miss Brown asks her to see how many children are in the bathroom. Seriously Ellen counts them: two are using the toilets, two are washing their hands, five more are waiting for turns at the bowls. "There are nine children," she informs Miss Brown, "so we'll need nine crackers."

"Did you count yourself?" asks Miss Brown.

Ellen is not sure. Conscientiously she returns to the bathroom, this time including herself in the total.

"We need ten crackers," she says when she gets back. "And another for you," she adds. "That makes eleven."

Irene is getting sharper at this, too. One morning she helps Mr. Andrews set out paints on the easel. He is preparing three jars for each side. One by one, Irene carries the jars, careful not to jiggle or tip them. Mr. Andrews asks her to put the blue and yellow and brown on the far side of the easel and to start the nearer side with green.

"Now we have three colors on one side, and only one color on the other," she observes. "You have to mix two more." She is beginning to put these magical numbers into worthwhile use.

The following year, we find Ellen among the kindergarten group. She is now well over five. She has filled scores of tin cans with sand. Her array stretches in several parallel rows around the sandbox.

"Miss Hoagland!" she calls. "I have eighty-three cans! Isn't that a lot?"

Miss Hoagland begins to count, just to see how close Ellen has come to the true total. Ellen continues with her work. By the time Miss Hoagland has finished counting, several more cans have been added to the line. Miss Hoagland's total is ninety-one. Ellen's addition, if not exact, could not have been far off. Many experiences in the year just past have given her closer familiarity with numbers.

Kindergartners are introduced to stories and games which give further impetus to this awareness of number. "Counting Katie" fills the need and makes an early appearance on their book shelves. A favorite game among fives is one in which rings are tossed in order at a numbered board. Sorting out equal amounts of crackers, glasses, and napkins for the midmorning snack is a sought-for privilege. One sometimes hears an alert child of this age say, "There were eighteen here yesterday. Two children must be sick. I only count sixteen today."

When children, just turned four, come out with startling facts like "seven and seven are fourteen," and "three times two makes six," teachers do not rush to the conclusion that a mathematical genius is in their midst. After nodding or saying, "Yes, that's so," they mark it down to the influence of an older brother or sister. Such advanced knowledge has no real meaning to these young children. They are only parroting what they have been told. Pity Anne, whose father is determined to make her a musical prodigy. Her head is full of sentences like "Two quarter notes make a half," and "Two halves make a whole." It is no wonder that she avoids singing time and refuses to listen to stories. She is afraid that all things an adult does with her will be on this same confusing plane.

If counting concrete objects is a challenge to children, how much more confusing must be the concept of Time! Many amusing quotes involving this perplexing dimension dot teachers' files. Three-year-old Betsy was overheard talking with a crony, as they sat quietly in the outdoor tunnel. It was early March.

"Would you like to come to my birthday party, Flora?"

"When is it?" was the eager response.

"In October."

"Oh," said Flora, "that's pretty soon, isn't it?"

"Yes," Betsy agreed cheerfully, "and I want you to come because you're my best friend."

Teachers of threes and fours are inured to paradoxes like, "I am going to get a haircut yesterday," "Tomorrow my daddy came home," and "Mommy is taking me to the St. Patrick's Day Parade because it is Easter."

"My daddy is ten years old, but Mommy is fifty-forty years old," announced Johnny. Despite her long experience with these astounding threes, his teacher found herself grinning from ear to ear.

Tommy, now four and a half, comes to Miss Platt with furrowed brow and announces, "In three more tomorrows, it will be Friday." Since today is Tuesday, he has somehow come through the maze successfully. The following Friday, he shows her a toy watch. "I got this yesterday."

"Oh," she replies, "I thought your mother said it came Wednesday."

"That was yesterday," Tommy says, but he is not really sure.

"No. Yesterday was Thursday," Miss Platt informs him.

"Oh," says Tommy, puzzling it out. "Well, then, yesterday was Thursday, and Thursday's yesterday was Wednesday." Quite right!

A year from now, he is still likely to make mistakes about the calendar. Then the sequence of months will be the problem. One may hear him declare, "I went to camp last summer—in the month of January," or "I always go in summer. That is in Easter." But by the end of the kindergarten year, it is not uncommon to hear such wisdom as: "When the big hand goes from twelve to six, it is a half hour. When it goes back to the twelve it's a whole hour. This is how long my nap is." By that time, days and hours, at least, do not pose such problems as they once did. Things are beginning to fall into recognizable order.

Through occasional excursions into areas outside his own classroom, the maturing child catches a glimpse of the varied pursuits of the adult community, of the many people on whom his comfort and his safety depend, and of the great, busy and heterogeneous world that encroaches on every side. He may pay visits to the grocery, the fire station, or a neighboring church. His perspective widens as his interest grows. He becomes aware of the many ways people differ from each other. He is the only child in his group whose father is a jeweler. Danny's father is an artist; Marge's dad sells automobiles; Jamie's works in an office downtown. He eats lunch at Cynthia's house and makes the discovery that finances affect people's modes of life: Cynthia's mother has a maid who washes dishes and serves meals for the family. When he gets home, he asks his mother why she doesn't have a maid, too. "We don't have enough money to hire one," she explains. "Cynthia's mother and father have more money than we do."

At school, some differences which seem plain to adults are less obvious to the children. Threes and young fours are seldom aware of contrasting racial characteristics unless these are pointed out by adults. Robbie, who is almost five, and one of three black children in his group, made this discovery in a conversation with his mother at home.

ROBBIE [*looking at the faces of two children in a picture on his box of water colors*]: They have paint on their face.

HIS MOTHER, MRS. WILLIAMS: Why no. What makes you think so?

ROBBIE: Because they are white.

MRS. WILLIAMS: But, Robbie, some people *are* white. This is their color. Do you know anyone who is white?

ROBBIE: Well, maybe Marjorie [*one of his friends at school*] is white. I don't know. How many colors are there? Green? Purple?

MRS. WILLIAMS: No. Only brown, yellow, and white. And that is only the color of the *skin*.

ROBBIE: Well, hair is red.

MRS. WILLIAMS: Yes. Hair can be a lot of colors—red, yellow, white, black, and brown.

ROBBIE: I have a song "What Makes the Red Man Red?"

MRS. WILLIAMS: That song is about Indians. People call them red men, but really they are brown with a reddish look.

ROBBIE: But all people are red inside. Their hearts are red. [*He has a book called* What's Inside of Me, *which shows the insides.*]

MRS. WILLIAMS: Yes, Robbie. Inside, everyone is red. That is, they all have red blood, and bleed red when they cut themselves.

By the time most children reach kindergarten, experience has taught them that there are distinct differences in color of skin. These differences are accepted in a matter-of-fact way unless undue emphasis is placed on them by grownups. Shaila, a five-year-old girl from India, brought a lovely, dusky-faced Indian doll with her to school. She and her friend, Eleanor, were the first to arrive. Eleanor had brought a doll, too, so they decided to play together in the doll corner. Eleanor noticed Shaila's Indian doll. "That doll sure is pretty," she said. "It matches your skin."

"And yours does, too," Shaila observed correctly.

Eleanor laughed. "That's right. They both match us. That doll is sure pretty. Could I hold her a little bit?"

Shaila, busy draping herself in some scarves and a dress-up gown from the school's wardrobe, for the moment ignored Eleanor's request. Suddenly she changed her plan of action. "Put that doll down, Eleanor," she said. "And, here, I'll take this off, and you put it on." She unwrapped the scarves and the robe, and helped her friend get into them. Only now that Eleanor was dressed in an approximation of Indian garb did Shaila exchange dolls with her.

Eleanor looked closely at the Indian doll. "Shaila, why does she have that net on?"

"So her hair won't be messy."

"Why don't we take it off, and then put it back on?"

"We can't," Shaila decided. "I don't know how."

"Let's see if the dolls will play together," was Eleanor's next suggestion. She suddenly gave an infantile screech and explained, "Your doll is screaming." She also gave the doll such a violent lurch against her chest that one of its long eyelashes was pulled off. "Shaila," she exclaimed anxiously, "What happened?"

"To her eyebrow?" said Shaila without undue concern.

"It came off."

Eleanor next became annoyed by the gown and silk scarves, which were somewhat confining. "Why don't *you* wear it?" she suggested.

"What? The sari?"

"These scarves." She pulled at them.

"They aren't scarves," Shaila corrected her. "That's a sari."

"What's a sari?"

"That's what Indian ladies wear."

Eleanor remembered seeing Shaila's mother wear a sari when she came to call for her at school. "Why don't *you* wear one?" was her sensible query.

"I don't know."

"I wish I could take this doll home."

"I wish I could take all your dolls home."

Both children absorbed more from this exchange than facts about each other's skin color and customs of dress. They were developing basic attitudes of respect and friendship that have a good chance of lasting through life, though Shaila will return to India and Eleanor will remain in the United States. Thus, if it can be said that the child's home is the hub of his universe, surely one can say that his school experience helps direct the spokes outward in every direction toward the wide circumference of the world.

14

Deep Thoughts and Special Days

Mrs. Bernstein is Jewish and has been careful to place her daughter, Kathy, in a nursery school which has no special religious affiliation. She is interested to hear that Kathy's best friend at school, Ahmed, comes from a Moslem home, and when Kathy asks if he can come home for lunch, Mrs. Bernstein is happy to give her permission. One can imagine her surprise when she hears the following conversation, spoken earnestly between bites of peanut butter sandwiches, by the two young five-year-olds.

AHMED: The king of the whole United States is God.
KATHY: And Jesus was his deputy.
AHMED: He was a very good man.
KATHY: I know. Everybody prays to him.

Mrs. Bernstein begins to wonder what kind of religious instruction is going on at school. When she brings up the matter with Kathy's teacher she finds that there has been no emphasis placed on this subject by the staff. It is, however, an inescapable topic in our culture, and children are bound to come to grips with it. They discuss it along with other topics of interest, offering what they have heard, and considering their friends' opinions. By way of example, Kathy's teacher shows Mrs. Bernstein the transcript of a conversation among some of Kathy's friends overheard only the day before:

LAWRENCE: The world can fly, and it really *is* flying.
JIMMY: If this school could fly, it could go all around the world.
ERNEST: Without even breaking?
JIMMY: If it was walking, wouldn't that be funny?
ERNEST: You could only move it with a crane. Sometimes they can knock buildings down with it.
LAWRENCE: I know that. Old Tommy [*not at school today*] is coming.
JIMMY: Where?
ERNEST: Let's play cowboys.
JIMMY: No. Let's talk about the world.
LAWRENCE: How can anything lift up this world?
JIMMY: God can. He can do anything.
LAWRENCE: He can't lift up the whole world.
JIMMY: Yes, he can. He's so strong he can lift it up with one finger.
LAWRENCE: No, he can't. You know why? Because he's little. He couldn't lift up a school.
JIMMY: Yes, he could.
ERNEST: No. Because there are no schools up in the air. Let's jump. [*They all jump.*]
LAWRENCE: Let's talk about the world. Do you think God could lift up a school?
ERNEST: No.
LAWRENCE: Do you think a crane could lift up the school?
ERNEST: Sure. [*He jumps again.*]
JIMMY: You can't jump a hundred miles.
LAWRENCE: You can't jump to another city.
ERNEST: If you could fly, you could.
JIMMY: I'll bet you couldn't jump a hundred billion million.
LAWRENCE: Let's talk about airplanes. Do you know they fly by rudders?
ERNEST: They have motors.

JIMMY: If they don't have motors, they crash down.
LAWRENCE: Gliders don't. Gliders are shot out from cannons.
JIMMY: You know what? Helicopters can float on water.
LAWRENCE: Helicopters can bomb battleships.
JIMMY: They don't have bombs.
LAWRENCE: They have shooting guns.
ERNEST: A bomb can break anything.
JIMMY: It can break down this whole school.
ERNEST: Wouldn't the teachers be surprised!
ALLEN [*who has been eavesdropping*]: We could put a bomb here and the teachers would be surprised.
ERNEST: We could put it here before we came.
JIMMY: If we could fly, wouldn't that be funny?
ERNEST: Wouldn't the teacher be surprised if we flew over on her head?
JIMMY: I know who built the ocean.
LAWRENCE: God.
JIMMY: No—Jesus.
LAWRENCE: First it was the Indians. Then the Pilgrims.
JIMMY: Jesus is true, and he can walk on water.
ERNEST: He's a little baby. How can he go in the water?

School offers the child an ideal opportunity for such free exchange with people his own age. The youngster whose parents have given him specific ideas on religious themes comes face to face with one who has heard nothing about God, or who has a number of questions about Him. It is best if he can discuss religion as naturally as he can other topics, asserting and questioning and approaching it from various directions. If adults answer his questions about God or death or religious observances with catch phrases or with fragments of grownups' dogma, the child is likely to go repeating what he has been taught, to hold to it tenaciously, and feel little need for further inquiry. Luckily, the salutary effect of daily give and take among his peers can often hold the door open for the child's future growth.

Five-year-old Martha came to school one day with a big piece of paper on which she had pasted various pictures pertaining to Christmas. She joined her friends at the crayon table and proceeded to lecture them on the meaning of each picture on her paper. A teacher moved closer to observe.

"Santa is a spirit, and a spirit is God, and God helps Jesus," Martha was saying. "God helps everybody around the world so that nobody gets hurt."

Gerald had been listening impatiently and, at this point, interrupted with the sensible observation, "A boy rode a bicycle, was hurt by a car, and was killed, so . . . so don't believe everything you hear."

This did not faze Martha who continued to intone, "God is a spirit, and a spirit don't die."

"Anyway," Janet said, looking up from her drawing, "Santa isn't a spirit. It's a person."

"Yeah." This, from Tony. "It's a mommy or a daddy dressed up like Santa."

But Martha's parents had told her that Santa was a spirit, and she would not budge from this opinion. Janet finally interrupted Martha's repetitions with, "Wouldn't you know whether your father knows or not, whether Santa is real or no? My father says Santa is real. Santa is a father or a mother." Her information had come from home, too, and she was just as confident in her parents' judgment as Martha was in hers. Things had reached an impasse for the moment. Perhaps someday Martha and Janet will arrive at middle ground. After all, people do dress up to look like Santa, but the spirit of love and generosity he represents is more important than his red suit and white whiskers.

Parents of young children are well-advised to be ready for all kinds of probing questions. It is hard to tell in advance what is going to start this flow of curiosity. A three-year-old, looking through a magazine with his father, saw pictures of Benjamin Franklin and several of his inventions. "Who is Benjamin Franklin?" he asked.

"He's the man who made all those things," his father

replied, unaware of the direction the conversation was about to take.

"Can I see him?" was the next question.

"No," the father laughed. "He lived a long time ago."

"Where is he now?"

"Why, he's dead." And now the father was forced to continue answering questions, some of which he felt squeamish about, others to which he wisely admitted he had no answers. He was annoyed with himself for not having had more definite ideas in mind, for he had known all along that his son would put him on the spot sooner or later. Parents who consciously reject organized religion for themselves are no more exempt from such experiences than are others. A day will come when they, too, will be confronted with their children's queries about death.

Whatever the parent's personal convictions, it is wiser to admit to them honestly than to gloss them over or invent something that seems more palatable to young children. Children sense what they do not understand, and if Daddy answers their questions with statements he doesn't believe, this evasion is communicated to his children, who react with puzzlement or anxiety.

Mrs. Sutton came to Francie's teacher with concern over her five-year-old's fears about death. "I don't know why Francie should be so upset," she said. "I've told her again and again what a nice place Heaven is, and how pleasant it must be to go there."

"But what do you actually believe?" asked the teacher, hearing no real conviction in the mother's tone.

"Oh, if I told Francie *that*," Mrs. Sutton admitted with a shiver, "she'd be scared to death."

Actually, "that"—whatever it was—was exactly what she had told Francie, not through her words, but through her transparent tension, for by trying to hide what she felt she was actually proclaiming it to her child more clearly than words ever could.

Teachers in a nonsectarian nursery school should be prepared to discuss these topics, which one might consider more typical in a parochial school. Miss Haley's kindergarten group had voted that if one of them brought a story to school and asked a teacher to read it, it should be the first one heard in the book corner. One day, James brought a large collection of stories on the life of Jesus. James claimed his right, and Miss Haley announced to her group, "We'll read a story from James' book first."

"I want you to read *all* of them," James demanded.

"Well, that really wouldn't be fair," Miss Haley told him, "because we all have to take turns choosing stories, and many children want more of the *What's Inside of Me* book."

At this point, Winifred and Sharon started looking at other books, pointedly ignoring James' volume. Miss Haley called them by name and said that the group was waiting for them.

"We used to be able to look at other books if we didn't want to listen," Winifred complained.

"That's true," Miss Haley admitted, "but remember we had a discussion about that, and now we all have a discussion or story together."

"Because we'll soon be in school, and that's how they have lessons," Bill asserted wisely.

Sharon resorted to blocking her ears with both hands. Winifred continued with verbal resistance: "Well, I'm not going to listen because Jesus isn't true."

Miss Haley saw a discussion looming before her, willynilly. "Before we read the story," she began, "we really should talk about that. Everybody knows that Jesus was a real man who lived a long time ago."

"And he was magic!" James broke in.

"Well, he did many kind things," Miss Haley amended, pointing to one of the pictures in the book. "He was able to help people like these walk. And because he did so many good things some people thought he was special. But some people didn't think he was special."

James popped up, "I think he's special."

"I don't." Winifred was still miffed.

Miss Haley read some of the story and got to the point where Jesus was being led away by the soldiers. Carl interrupted with a question: "Why did the soldiers take Jesus prisoner?"

James was ready with an explanation, "The soldiers wanted to be special like he was."

"Some people believe and pray to God," Winifred added, suddenly growing interested in the subject. "My grandmother does. Some grownups think that God is really true, but most children believe in Santa Claus."

"Well, I want to know what *you* think." James turned to Miss Haley.

His teacher, knowing that her group was composed of various religious and racial strains, felt it best not to put the weight of her opinion behind one side or another. She countered his demand with a question. "All the people who believe that Jesus was very special are called . . .?"

But no one responded, so she was forced to answer her own question. "Christians."

"I'm Jewish," said Sharon.

"And I'm Jewish," said Bill.

"That's it. The people who are Jewish think that Jesus was a good man, but not special," Miss Haley continued, "but all the Christians think he was."

"I think he was special," said James. He was backed up by Stanley, who said, "So do I."

"I don't," Bill stated.

"I don't think he's *so* special," offered Tony.

"I'm Jewish," said Rachel, "but I think he's special."

Miss Haley read only half of the next paragraph before she was interrupted again, this time by James. "There's no jail," he pointed out. "He's tied to a real cross."

"He was hammered," Perry corrected him. All the children looked closely at the picture of Jesus carrying the cross.

"Why is he doing that?" Carl wanted to know.

"In the olden days when someone did something that the people didn't like, they put him on a cross," Miss Haley explained. "What do they do now?"

"Tie him up and put him behind bars in jail," Bill said with gusto.

"They don't tie them up," Miss Haley reminded him, "but they do put them in jail."

Dicky, high-strung and unpredictable, interjected the sensible comment, "They have handcuffs," but at once he began to make silly grimaces. "You know what?" he said in a squeaky voice. "God has a little house up in the sky, and when he wants to come down he slides down and visits you."

His humor was received with appreciative giggles and guffaws. "You know Dicky is just fooling," Miss Haley remarked. She went on a little more with the story and came to the place where a crown of "branches"—the book hedged on this gruesome detail—was placed on Jesus' head.

Allen stopped her: "I thought that a crown was what people wear when they become famous."

Miss Haley nodded. "Kings and queens wear crowns of gold and jewels like the one Queen Elizabeth wore, but this crown was just made of branches."

"I think of Jesus so much," said Rachel, "that sometimes I wish I was Jesus, too."

"Lots of people do try to be like Jesus," Miss Haley told her.

"I always try to be like Jesus," James declared.

"Well," Dicky put in with a hostile look, "I sometimes like to pretend I'm the soldiers that got him." He looked at Miss Haley to see her reaction.

"That's how it is," she said mildly, knowing that he needed support these days, as an antidote to his feelings of worthlessness. "People often like to pretend they are different things, according to how they feel."

Winifred added, "I wish I was a prisoner."

"Then you'd just have bread and water to eat," Miss Haley teased her.

"I'm glad, because I hate my food," Winifred retorted. A minute or two later, though, she was munching her snack with obvious relish, while the conversation around her shifted to a discussion of marriage and the atom bomb.

Though Miss Haley's class got into this discussion as a result of the book James brought to school, the subject of religion had come up many times before, often in the doll corner or on the playground, where no adult comments were interjected. Similarly, at home there needs be no specific object or book to start the flow of comments about God, churches, death, and Heaven. These considerations are inevitable. Whether one celebrates religious festivals at home or holds to no specific religious creed he will be introduced to them anew through the penetrating questions of his own young child.

Most schools pay lip service, at least, to the festivals that dot the yearly calendar. The children's lively interest in Thanksgiving, Hanukkah, Christmas, and other great church days demands some response at school. It would be no more realistic to ignore them there than it would be at home. But if they are to be celebrated at all, adults should make an effort to observe them in ways that have meaning to children.

The first of these special days to claim the attention of Miss Lark and her three-year-old group is Halloween. A day or so before the day itself a few horrid masks, grotesque costumes, and paper jack-o'-lanterns find their way into her room. She allows herself to be properly impressed, suggests that the masquerader show his skull or witch's rags to his friends, and then requests him to put the disguise into his clothes locker. There, it is likely to be forgotten until the end of the morning. The witch's gown might trip up a busy housewife in the doll corner, and the skull would restrict the vision of some intrepid fireman rushing to the rescue. Anyway, Miss Lark knows that these gruesome items mean little to her three-year-olds. If someone at home, perhaps an older brother or sister, had not sparked this interest, her group would be content to let this day, with its synthetic horrors, slip by unnoticed. In a few more years, when little Judy can be sure that the flapping ghost at her window is really only her brother, and when a cloth mask no longer changes her father into a terrifying stranger, she will have more fun with dressing up in frightening things.

On the other hand, the pumpkins that Miss Lark selected at the corner fruit and vegetable stand can be put to worthwhile use. She has taken two fine plump ones, washed them, and put them on a low table where the children can lift, poke, and sniff at them time and again. Even when they have attained the sophistication of kindergarten, they will still want such an opportunity to appreciate the pumpkin in its natural state. For some children this experience may be enough. One year no one asked for a chance to turn the pumpkin into a jack-o'-lantern, and Miss Lark did not urge it on her group.

Judy's father has already fixed her a jack-o'-lantern at home, so she asks Miss Lark if they can do the same thing at school. Several other excited voices demand a chance to tell how their daddies cut pumpkin faces out at their houses. At last Miss Lark gets the interested children around her and lets each one say what he wants to about the job at hand. With a black crayon she marks a circle around the stem, then brings out a sharp knife and slips the blade into the firm orange skin. Each child in turn helps her cut slowly along the line until the circle is complete. This job is done with care. Miss Lark allows her children to push the top of the knife while she holds the rest of the handle. In another year or so they will be ready to do the job more independently, but for now, this way is safest.

A concerted gasp is heard as the top is finally pulled loose from the rest. "What a lot of seeds!" "What a funny smell!" Now everyone gets a chance to scoop out the seeds and the stringy pith with a spoon or with his hands, depending on his reaction to the consistency of the pumpkin's innards. Miss Lark puts this whole mass into a dish and saves it for later.

Serious decisions are made concerning the shape of eyes, nose, and mouth. Shall the eyes be round or pointed? Shall there be teeth? Danny insists on ears, too. A crayoned sketch on the uncut surface settles all last minute arguments. Miss Lark gets to work again, giving each eager assistant another chance to use the knife. The result is viewed with chortles and chirps of delight. Tommy watches as the triangular eye is pushed out. "It looks like cheese," he says. Everyone bends near to watch the candle set into place. When it is finally lighted, a spontaneous song arises: "Happy birthday to you . . . happy birthday, dear pumpkin, happy birthday to you." Later, during rest, the glowing features hold the attention of the most noisy child. Donald, usually silly and active, settles himself near the jack-o'-lantern and watches solemnly as the candle burns down.

The pumpkin can serve other duties as well. In groups older than Miss Lark's, its meat may be cooked by a number of associate chefs, some of whom have already sampled it raw. The final result is a delicious pumpkin custard pudding.

Some children in Miss Tong's four-year-old group wash the seeds and set them on a saucer for everyone to see. Miss Tong has collected a multitude of small jars, and has squeezed rectangular pieces of blotting paper into each one. The blotting paper fits tightly against the glass sides. The children are given a seed apiece, and they carefully slip them down between the paper and the glass, where they are plainly visible. Miss Tong has brought some dried beans and peas from home. These are compared with the pumpkin seeds and added to the jars. A bit of water— enough to moisten the blotting paper—is poured in, and the job is at an end. The fun and interest, however, have just begun, since now the children may take them home and watch them grow. For the next few weeks, Miss Tong and her staff will be informed, "None of my seeds sprouted yet," or "My bean is the biggest, but my pumpkin has a longer root."

Sometimes, before she throws a jack-o'-lantern out, Miss Tong shows it to her children as it slumps forlornly on a saucer. Mold has all but eaten it away. Some of them touch it, "Oh! It's all black and hairy!" "Its eye is gone!" That is its final bow.

The celebration of Thanksgiving is attended with unique problems of presentation. Perhaps its essence is best captured in pictures of the great nationwide harvest—or better still, in its actual fruits and grains and vegetables—for which everyone is thankful in the fall. Children who live near Jewish places of worship are fortunate, indeed, for they may be treated to a view of the magnificent Sukkoth booths and displays which usually appear some weeks in advance of this time. The sheaves of wheat, great clusters of grapes, mounds of pumpkins and squash, red apples, and varicolored ears of corn are massed in such eye-filling and mouth-watering profusion that just to look upon them evokes a sense of well-being and wonder.

No matter what one may do to focus enthusiasm on its historical basis, Thanksgiving remains for New York children the time of the Macy Parade, and for American children everywhere a day for visiting relatives and eating turkey. Their historical perspective is primitive; further back than "when Mother was a little girl" is hard to imagine. Yet real interest in the story of the first Thanksgiving can be aroused among fours and fives by a simple, graphic telling. Using crayons, Miss Terry draws pictures on an easel to represent the English King, the *Mayflower*, America without skyscrapers and automobiles, some Indians, and the first crude dwellings on the New England shore. These rough drawings clarify a few of the differences between life "long ago" and things as they are now. Miss Terry tells the story in an up-to-date way. Parents report that the whole tale comes home. They are informed that the king would not allow these people to go to the church they liked best; that the *Mayflower* had no iceboxes and that people got sick from the miserable conditions on board; that landing on a cold, unsettled shore the Pilgrims might all have died but for the kindness of some local Indians. Miss Terry's children can also explain in detail how the Pilgrims were taught to plant corn. They tell of the big feast to which the friendly Indians were invited, and where God was thanked for helping them through a troublesome time.

But it is toward the joyous festivals of Christmas and Hanukkah that children look with the greatest anticipation. Radios and television start the Christmas fever long in advance of the day itself. There is a Santa Claus in every large store, and many a street corner boasts its jolly man with his red suit and clanging bell. Excitement mounts as the season approaches. Aunt Edna and Uncle Will are coming to visit, and Susan's two-year-old cousin is to be her guest for over a week. The commercial aspects of this great church holiday are everywhere. Window displays dazzle the eye; popular singers croon "Jingle Bells" and "Silent Night." When Tony hears his grandmother mention going to church to celebrate the day, he announces, "*We* go to the five-and-ten at Christmas."

Some families look enviously across the ocean, where Christmas Day is devoted to religious observance, while a separate day (like St. Nicholas Day in Holland) is spent in merrymaking and exchanging gifts. The happy Jewish festival of Hanukkah has been less tarnished by cheap commercialism.

The school where Miss Thayer teaches is almost equally divided between Christian and Jewish children. The nursery staff has spent great thought on deciding what is meaningful in both of these festivals at this young age. First of all, they will try to avoid overstimulation, tension, and too much talk. Miss Thayer wants to introduce a few songs to her four-year-olds, and plans to start right after Thanksgiving so that the children will have plenty of time to become familiar with them before the holidays. But as she sorts through some of the old Christmas carols, she runs into an unexpected snag. Until the recent staff meeting, it had never occurred to her how sentimental many of them were, and (even worse from her point of view) how many of them interjected somewhat doubtful religious concepts. Her aim has always been to widen perspectives, yet her favorite Christmas hymn, "Away in the Manger," suggests a localization of Jesus somewhere above the clouds. She reads the phrase, "look down from the sky," and slowly turns the page. She has to reject some others, too, because of their preoccupation with angels. She did not encourage belief in witches at Halloween, nor will she bring up an egg-laying bunny at Easter, so why should she foster an interest in supernatural beings at Christmas? She knows that other teachers may not share these qualms, but as long as she feels so strongly about them personally, she will go on seeking songs that fit into the spirit of the rest of her year's curriculum. Finding songs which her children can understand and through which their thinking can expand is one means of providing experiences in which they themselves can take part.

Hanukkah songs prove somewhat easier to find, and she soon has two or three that mention the spinning dreidl and the exploits of the brave Maccabees, without becoming involved with miraculous events. She takes her fours to a corner and sings without accompaniment at first. Later she brings out her Autoharp and strums it as accompaniment, sitting cross-legged on the floor. In a week or so, some of her children know both words and music; some sing along spasmodically; the rest show their interest by tapping feet or humming rhythmically, though out of tune. A week before the holidays begin, all of them make lusty sounds as they sing about the glowing lights, and temper their vigor with quietness in the verses of "Come Softly, Tread Gently," another favorite song. Katie brings a Menorah to school and tells, as well as she can, about the lamp that kept burning long ago. Adrian brings a shiny star to put on the Christmas tree in his room. He isn't sure what a star has to do with Christmas, so Miss Thayer brings it up in the book corner that day, and he is given fairly accurate answers by some of his friends.

Miss Thayer feels hampered by the poor quality of stories about these two holidays. "The Night Before Christmas" remains the only child's classic concerning the nonreligious side of Christmas, and it is full of unfamiliar words. Many modern presentations of the story of the Nativity are excessively sentimental. The Biblical narratives as they stand are not particularly satisfactory for four- and five-year-olds at school, though children may enjoy an opportunity to hear them read if it gives them a chance to share in an experience that their parents enjoy. Miss Thayer's Jewish children fare slightly better with some factual stories concerning the Maccabees, but the Torah passages suffer from the same drawbacks as do sections from the Christian gospels.

Children in Miss Thayer's groups often use rhythms as a way to become familiar with the basic elements of each story. In this way they have an active role in the telling; some of them are even able to suggest the episodes in proper order. Theologians might quibble with details, but no one who watches these dances progress can fail to catch their luminous spirit.

Miss Thayer tries not to overemphasize the Nativity story, however, since too much stress on Jesus' birth is likely to detract from the greatness of his active life. One of her children asked, "Didn't Jesus ever grow up? Every Christmas he is still a baby."

It is hard for adults to realize how literally their explanations are taken by children. Especially in areas which the child is unable to explore or prove by his own abilities, the most casual word dropped by his parents or teachers may be snapped up as a final truth. Thus, Santa Claus may be equated or confused with God, particularly among children who have been told that both are "spirits." Winifred says, "Some grownups think that God is really true, but most children believe in Santa Claus." "Santa Clauses know everyone," remarks Angelo during rest period. "They even know God. They know everything. You can't fool any Santa Clauses."

Stories about Santa appear among tales dictated by four- and five-year-olds. Some of them reflect the spirit of overpowering commercialism. "Santy Claus came down the chimney with his reindeers. He unpacked. Then he put the toys under the Christmas tree. Then back to Macy's!" "We saw a million of Santy Clauses down at Woolworth's. They're all for Christmas. First it goes to Macy's and then to my house." "I saw seventy-six Santa Clauses at Woolworth's, and then they came up the chimney and I chased them out the window."

A great argument as to how Santa Claus gets into the house is part of one story dictated by city children. Ellen said, "It isn't true that Santa Claus comes down the chimney. He comes up the elevator." She was corrected by Ross, who asserted that, "If you live in a flat house, he don't come up the elevator. He goes down in the cellar and opens the cellar door and then goes upstairs and into the kitchen and then he goes thump into the living room." This story ended when Santa "banged his head on the chimney and the people got mad and they waked up and didn't see anything. They just seen something moving back and forth in the chimney. That was Santa Claus moving his feet. Then they saw something going over the trees, wiggling. That was Santa Claus."

At one church school, a boxful of little red hoods and capes await the Christmas season, when they will be donned by eager five-year-olds who boast a memorized repertoire of six or seven carols. These children bring music and cheer to cooks, mechanics, ministers, and office personnel throughout the entire building, and their annual visit is remembered by everyone as a moving and joyous experience. The shining faces peering out from pointed hoods are proof that these children find conscious enjoyment in sharing their own talent and good will.

A bare evergreen tree is brought early one morning into Miss Allen's classroom. It is one of the great moments of her school year to see the children's delight as they enter and find it standing there. They prance around it, relish its fresh smell, conjecture as to how it came in. Her fours and fives build a block structure around it and route roads for toy autos under its branches. They lie on their backs and look up, touching the needles; some pretend they are animals that live among its roots. For a full day they are happy to appreciate the tree for itself. But soon, Carol says she wants to decorate it, and the fever spreads rapidly. Colored paper, paste, strings, tinsel, and bits of wallpaper are added to the usual supply of art materials, so that the children can make any kind of decoration they wish to put on the tree. Younger children would be content to hang tinsel on the branches within reach, but these fours and fives are ingenious at inventing ways of reaching the heights. The end of the day finds their tree gaudy with large drawings stuck here and there, half hidden by dangling bits of silver pasted onto green or red paper. Some artistic souls have fashioned flowers and stars that seem to blossom from the end of each branch. Crude Santa Clauses and just plain people have been cut out and strung up at random. The whole picture looks comical, disorganized, or simply mad. But this external impression fails to take the really important factors into account. It overlooks Georgia's concentrated stare as she applied just the right amount of paste to her bit of purple paper, and her satisfaction when she had hung it on that branch so high that it took a chair to raise her to its level. That hodge-podge of color stuck on the very top was Donnie's first piece of art work. Gerald, who licked his lower lip as he cut so painstakingly, had never used scissors before. Like the other children in Miss Allen's group who made decorations for the tree, he now views it with personal pride. When his mother later took him downtown to see an artistically decorated tree, she was amused to hear Gerald say, "It's very pretty. It's almost as nice as my tree at school."

The climax of the carefully planned Christmas program at one church nursery school comes in a visit to an adult meeting hall. There a simple but impressive ceremony takes place. Each group has its own time to enjoy the large room, empty except for a beautiful tree and a crackling fire in a fireplace at the far end. An expanse of soft red carpet, the glittering tree, and the sounds and smells from the fire invite the children to step forward. Records of traditional carols play as they walk toward the fireplace and admire the tree. The teachers follow the children and sit on the floor behind them. After a few minutes the records stop playing and one of the teachers sits in front of the fire, ready to accompany the older groups on the Autoharp as they sing the songs they have learned. The smaller children do not attempt group singing here. An atmosphere of real happiness is reflected in clear voices, on the upturned faces of the children seated on the red carpet, and among the teachers as well. One after another the songs are requested and sung. Some of the favorites are repeated. Their singing done, the group walks out slowly to the tune of a rhythmic carol. That is all. But these ten or fifteen minutes reaffirm what their teachers have tried to express since the first day they sat down to sing the songs together. Without words, the festival has come to mean something that everyone can feel.

Hanukkah, the joyous Festival of Lights, takes its important place in the religious calendar of the Jew, but its celebration can hardly be called the cornerstone of his faith.

For the Christian, Christmas is a different matter: it marks the birth of the central figure of his faith. Consequently, a meaningful presentation of the one, with its persuasive twin stars of light and freedom, is somewhat less complicated than a comprehensible explanation of the other, with its mysteries of incarnation and redemption. It may be difficult for the adult to explain the meaning of Christmas to children, but it is not beyond his reach to create the proper emotional tone for the celebration at home.

When Peter asked, "Christmas is like a birthday, but whose birthday is it?" his mother replied, "It *is* the celebration of a birthday—Jesus' birthday. We cannot give presents to him, because he lived long ago. But we can give things to each other, to remind us of his birthday and to make each other happy."

The story of the Nativity contains elements that are bound to elude children, but Easter's theological complexity poses an even thornier problem. Again, it is important that what adults do or say must be along lines that children can respect as they grow older, but not so wordy or diffuse that it has no meaning for them now. The staff of one church school went to great pains to prepare a chapel service at Easter for their youngest children. At its conclusion, a four-year-old boy asked, "Who is Mr. Easter?" Most nursery schools wisely content themselves with cultivating an awareness of rebirth in nature, an element which is common to the spring festivals of all the great faiths. Concentration on the details of Jesus' suffering and death and rising again is likely to mystify and confuse the young child. A number of weeks after Christmas, four-year-old Ralph urged his teachers to dance out the story of Jesus. The group accepted his idea and acted the Nativity as they had done before.

"Now let's do the Last Supper," called out Jack, one of Ralph's closest pals.

Asked what that was, he explained, "Jesus asked his

friends in to dinner. And they ate and ate. And that's all."

Jack was the son of a minister; what had no doubt been intended as proper instruction was rendered meaningless by a mind too young to digest the significance of what he had been told. The Last Supper, however, suggested something more to Ralph, who suddenly burst out, "Then the bad men got him. They hammered him. They put nails in him and hammered him on a cross. I saw it in a picture in a book at home." Ralph's expression of distaste and worry, his attitude of perplexity, and the look of surprise that swept over the rest of the group were sufficient proof to his teachers that the story of these cruel events did not need to be introduced so soon.

Depending on how far advanced the season is at Easter, there may be many or few indications that spring is really at hand. If Easter comes early, schools may want to provide crocus or narcissus bulbs for the children to plant in flower plots. The miracle that brings blossoms from a brown, dried bulb is as full of interest for the teachers as it is for their groups. Miss Lark's children take this opportunity to plant the pumpkin seeds they have saved since Halloween. All that is needed for success is judicious watering and patience. More examples are all about. Buds have begun to swell on the trees. A branch brought indoors and set in water will soon put out leaves and demonstrate in a short time what is happening more slowly outside. Grass is turning green in city parks, on suburban lawns, across wide fields and prairies.

If adults are honestly enthusiastic about noticing these changes, the children are quick to respond and find enjoyment in the world reawaking about them. Cocoons are brought in, and a whole group awaits the emergence of a moth. Everything begins to take on fresh meaning. Weather changes, clouds, the first worms on the sidewalk after rain—they are all noteworthy and occasion much serious discussion. Once aroused, this interest opens up new causes of wonder, explains old mysteries, and alerts the children to the discovery of facts about themselves and the world around them.

"The pumpkin grows from a seed. I growed from a seed, too! Everything growed from a seed," proclaims four-year-old Tommy. The return of spring has brought his Halloween experience into sharper focus. Roger remembers how in the fall he loved to chase leaves as they fell, and bury himself in the drifted pile by the jungle gym. Now he watches the opening buds with new awareness. He suggests a dance about them; after his idea has been followed through, Susan suggests "bulbs," and Jane asks for "babies." They are surprised to find some similarities in the way everything starts.

The traditional aspect of Easter has little place in a curriculum for the young child, but in his eager interest about the world and his own place in it there is something basic to all the great faiths. Eastertime and the coming of spring offer the most dramatic illustrations we have of the miracle of rebirth and the continuation of life.

"Rig-a-jig-jig and away we go." **15**

Birthdays and Good-bys

The celebration of a child's birthday is of far greater interest to him than all the religious and historical festivals rolled together. This is an occasion which has important significance for him, since its only excuse for existence is the momentous fact that he was born on that particular day. His attitude toward this event changes noticeably during the nursery school years. It varies from uncomprehending acceptance in the youngest groups to the excited sociability of kindergartners. Before the end of their nursery school careers, children come to view their birthdays not just as colorful performances of which they are the stars, but also as important yardsticks by which to measure their progress and the passage of time.

Just a minute ago, Miss Ellis pulled the curtains across the windows of her four-year-olds' classroom. Now she looks around to be sure that everything is ready: four tables arranged so that they focus upon the round one at the far end of the room; a candle on each table; napkins, milk, and cookies at every place. She lights the candles and goes to the book corner to find Jane.

"Who would you like to have sit with you at your table, Jane?"

"My mommy." Jane stretches out her arm to touch her mother, who is listening to a story the group has requested.

"Well, besides your mother? What children?"

Jane decides on her three closest cronies. Since there is one more chair at her table, she chooses Bobby, who happens to be sitting next to her, to fill in the extra place. The five children and Jane's mother settle themselves at the round table, and the rest of the group mills in. There is much scrambling for chairs. "I want to sit next to Josie." "But that's *my* mat." "Where should I sit?" Earlier in the day, many children had made colorful place mats for the party. Wallpaper, scissors, paste, crayons, and manila paper were used to make a variety of types—some symmetrical and intricate, others formless and jumbled. Now a great search goes on to find the right mat. Extra ones have been made so that there is a special decoration at each place.

Jane looks about, her eyes reflecting the glow of the candle at her table. This is her birthday. She is five years old! Jane's mother looks at her with a little concern. Will she giggle or fidget or cry when the group sings "Happy Birthday"? The teachers will be aware of her behavior, too, for the way she faces this situation will give them a good indication of Jane's inner reserves.

The final stragglers have found their places. Everyone is eager to touch the cookies. Ordinarily the midmorning snack is informal, and one may eat when he likes, but this is a birthday. First, a lusty chorus goes up: "Happy Birthday to you!" Jane looks directly into her mother's eyes, drawing her poise from them while the singing lasts. The song ended, eager fingers reach for the cookies, and a hum of conversation begins. No formality surrounds the end of Jane's party. As the children finish, they make for their blanket lockers and prepare for rest. Jane blows out the five candles.

While the children are resting, Jane's mother helps put the tables and chairs back into their regular places: the round table into the book corner, the formica-topped one by the window, and the three wooden ones together by the crayon shelf. She is amazed by the festive spirit that resulted from such little bother. Candlelight, the simplest cookies, homemade mats, and waiting to eat until "Happy Birthday" was sung seem to have been the main elements. Yet since the first birthday of the year, Jane has described these parties at school as really special occasions.

"It makes me mad to think how much effort I wasted on Jane's party at home," her mother states ruefully. "Half of the children didn't touch their ice cream, and nobody seemed at all impressed by the cake. By five o'clock, I was a wreck. Judy and Nancy were crying when their mothers came for them. Why, you would have thought these sugar cookies were something they'd never had before, the way they ate them today! And they behaved like angels. You know, yesterday was Jane's real birthday, but I can tell that this party was as important to her as the big one. I could kick myself for going to so much trouble. Next year, I'll ask her to limit her guests to five or six, and they can dress up or play some simple games. No more "Drop the Handkerchief" for me until she's old enough to keep the rules straight. And another time, I won't serve anything but milk and cupcakes. I wish you could have seen my house last night! Napkins and paper hats and confetti all over! I wouldn't do it again for the world."

Of course, at school refreshments are limited to a minimum. For one thing, it is hardly advisable to stuff children with sweets an hour and a half before lunch time. But teachers also want to avoid the competitive spirit that prompts each mother to make her child's party more colossal than the rest. No doubt some of that is to be expected at home, but by talking things over with parents beforehand, one can do away with it altogether at school. There, the humblest cookie, and, at most, a napkin, are sufficient.

Everyone is served alike. The birthday child generally receives only two extras: the right to blow out the candles she has chosen and the honor of having the group sing to her. By making an effort to arrange the tables differently for each party, and by decorating them with shells, toys, or flowers, the looks of the room can be varied somewhat, but the general effect is always the same.

The importance of the five-year-old birthday cannot be overstressed. For these children, it is the event of the year, surrounded with more glamor than Christmas. "How old are you?" "I'll be five April twenty-third." "I'm five, so I'm bigger. I'll be the boss." "When I'm five, I'll know how to climb the jungle gym." It is like the millennium. For four-year-olds, life begins at five.

What a different atmosphere surrounded a similar event two years ago! When Jane's third birthday arrived, it was a day like any other as far as she was concerned. If no one had mentioned it, she would have been content to let it slip by without any fanfare at all. At school the celebration was simple indeed. Little was done to disturb the usual sequence of routines. An unchanging order of events provides comfort and reassurance for the very young, so care should be taken to avoid unfamiliar procedure, even on a special day like this. After she had finished in the bathroom, Jane sat by her teacher and listened as usual to a story, while tables were prepared for her party. Napkins and milk glasses were set before each chair. Candles were lit and put into place. Near each candle sat a pitcher of water. Twos and young threes are likely to move quickly and without warning, so it is best to be ready for any emergency! Chubby hands may reach out toward the flame and knock the stablest candlestick across the table. Teachers are careful to sit close enough for effective action.

The story ended, Jane stood up and rushed to the table. Her mother, fortunately able to be on hand for the party, waited until Jane had chosen a seat, then took a place beside her. Moving at a great variety of speeds, the rest of the children at length found spots to settle in, too. One of the teachers suggested that it was time to sing "Happy Birthday" to Jane. The guest of honor sat placidly staring at the candle before her. Her lips formed the proper sounds, and Jane sang happily to herself with the rest, unaware of any incongruity. Cookies were distributed and everyone munched seriously, too much absorbed in the process of eating to trouble with conversation. Once or twice, a candle had to be lit again. Ultimately, Jane was called on to blow them out. Backed up by a puff or two from her mother, she was able at length to extinguish them. The party over, she found her cot in its accustomed place and curled herself upon it for rest.

Four-year-old birthdays assume more importance and acquire greater social significance. Teachers may find it wise to divide a large group of wiggly threes and fours into two sections. The birthday child then celebrates with one group, but the attention of the other children is drawn to the fact that he brought the cookies and the napkins. He is likely to receive congratulations from this group all the rest of the day. At these parties much talk goes on about ages and sizes. "I'll be four in May," says Jamie. "But I'm bigger than you," is the stout reply of his younger friend. Is it true that you can be smaller even if you are older?

Much interest is still focused on candles and cookies. By the end of this year, almost everyone has learned to accept the rule that only the birthday child may blow out the candles. He may ask a friend to sit beside him, for his playmates are beginning to assume importance in his eyes. They talk chummily between mouthfuls of cookie. Almost any special celebration is likely to be regarded as a birthday by these children. One Halloween, teachers were asked, "Did the pumpkin bring the cookies?"

Still a different spirit characterizes these occasions in kindergarten. By the end of the year, many of the children there have turned six. They feel very grown-up indeed. Much of the responsibility for their parties may be delegated to committees. These self-appointed workers often go to great pains to create things of beauty for the tables. If the birthday child has brought lollipops, little rings may be cut and pasted to hold the sticks in an upright position at each place. Tiny designs may be colored and stuck to the milk glasses. Fancy mats or table decorations flower under several pairs of steady fingers. Place cards are made now and then, for these children have become highly conscious of the importance of the alphabet. Painstakingly, they write each child's name, listening intently as the teacher spells it out. It is a matter of pride to them all that they can find their places quickly by recognizing letters on the cards. Perhaps the birthday child is given an opportunity to choose games or stories just before or just after his party. Schedules may be flexible now, easily adaptable to the requirements of the day. Blindfold games are popular among this group; the guest of honor may try to guess the identity of a friend by the sound of his voice, or recognize an object by feeling or smelling it. In ring games, he is the central figure. The whole group responds to his suggestions, for everyone may be expected to cooperate in making this occasion a success. His mother watches from her chair on the sidelines. She is a welcome visitor, but no longer as necessary as she was a year or two ago. She looks at her son's lengthening limbs. She sighs when he smiles, for where his baby teeth used to be, there are gaps that would look better on a jack-o'-lantern. "I'd better face it," she thinks. "He is growing up."

Growing up, among nursery school children, is clocked not only by birthdays, but as well by the group in which one is placed. As the end of the school year approaches, the older children begin to look with added interest at the teachers and the classrooms they will advance to in the fall. A little clique of children, all nearly four, meets in a packing box on the playground to discuss plans for the future:
"I'm going to Gran's farm this week end."

"I'm going to the beach."

"Oh."

"And next year, I'll be in Miss Sargent's group."

"So will I!"

"Teenie will, too."

"But not Bill. We won't see Bill, will we?"

"Goodie! We don't like Bill, do we?"

"But you like *me*, don't you?"

"Yes. And you like me, too. You're my very best friend."

Such little circles will form the nucleus of Miss Sargent's group next year. For these children it is a comforting thought to know that they will not enter the four-year-old group as strangers. Margaret and Brian will be there, too. Maybe even the odious Bill will not look so bad, for at least the familiarity of his face will be a point in his favor.

Among kindergartners, end-of-the-year excitement is particularly high. From now on there will be no more daily climbs on the outdoor jungle gym, no regular return to the familiar rooms. First grade, with its new experiences and strange faces, lies ahead.

John has heard his parents speak anxiously about next year's schooling. They are not happy about the neighborhood public school, and all the private schools ask tuitions that are impossible for their budget to assimilate. They have applied for a scholarship in one of them. What will they do if John is not given help? Ellen's parents are satisfied that the public school near them is their best bet. Roger's big family has moved to the suburbs to solve the children's schooling problem. Some children learn with relief that one or two old pals are enrolled in the same school they will attend. Others will follow older brothers and sisters into classrooms about which they have heard many a story. Whatever the final decision, the subject has been discussed so often at home that every kindergartner is highly vocal about his plans for the fall.

Teachers will listen eagerly for reports about these alumni. Since first grade is always quite a step, no matter how well prepared in kindergarten, the ease with which it is taken demonstrates how worthwhile their nursery experience has been. With few exceptions nursery school graduates make better-than-adequate adjustments to first grade. Whether they enter traditional, very conservative schools, or others of more progressive leanings, they are well equipped to face the challenges any of these types may present. Qualities of self-reliance, manual and bodily skill, social understanding, and poise are of prime importance regardless of where they are put to the test.

Tommy, who is almost three, is cavorting on the grass near the sandbox. His birthday will be next week, but whether that means it is close at hand or a long way off is a mystery to him. Of even less importance is the fact that today is his last day of school until he enters the three-year-old group in the fall. His mind does not grapple with this problem as he pauses for a moment to stare at the clouds overhead. It is, in fact, no problem to him at all. He has never changed to another group before, so its attendant worries do not occur to him. Nor can he imagine a day much different from the ones just past. Time ticks on unnoticed as he rolls over on the grass and examines an ant that is scrambling through the leaves near his fingers.

Mrs. Roberts, a parent participant in the four-year-old group, can hardly keep her eyes open as she stands by the digging patch. The day is warm, and she has sought the shade of a sycamore tree. She yawns a deep and satisfying yawn.

"My! You folks really have it easy nowadays," she says to Miss Sargent. "Beautiful mornings, no trouble at all with the children—what more could anyone ask? As a matter of fact, I don't think you need a mother around to help. Here it is eleven-thirty, and except for getting ready for the party, there hasn't been a thing to do."

Miss Sargent smiles. "In a way, I guess you're right," she says. "The group is pretty independent. I think you saw the only fight that broke out this morning, and you noticed how it took care of itself. And no one has been hanging around for lack of something to do. Yes, you are right. This is the time to enjoy the results of our year's work."

While Miss Sargent's staff does not relax its alertness to what is going on, they feel an end-of-the-year glow. With justifiable satisfaction they notice the growth that has taken place in every child. From a purely physical standpoint, the group is more active and better able to fend for itself than at the start of the year. Individual examples are easy to single out. Antonia waited until only two weeks ago to attempt the highest rung of the jungle gym; perhaps a consciousness that time was running out prompted her last-minute efforts. Whatever the reason, there she is now, waving happily from the very top to a friend below. Little George, who used to complain, "I don't know what to do now," has not had an idle minute since he ran in at nine o'clock. Miss Sargent would like to have had another month or so with Susie and Ellen; they have just begun to come out of themselves. The kindergarten next year will take them where they are and try to follow through what she has begun.

When she considers what has been done in the course of the last nine months, she recognizes how unprofitable her efforts with any child would have been without the willing support of his parents. How hard it was for them, in the face of a thousand-and-one setbacks, to do the job they wanted to do! Their friendliness has been one of her greatest assets and one of her deepest satisfactions.

Quite apart from individual progress, she can now look upon her group as a whole. Though at the beginning of the year the children played singly or in small exclusive cliques, she finds now that these groups have melted and changed. A cluster of eight boys is using the wagons for fire engines. They accept each other's suggestions and put bossy William in his place with a few well-chosen remarks. The girls, instead of standing around idly, are working together, coating the jungle gym with water "paint." It is the White

House, and when it is completely painted, Mr. Williams and Miss Sargent are invited in as the President and his wife. Miss Bruce, the student teacher, is asked to be a visiting princess. What delights the teachers is the comfortable atmosphere that is fairly visible throughout the group. It is friendly, honest, and together.

This feeling of belonging to a larger framework than family and relatives is clearly illustrated by bringing it back to the individual level. Adele provides a dramatic example. In the fall, she and her teacher walked into the garden plot that adjoined her church school playground. All about were flowers in gorgeous bloom, the result of patient labor on the part of the church gardener. Children were allowed in this spot for quiet walks and stories. Adele looked around her with delight. Then, in all seriousness, she asked, "Is this *my* garden?" The teacher replied that it belonged to the church and the people who went there on Sundays. Adele responded with this shocker: "When will the people die so they can give it to me?" Lack of sensitivity to others is typical of young children, but Adele seemed almost totally wanting in respect for other people's rights. Throughout the year, she bumped constantly into social troubles because she refused to take other children into account. The staff was finally rewarded at the end of May when her mother came to them with this story:

"Which boy is Walter? Oh, I see. Well, I want to tell you something that made me feel very happy. Adele asked me yesterday if she could invite Walter to her birthday party. I was surprised, because I know she has never mentioned him before. I asked her why she wanted him to come. Do you know what she said? 'I feel sorry for him. He's never invited to anyone's party.' Of course we invited him. But I was so pleased, and I thought you'd like to know."

The matter-of-fact friendliness with which adult visitors are accepted is further proof of the children's maturing social sense. One hears no "Get out of here, dirty snot nose," sees no spiteful kicks. Without being lectured about it, the children have discovered more successful techniques of winning pleasant responses from grownups. When, on this last day of school, Miss Sargent and her four-year-olds sit together at tables decorated as if for a birthday party, the school's director and her secretary are included as guests. Their invitations came from the children and resulted from honest regard rather than from any adult-imposed sense of courtesy.

A hot breeze blows through the curtains and causes the candle flames to flicker and smoke. The children have just come from the pool. Their faces are eager. This is the last graham cracker—this, the last glass of milk—until school begins again in the fall. And fall is a long way off. Anybody knows that. Before they start the snack, they sing a good-by song. The tune is the one used for birthdays; they decide on words to fit it. A few minutes later, crackers and milk are no more.

The last contribution to their book of stories is a group letter. It will be sent to all the children who have left before the end of school. Miss Sargent and her brood adjourn to the book corner to tell their absent friends what they are going to do during the summer. Summer lasts a long time. Will school ever begin again, really?

Dear Josie, Ellen, Stephen, Dickie, and John:

ALICE: This summer, I'm going to Texas when my brother and sister are at camp. I'm going by a sleeping train. It will take one whole day and a night and another half a day. I'm going to visit Grandma. I'm going to play with my cousin; it's a girl and her name is Mary Laura.

VIRGINIA: I'm getting two black puppies that are both going to be boys. We're going to fix a rickety-rackety old kennel up right in front of our house. Up in the country there is a big apple orchard and a barn with upstairs and downstairs. We have a big field; we play there. I have a vegetable garden: carrots, parsley, corn, watermelon, and cucumber. We have our very own road at the country, and we have an old cottage. We have a garage of our own.

JACKY: Do you know what I'm going to do at camp? Do you know what they have at camp? A hay wagon, and you get rides in the hay!

ADELE: We might look for houses, because we've started to look for houses already, and we missed a lot of Sundays.

MARGARET: All I'm going to do is come to Summer School.

ROBERT: I'm going to move this summer. We have seven-and-a-half acres and a stream, but not big enough for a boat.

DOUGLAS: I'm going to summer camp. It isn't really a camp— it's just a church where my mother is going to teach, but they call the church a summer camp.

EDWARD: We have a camp, but our neighbor is a farmer. I run a tractor up a hill. I milk the cow, and I squirted Milton a little bit with the milk. If you ever come with us, you can see Milton.

Good-by!